Living in the Margins

LIVING
IN THE
MARGINS

Intentional Communities
and
The Art of Interpretation

TERRY A. VELING

Foreword by Thomas Groome
Afterword by Bernard Lee

Wipf and Stock Publishers
EUGENE, OREGON

Wipf and Stock Publishers
199 West 8th Avenue, Suite 3
Eugene, Oregon 97401

Living in the Margins
Intentional Communities and the Art of Interpretation
By Veling, Terry A.
Copyright©1996 Veling, Terry A.
ISBN: 1-59244-091-6
Publication date: November, 2002
Previously published by Crossroad Publishing Company, 1996.

Picture two lovers side by side
who sleep and dream and wake to hold
the real and the imagined world
body by body, word by word
in the wild halo of their thoughts.

Gwen Harwood

CONTENTS

FOREWORD

There are many ways to describe ourselves as human beings, but "hermeneutes" will likely always ring very strange and never as a compliment. Inelegant as it may sound, that, among other things, is precisely what we are. To be a "human being in residence" is a perennial act of hermeneutics; we ever endeavor to interpret and explain the life around us and the cultural world left by those who went before. Existentially and by necessity, to be human is to be engaged in hermeneutics.

But hasn't this always been true, so why the fuss of late about hermeneutics? If so human, why have we not attended to it before? It is amazing how quickly the term has come into common usage, almost to rival some of the strange terms that have avalanched us from cyberspace. Only twenty-five years ago even the prestigious *Encyclopedia of Philosophy* didn't have an entry for the term. Now it is like a "buzz" word throughout so much literature of all kinds, philosophical and otherwise.

What the theory of hermeneutics tries to systematize, of course, has always been an aspect of living humanly. The first philosophers to reflect systematically trying to make sense out of life and to inherit the "sense" made by a previous generation that they found congealed in their symbols of tradition were in fact doing hermeneutics. But, amazingly, only recently has this universal act of interpreting and explaining been developed into something akin to a science. Though still in its infancy, hermeneutics as a theory to aid interpretation has made huge progress. However, it continues to be perceived largely as the preserve of experts, and a foray into its technical literature will readily demonstrate why. But we cannot afford to leave it there. Perennial "hermeneutes" that we are, what a benefit it would be to have access to the wisdom of a concerted science that attempts to offer theoretical clarity, practical criteria, and reliable ways to proceed with interpreting our lives.

Though hermeneutics is usually referred to as the science of the act of interpretation, the Greek *hermeneuein* means both to interpret *and* to translate or make something understandable in a context for which its meaning is not immediately self-evident. Paul Ricoeur points out that all of our interpreting is done with an eye to explanation; though distinguishable, they are never separate activities. It is interesting to note too that the Greek god Hermes was the divine messenger but was also *to explain* the message of the gods to its recipients. And Hermes was a god of fertility; likewise, as Gadamer insists, the hermeneutical act should fuse into a new moment with a practical wisdom to it. All three aspects are retained in the contemporary meaning of the word; hermeneutics is the art of *interpreting* texts and symbols, but at best this is done with a view to *explaining* them in ways that make sense and give *new life* to self and others.

As might be expected in the history of Western thought, hermeneutics was originally focused on the interpreting and explaining of the Bible and was closely correlated with biblical exegesis. However, Dilthey, Heidegger, and other recent philosophers broadened hermeneutics beyond written texts to include attention to any symbol or expression of human self-awareness; the whole symbolic world is now its agenda. And yet hermeneutics has retained its moorings in its original religious context, where the interpreting of sacred texts is an "eternal" enterprise. The emerging awareness in the "divine" disciplines, however, is that hermeneutics is more than the concern of Biblical exegetes; all theological specialties must attend to it. Further, it must become a competent art—a modus operandi—among the church's religious educators and pastoral ministers. To render our ministry, we simply must become intentional and well-informed "hermeneutes."

All the functions of ministry help to mediate between people's everyday lives and the "texts" of a faith tradition. This whole process of mediation must be suffused throughout—at every turn—by reliable hermeneutics. To mediate well the minister must enable people to interpret their lives from a faith perspective, to interpret the texts of tradition from the perspective of their lives, and to integrate the two—their lives and their faith—into a creative and meaningful synthesis. Thus, to be well versed in hermeneutics would seem like an imperative for theologians, religious educators, and pastoral ministers. Just as we turned to psychology some fifty years ago, and more recently to sociology, so, without repeating the mistake of expecting a panacea, we must now turn to the literature of hermeneutics for insights essential to our work. This need is heightened further by the exigencies of our "modern" world, where much from the past can

seem so strange and needing to be made "familiar"—interpreted and explained—
again.

The fact remains, however, that to become au courant and competent in the art
of hermeneutics is a complex chore for the busy pastoral minister or religious
educator. To begin with, the literature on hermeneutics has literally exploded,
and so too, apparently, has the complexity of its considerations. For example,
awareness that knowledge is a social construct, that it is shaped by the social context and personal interest of the knower, has heightened the complexity of interpreting and explaining any "text" of life. Or again, that we are capable of
"reading into" our own lives or into texts from another time what we want to
"find" there is now a common awareness, and yet how are we to proceed without
falling prey, on the one hand, to total subjectivism that simply manipulates the
"text," or, on the other, feigning "objectivity" and remaining blind to our own
subjectivity? Within the hermeneutical act itself, can we ever really know the   Caution
mind of an original "author" or audience; can we even know our own minds
without self-delusion? Or how can we maintain a healthy skepticism toward
absolutist interpretations, and yet without falling into the paralysis of total relativism? These and many others like them are crucial questions for human well-
being; how we answer them has much to do with making and keeping life human
for ourselves and others. One hope of tackling them appropriately is to have
access to the insights of hermeneutics!

So, as religious educators and pastoral ministers we are faced with the urgent
need for a working knowledge of, and some art in, hermeneutics, and yet with the
daunting task of taking on a very complex and controversial literature. It is precisely at this juncture that *Living in the Margins* becomes an invaluable resource.
Terry Veling has read and summarizes for us here much of the best contemporary
literature on hermeneutics; he has done so succinctly and in very readable language. Of particular benefit is that he locates his review within the context of
community, with the underpinning question throughout—what kind of hermeneutics can best serve the shared life of an intentional faith community? We can
say that community is his own hermeneutical lens, but what an added asset this is
for people concerned for the life of the church in the world.

Undoubtedly, he makes his own compelling proposal, leaving no doubt that
when it comes to interpreting texts his own preference is to "live in the margins."
Even this will be helpful to the reader. You will find yourself employing the
hermeneutical principles that Veling enunciates to interpret his own text, and the
sweep of his review will provide the resources to agree or disagree with him. In
the process you will discern your own hermeneutical principles and reformulate
them as you deem needed. This is surely a tour de force.

Living in the Margins will provide theologians, pastoral ministers, and religious educators with an invaluable map through a maze that they must navigate themselves and help others to travel as well. I wish I had such a compass twenty years ago; it would have saved me a lot of time—and some wrong turns along the way!

                              Thomas H. Groome
                              Professor of Theology and Religious Education
                              Boston College. Summer 1995

PREFACE

It has always struck me as strange that most writers write their introductions or prefaces at the end, after they have finished writing the main text. A strange paradox: we take what is written and proceed to introduce it, as if it were yet to be. So one wonders: where was the real beginning if it was reached only by the end, or the real end if it had to be placed at the beginning? This intriguing phenomenon is perhaps a good example of a "marginal text" — one that is written in the interplay between text-written and text-yet-to-be. It presumes the latter, but only in the light of the former. We are always introducing the "new" in the light of what has been written, commenting on the "old" in the light of what yet needs to be said, questioning the "whole" in the way endings always seem to end-up as beginnings.

The following work is dependent on a vast web of texts and scholarship that has gone before me. It is a part of what Henry Nelson Wieman refers to as "the creative event" that emerges from "the meanings gathered by a million others."[1]

Words that reach the furthest are dependent on an immense book, dependent itself on every striving word.

Postmodern writers often speak of the generative power of "intertextuality," which unleashes textual meanings into a vast, dispersed range of new and unexpected contexts. The power of a text lies less in its original historical context than it does in its intertextual "play" — its uncanny ability to wander and join other texts, sometimes turning up in surprising places. Writing, therefore, actively "weaves," "fabricates" and "spins" the text, producing new meanings and new readings in freshly persuasive ways.

I draw on the insights and strategies of many writers and thinkers, not so much to form a coherent synthesis or representation of all their ideas, but to argue for a specific reading of things. Moreover, I believe it is possible to engage the insights of particular thinkers without necessarily adopting each one's whole system of thought. I recognize that there is much I write that others will dispute. My readings of various thinkers could be more nuanced, and there are many times I feel that I miss the mark in what I write — that looked at from another angle, things could perhaps be put differently. Yet I am willing to live in this "margin of error," because there is no truth-telling that is not also a "lie." We never quite make the mark, except perhaps for the purposes of measuring the size of our questions.

This work has two "readers" in mind — members of the academy and members of intentional Christian communities. I write between these two worlds, and I hope that my writing can serve as a bridge between the rigorous demands of the academy and the issues and concerns of intentional communities. I like Walter Brueggemann's idea of "funding the imagination," when he writes: "the task is to *fund* — to provide the pieces, materials, and resources out of which a new world can be imagined. Our responsibility, then, is not a grand scheme or coherent system, but the voicing of a lot of little pieces out of which people can put life together in fresh configurations."[2] I want to excite the imaginations of intentional Christian communities, to let them see new possibilities, to legitimate their visions and their marginal space, to give value and hope to what they are doing for the life of tradition and the life of the world.

My hope is that the following work can be an exercise in persuasive and "passionate scholarship."[3] Along with Alfred North Whitehead, my confidence lies in "the power of humanity's spiritual adventures — adventures of thought, adventures of passionate feeling, adventures of aesthetic experience."[4] The commitment of this work is both to the community of scholars (the academy) and to members of intentional Christian communities (the marginal *ecclesia*) straining toward an unforeseeable novelty: "The death of religion comes with the repression of the high hope of adventure. . . . It is the business of the future to be dangerous."[5]

It is not always easy to hold together diverse interests such as hermeneutics, religious education, and intentional Christian communities. Hermeneutics, like any specialization, can either be a limitation that "narrows," or a point of entry that "opens up." In my case, it has definitely been the latter. In both academic and pastoral contexts, I find that my interdisciplinary interests in theology, hermeneutics, and education have proved a wonderful mix for engaging a variety of contemporary issues that are of concern both to the academy and its intellectual pursuits and to the social and cultural realities that shape the questioning and concerns of people in their everyday practices.

Perhaps there are many of us who, in our ordinary lives, find ourselves somewhat suspicious of theories and impatient with complexities that academics seem to revel in so much.[6] However, there are deeper questions that affect our lives and, while they may at first appear far removed from everyday practical concerns, they are really "as basic as bread" — things like who we are, what we can know, how we should act, where we are going, and so on. Mary Boys, for example, reminds us that religious education is an ancient practice, concerned as it is with humanity's way of naming the sacred and being-in-the-world, with wisdom and knowledge, stories and rituals, anxiety and suffering, wonder and celebration. Religious education, as such, cannot simply focus on questions of "how to?" Rather, it must inquire more deeply by asking: "What does it mean to educate religiously?"[7] In other words, what does it mean to belong to a religious tradition, at the heart of which lies the questioning of where we have come from, who we are, and what we are called to become.

To focus on questions such as these is to recognize that we only attain a sense of the "whole" through our participation in what is "particular" to our own specific situations and places of belonging. "The concrete is the particular, yet the concrete is not only the particular — my experience, my friends, my community, my tradition. The concrete is the all reached through the particular."[8] There is no other way to approach a vision of the whole except through our belonging to particular traditions. According to David Tracy, our particular ties and attachments both reveal and conceal the hiddenness of the whole as we

embark upon a journey of intensification into the concreteness of each particular reality — *this* body, *this* people, *this* community, *this* tradition, *this* tree, *this* place, *this* moment, *this* neighbor — until the very concreteness in any particularity releases us to sense the concreteness of the whole as an internally related reality through and through.[9]

The "focal meaning" of this work is inescapably tied to my own particularity as a white, middle-class, educated, Western, Catholic Christian, who feels both "at home" and "not at home" with all that blesses and binds me, all that says "yes" to me and all that says "no," all that already is and all that lies hidden and yet to be.

I would like to express my heartfelt gratitude to three "large spirits" who have been both mentors and friends to me: Tom Groome, Bernard Lee, and Michael Cowan. My thanks also to Mary Boys and Tony Saldarini, who supported and encouraged this work from its most tentative and earliest beginnings. I feel grateful also, along with Mary and our children, to have spent such wonderful time as members of the New Orleans intentional Christian community (affectionately known as house church) — to Cinny, Mike, Michaella, Billie, Vahae,

"The gift of others enriches. It foreshadows the gift of oneself." (Reb Alan)[10]

(from a letter to a friend: "I was struck with the way your words highlighted my time with you as a time of an immense beginning. . . . So many new directions, paths and possibilities found their genesis with people just like you. It strikes me how much large, generative futures are depen-

dent on equally large, generative places of beginning. . . .")

We sense that "thinking can become thanking, that silence does become, even for an Aquinas when he would 'write no more,' the final form of speech possible to any authentic speaker."[11]

Bernard, Ed, Jim and all the community, our thanks! My thanks also to the many friends and conversation partners who have been part of my life, people such as Chris Murphy, Paul Finlay and Catherine Melville, Peter Mudge and Gwen Wijenburg, Mike and Monica O'Brien, Jim and Ursula Cranswick, Evelyn and Jim Whitehead, Anne Tuohy, Gerard Hall, and so many others who cannot all be named here.

With much love and affection, I would like to thank especially my parents, Ben and Brenda, for their unfailing support and encouragement. Also, to Antoine and Sue Veling, for being there while we were away; to Bernie and Maureen and all the members of the O'Brien clan; and to my conversation partner par excellence, Mary, and our children — Joel, Simon, Reuben, and Asher.

This work would not have been possible without the encouragement and financial support I received from the provincialates of the following Australian religious congregations, all of whom were willing to share the burden of risk-taking for the sake of a more hopeful future: Good Shepherd Sisters, St. John of God Brothers, Marist Brothers, Marist Fathers, Daughters of Charity, Mercy Sisters of Brisbane, Good Samaritan Sisters, Pallottine Fathers, Missionary Sisters of the Society of Mary, Carmelite Fathers, Sisters of St. Joseph, St. Columban's Mission Society, Archbishop Francis Carroll and the diocese of Canberra and Goulburn, Cardinal Edward Clancy and the Archdiocese of Sydney. Similarly, in the United States, Mary and I found kindred spirits who were willing to offer their support and to urge us on when things became difficult. Our thanks to Bill Neenan, S.J., Academic Vice-President of Boston College; to James Carter, S.J., President of Loyola University New Orleans; to the Praxis Fund established by Thomas Groome and Colleen Griffith; and to the St. Joseph Foundation.

The book occupies an immense space indeed, and, in the end, one can only feel its silence and its yearning with a large measure of gratitude.

"I spent all Spring — waiting for words to sprout,
all Summer — watching them grow,
all Fall — raking them up,
and all Winter
in silence."

Terry Veling
Spring 1995

NOTES

1. Henry Nelson Wieman, "Creative Good," p. 59.
2. Walter Brueggemann, *Texts Under Negotiation,* p. 20.
3. Elizabeth Kamarack Minnich, *Transforming Knowledge,* p. 163.
4. Alfred North Whitehead, *Science in the Modern World,* p. 207.
5. Ibid., pp. 192, 207.
6. For a further commentary on this, see Raymond Canning, "Sharpening the Questions," in Peter Malone, ed., *Discovering an Australian Theology,* pp. 25–45.
7. Mary Boys, "Religious Education: A Map of the Field," in Mary Boys, ed., *Education for Citizenship and Discipleship,* pp. 100–101.
8. David Tracy, *The Analogical Imagination,* p. 257.
9. Ibid., p. 382.
10. Edmond Jabès, *The Book of Questions* (Vol. 1), p. 200.
11. Tracy, *The Analogical Imagination,* p. 385.

INTRODUCTION:
THE MARGINAL SPACE
OF INTENTIONAL
CHRISTIAN COMMUNITIES

This is a book or, rather, the hope of a book written and rewritten night after night, as if it could not come about by writing alone, as if it were happening elsewhere, far from my pen, without my patiently awaited words, with other words, other dreams, by other routes, during other rests, with other screams, but with the same silence. . . .

I have gotten used to proceeding by words and in the wake of an unknown word.

I have always preferred being on the margin because it gives a perspective which allows us to judge, imagine, love, live within the moment and outside it, free, but with the freedom of a slave who dreams of it. . . .

Where can the book blossom except in the book? The sacred is within us, deeply anchored.

"Ah, who will ever count the centuries examined in the margins of our books?" wrote Reb Amit.

I myself have tried, in the margin of tradition and through words, to find again my fountainhead.

So weighed down with centuries, the book you unearth.
Each of your sentences makes it younger.

Writing a book means joining your voice with the virtual voice of the margins. . . . The deepest expression of the book . . . lets the margins breathe. . . .

To muddy the water with a bit of ash.
Allow the unforeseen, the chance event.
Dethrone the system.
Get the seal of approval from the possible.
Make wide, wide the margins.

Edmond Jabès

The experience of "living in the margins" has become for me a guiding metaphor in framing this book around the themes of intentional Christian communities, hermeneutics, and educational praxis. In an effort to introduce each of these themes, this chapter will explore the marginal character of intentional Christian communities from three interrelated perspectives. The first perspective draws some contrasts between mainstream and marginal expressions of intentional community life to gain a better understanding of the social and ecclesial location of marginal communities. In the light of this, the second perspective explores some sociotheological insights concerning the tensional interplay between margin and center. Finally, the third perspective turns to the field of hermeneutics to introduce what will be a major player throughout this work. I suggest that hermeneutics provides an alternate way of looking at marginality; the space of the margins is a site of vital creativity, a creativity that is generated in the ongoing interplay between belonging and nonbelonging, attachment and alienation, tradition and innovation. Rather than seeing marginal space as a typically narrow, withdrawn, alienated space, we need to allow the margins to breathe, to be the very life and breath of the book — to make wide the margins. I believe intentional communities can purposefully claim this marginal space as their own and in this way become intentionally marginal rather than peripherally marginal. As such, the third perspective introduces some key educational issues facing marginal Christian communities and asks, What insights can hermeneutics bring to the intentional life of marginal Christian communities, to their educational praxis?

The Social and Ecclesial Context
of Intentional Christian Communities

Small Christian communities have become widely recognized as significant expressions of Christian life emerging in a variety of cultures and contexts throughout the world.[1] They go by many names: base ecclesial communities, basic Christian communities, small Christian communities, home/house churches, and so on.[2] These are *communal* expressions of Christian gathering and need to be distinguished from *small groups* (such as Bible study groups, support groups, and so on). Given the breadth of small-community initiatives taking place today, my interest lies primarily with communities that are located in Western, middle-class cultures. In order to name these communities, I prefer the term *intentional Christian community*. I also employ the term *marginal Christian community* to designate those intentional communities that have adopted a critical distance from mainstream church life. Generally speaking, I am referring to small, intentional communities (approximately twelve to twenty adults, along with children), who gather on a regular basis (at least biweekly) to seek genuine ways of being together as Christian communities: committed to mutuality and inclusiveness, attuned to the sacred texts and rituals of their tradition, and engaged in the world as communities of public presence in culture and society.[3]

I am also using the word *intentional* to distinguish the life of small communities in the relatively affluent, middle-class cultures of Western societies (my own experience being that of Australian and United States culture) from the life of those communities situated in Third World contexts and generally referred to as *basic* or *base* communities. *Intentional* means "deliberate," "attentive," or "actively pursued." Small-community life does not come naturally for members of Western, individualistic cultures. It is something we must consciously choose and consistently work at.[4] Moreover, we are less likely to be drawn into small-community life out of the urgency of oppressive social conditions, as has been the case for small-community movements in Latin America and other Third World countries. Rather, intentionality reflects the need for a continually focused awareness and critical engagement with the social, cultural, and ecclesial systems that shape our lives. Intentionality also highlights the commitment and endurance required of small-community members to create and sustain new patterns of Christian community as an alternative expression to existing church structures and as a means for public engagement.

Mainstream and Marginal Communities

Among intentional Christian communities located in Western cultures, it is possible to recognize two broad streams of development. One development we could name as "mainstream" communities, the other as "marginal" or "critical" communities. One development finds its primary location within the mainstream ethos and institutional structures of church life; the other adopts a critical distance from those structures.[5] We need to recognize, however, that we are speaking here of a broad, general distinction — one that serves a purpose mainly in drawing attention to the fact that there are many intentional communities whose character and way of being cannot be readily located in mainstream church life. A variety of books, articles, and programs have been written on parish-based small communities, even more on parish-based small groups. Little attention has been given to the many gatherings of intentional Christian communities taking place in contexts other than the mainstream ethos of Christianity. Nevertheless, it needs to be said that the mainstream/marginal distinction is not clear cut. There are many intentional communities gathering in mainstream parish settings whose sensibilities are also shaped by the strong, prophetic, cutting-edge claims of the gospel. They too, in their own way, are operating "on the edges" of existing ecclesial and social structures, trying to promote redemptive relations in their experience of church and society. Perhaps the mainstream/marginal distinction is more like a continuum, with intentional communities existing at various points along the line.

(i) Mainstream Communities

Mainstream communities are those intentional communities that clearly operate within the boundaries of mainstream church life. They operate primarily within the context of the parish, which is seen as the fundamental expression of church at the local level. The parish is usually regarded in official circles as the appropriate context for projects designed to revitalize church life. So while intentional Christian communities are clearly affirmed as a force for renewal within the church, this renewal happens within, and not outside of, parish life. Intentional Christian communities are viewed as a way of revitalizing the church through a revitalization of parish life.

A majority of parishes view small, intentional communities as one activity among many for reaching out to people and building community within the parish. In this context, small Christian communities usually coexist along with a whole range of other parish programs and activities. In many cases, however, they take the form of "faith-sharing groups" and represent a somewhat tamed, watered-down version of the more full-bodied concept of small Christian community. Australian sociologist Michael Mason suggests we need to clearly distinguish small groups from small communities. Often these terms are used interchangeably so that many parish-based small groups are misleadingly spoken of as "communities." Drawing on Mason's work, the following schema is helpful in distinguishing the life of small groups from the life of small communities.[6]

Differences Between Small Groups and Small Communities

Small Groups	Small Communities
Membership: Homogeneous, tending toward uniformity: persons of similar age, gender, specialization. E.g., youth, marrieds.	Pluralistic, bringing together persons heterogeneous in age, social standing, gender, religious practice. Open to families, children, youth, singles, elderly, marginalized/alienated.
Member's Role: Often just one of a person's many roles, e.g., learner.	Involves all aspects of the person: different sides of personality, capacities, and roles.
Duration: Temporary/transitory; often linked to a specific task.	Permanent/long term; an expression of constant, stable, social life.
Purpose: Specialized, responding to one aspect/problem, intensifying a specific dimension. E.g., prayer together, adult education, social justice.	Broad, to be church together — scripture/ word, eucharist/ritual, mutuality, social engagement. Integrating the fundamental dimensions of human life.
Commitment: Often contractual, for the duration of a learning program or task.	Cognitive, affective, moral; often unlimited or open ended in time.
Dynamic: Small group dynamic, often more satisfying to the articulate and those with group skills.	Community dynamic; neither family nor small group nor organization; open to a wider range of types of participation; less demanding of every person; may include small group components.
Intimacy: Superficial but often intense.	Deeper/richer and usually slower in developing.
Location: Usually a dependent part of a larger structure (e.g., a parish); does not aim for self-sufficiency; parish remains primary locus of belonging.	Ideally with a measure of self-sufficiency but not cut off from wider church structures; networking is important; exists as the primary locus of belonging for the member.
Examples: "Renew" groups, prayer/ Scripture groups, youth groups, justice groups, etc.	Parishes restructured as "community of communities"; some family/neighborhood and residential communities; lay-religious communities, intentional communities, house churches.

If some parishes view small communities as one activity among many in the parish, other parishes are committed to intentional Christian communities as a way for restructuring the entire parish, with intentional communities as the basic unit. Parish is still upheld as the primary expression of local church life, but current parish structures are seen as sorely inadequate and in need of significant reform and renewal. Intentional communities are not viewed as another program for renewing parish life; rather, they are seen as a fundamental way for completely restructuring the parish into a "community of small communities." As Arthur Baranowski notes, this calls for a radical decision in a parish's pastoral planning: "Continue with the present structure of the parish and do lots of good programs and outreach for the masses of parishioners *or* restructure the parish into smaller ongoing communities that are the church at a small level while maintaining the parish community."[7]

The decision to restructure means taking intentional Christian communities seriously. This is the obvious strength of the *restructuring* approach. Yet the very word *restructure* belies the hidden danger of employing a managerial, "top-down" approach to the development of intentional Christian communities. Developing a "parish plan with clear steps that deliberately moves the parish toward its ultimate goal"[8] suggests that intentional communities can be achieved as a result of long-term institutional planning. Yet we need to ask whether organizing an entire parish into small Christian communities would not be "tantamount to institutionalizing the de-institutionalizing aspect of community."[9] In other words, can a parish pastoral team organize for community to happen without stifling the decentralizing nature of community which is of its very essence?

This is a difficult tension to live with. On the one hand, we cannot deny the importance of a pastoral agent — not to impose something from the outside, but to encourage and facilitate what is there waiting to be brought into being. Yet we need to be cautious that the pastoral strategies we employ are not introduced in a managerial manner. This warning comes through strongly from those who have been closely involved in facilitating intentional-community life. David Prior, for example, writes: "One cannot *build* Christian communities: they must *grow* . . . from within their own resources. Endeavours to make them develop according to a predefined plan will stifle or even suffocate them."[10] According to Robert Banks, the result of a too structured and managed approach is usually this: "several communities run for a while then wither; some barely manage to survive; one community makes good — and the majority of people are truly insulated from ever attempting anything similar again."[11]

Whereas the "top-down" approach suggests that parishes can be broken down into small communities, the "bottom-up" approach suggests that small communities are built up into parishes. In Robert Banks's experience, this may mean starting with the networks of relationships that already exist in our local regions. It involves tending these, giving them a space to grow at their own pace, in their own way, and out of their own resources:

> It means being content with small beginnings and being prepared to wait for others to catch the same vision before proceeding further. Throughout, it remains an organic, not contrived, affair. Furthermore, the possibility that such tiny initiatives

may eventually reshape the life and structures of the whole congregation ought not to be ruled out. We dare not erect fences to hold back the Spirit.[12]

(ii) Marginal Communities

In contrast to mainstream communities, marginal or critical communities have intentionally chosen to remain outside formal structures, such as the parish, while retaining a strong sense of Christian community and public engagement, gathering as "home churches" with the Scriptures and the eucharist at the heart of their shared life.[13] These critical communities typically experience a strong call to place the social structures of both church and society under requirement of the gospel.[14] The word *critical* is important for these communities because they recognize that the Christian tradition contains many distortions that need to be filtered out. They also recognize that society is in need of critical transformation, and they experience a keen sense to want to make a difference in the world, to be engaged with the pressing social issues of our time.

Marginal Christian communities typically come into existence because their members have experienced a dissatisfaction over a long period of time with existing church structures. Such communities see the parish system as being in serious demise as a viable form of community life. Becoming increasingly large and impersonal, they do not believe the parish can function as a primary locus for religious belonging, and they see little hope in the efforts made to renew parish life. Intentional Christian communities cannot be manipulated or adapted as a means to an end, such as those who would view them as a means for renewing or restructuring parish life. Even in Latin America, where base communities are best known, fears are expressed that they are being coopted and assimilated into a dominant parish system that seeks to undermine their efforts to establish and consolidate themselves as a new ecclesial structure.[15] "The problem is one of wineskins," writes Robert Banks. "The old wineskins just cannot contain the new wine that is poured into them."[16] Is it possible to "pour" a biblical and early church concept of Christian community into a parish system with its own long and settled history and way of being church, which is so different to the small community way of being church? Jim Cranswick writes,

> By making the base Christian community subsidiary and using it to assist in the over-all pastoral plan for the parish it turns into a new and foreign organism trying to live in an old and tired body. This way of being church has its own authentic identity and needs space to operate effectively. It is always possible that given some autonomy and room to breathe and develop some BCCs may help to reshape the parish for the future. On general observation, however, those dedicated to preserving the parish generally look with some suspicion at those committed to "being Church" in

such a radically new way; and, in the long run, it may be stretching tolerance on both sides to develop a peaceful co-existence.[17]

Whereas mainstream communities retain a strong allegiance to the parish, with small communities being more like a subset of parish life, members of marginal communities see the intentional community to which they belong as their *primary* religious group, claiming their primary allegiance. If a parish or diocese has any viable role to play, it would be very much a *secondary* role of providing support and networking. Common to the self-understandings of marginal Christian communities is the awareness that when they gather, they are gathering *as church*. They do not consider themselves as parts or pieces of a larger entity we call church, but as genuine church, as truly ecclesial expressions.[18] This sense of being church represents what Peter Hodgson calls an "ecclesial freedom" to "revision the church" according to new paradigms that are nonhierarchical, participatory, and inclusive. He sees these new ecclesial visions emerging in Women-church communities as a sign of "ecclesial wholeness beyond all patriarchy, all clericalism, all misogynism"; in communities of the black church "as a paradigm beyond all racial prejudice"; and in the Latin American base communities "as a paradigm beyond all class oppression."[19]

For many marginal Christian communities, reclaiming ecclesial freedom has led them to explore new ways of ritual making and liturgical celebration. The eucharist, particularly, has become an important ritual expression in their communal gatherings.[20] Whereas mainstream communities see the Sunday parish eucharist as sufficient, marginal communities believe that the celebration of eucharist within an intentional Christian community is central to its genuine ecclesial status. As such, the radicality of affirming intentional Christian communities as basic instances of ecclesial existence needs to be stressed and compared with more limited understandings of small communities as communities of the Word, without eucharistic expression.

While we have seen a decentralization of access to the Scriptures, current institutional structures are not so willing to decentralize sacramental expression into small community settings.[21] Yet many intentional communities are instinctually recognizing the close link that exists between "breaking open the Word" and "breaking bread" together. For the breaking of bread is a deeply symbolic action expressive of the sacred story we share. Story and ritual, word and sacrament, are so intimately linked that it is hard to live in one without the other. Many intentional communities are going ahead with their eucharistic celebrations, quietly and without great fanfare, completing the process of biblical and eucharistic reclamation as central to the heart of basic ecclesial life.[22] Their own small-community celebrations of the eucharist have become important to these Christian communities because they are generally unable to tolerate the sexism and clericalism they experience in the mainstream liturgical celebrations. Moreover, ritual expression is an important way for members of marginal communities to collectively name their experience, to draw upon diverse symbolic expressions (such as goddess traditions, creation spiritualities, and so on), to form a counterculture to dominating and alienating structures, and to "midwife their liberation" from these structures.[23]

Perhaps we can gain a better appreciation of the sensibilities of intentional Christian communities as we listen to their own experience of what it means to "live in the margins." The following are some typical descriptions given by members of intentional communities.[24]

Many years ago I tried to work from within the system to bring about change but as I grew older I decided to let "them" catch up, while I got on with living my own vision of church in relation to the kin(g)dom.

Interacting with other Christians with whom I can pray and dialogue and break bread has re-energized me and rekindled my hope for church. It has enabled me to reclaim a Catholic identity which, at the present time, is important to me. I see much that is of value in the Catholic tradition, and because it is the tradition that nurtured me, I have a sense of rootedness in it and loyalty to it. I see my present position (i.e., outside the mainstream) as a valid statement to the church institution that all is not well, and as a witness to others that we can trust our experience and create options. We have stepped out of tradition in order to be true to that tradition which has formed us.

Having lived "on the margins" for most of my adult life, I like it "out here." It is much more alive, stimulating, fulfilling, open-ended, free, liberated. It gives one the independence to live and act in a more prophetic way. This may sound arrogant, but I know I'm not arrogant, but ready to look and listen and reflect.

We have a thirst for community. We want to trust our experiences and take responsibility for being church and celebrating eucharist in an authentic way. We also have a need to provide our children with an authentic faith community in their growing years. We do not want to subject them to the patriarchalism, clericalism, and authoritarianism we have experienced in the mainstream church.

We consider our community to be pro-active rather than re-active. We are seeking to be church, not merely to react out of alienation. We are church to one another. We offer each other a faith community that is central by providing eucharist, reflection, and action.

The parish to which I had given so much no longer had a place for me. I felt I could no longer support a church that seemed more interested in its power and status than in genuine commitment to seeking truth and justice. My questioning and challenging were construed as disloyalty, trouble-making, immaturity. I couldn't foresee any significant change or signs of hope for the future.

It is some of the brightest minds who have moved to the fringes. It is not that they want to duck the challenge of the gospel. It is that they are not finding it in the church. This does not mean break away, but it does imply a readiness to break out.

I think the terminology of "marginalized" communities underscores a definition that directly implies "the institution is center." For me, the question is more accurately: *why* have Christian communities emerged in such numbers? In the U.S. there are thousands and this is just the beginning. Why do these communities illustrate a *new center* to the church? What are the errors that the institutional church is making on such a widespread scale that people are searching out and forming their own bases of church?

Ecclesial and social reconstruction are critical for us and interrelated in an essential way. Since all oppression is interrelated, we cannot stand in opposition to one oppression (e.g., the oppression of women) without standing in opposition to all oppression — racism, homophobia, etc. We exercise a hermeneutic of suspicion and look at all levels of institutional expressions of church in our efforts to find the most liberating and authentic expression of Christian tradition.

Rebecca Chopp asks, "Are there anywhere signs of community, connection, relationships, and emancipatory transformation in and of the church?" It seems to me that a new ecclesial wholeness is being fashioned among intentional Christian communities. Chopp believes that "the possibility of speaking freedom, of proclaiming emancipatory transformation, resides in the reality that at the margins of modern Christianity there are communities that already proclaim emancipatory transformation."[25] These communities are determined to see themselves as communities living within the margins of mainstream church life, neither cut off nor attached, but rather claiming an alternative space for renewed, vibrant, and liberated ecclesial expression.

Decentralizing and Centralizing Poles: The Interplay of Margin and Center

In speaking of the normative hold of a religious tradition, Walter Brueggemann claims that we are not always called to the center; rather, we are also called to heed voices of marginality in the tradition that are away from the center, and to realize that these marginal voices are also shaped by the tradition "as dangerous stories at the edge which protest the center."[26] Brueggemann suggests that sociologically, "our interpretive context is 'the alarm of the border' pushing against the complacent center."[27] The question facing us is how the "settled centers of interpreted truth are addressed by the abrasive voices of challenge, assault, and invitation from the margin."[28]

Marginal Christian communities recognize that there are many ways in which the center no longer holds in their experience of tradition and society. They challenge dominant orderings of patriarchy in their quest for renewed feminist expression; they seek more inclusive and participatory structures over against hierarchical and clericalized structures; they turn their attention to ecological issues in the face of an overly technologized world; they are concerned with the causes of indigenous and Third World cultures in the face of dominant Eurocentric traditions. They are seeking alternate theologies, spiritualities, and practices, casting their "voice from the margins over the whole social-symbolic order, questioning its rules, terms, procedures, and practices."[29]

The marginal space of intentional Christian communities, therefore, is both rending and renewing. As Rebecca Chopp notes, it "comes out of the gaps and margins but also arises amid the dissolving possibilities of an order that can no longer be maintained."[30] For some communities, their critical attention is directed largely at the alienation they experience from the institutional church. Their concern is that the transformative vision and hope of the Christian tradition cannot take root unless it is embodied in communities that resist all forms of patriarchal and authoritarian structures. Others turn their attention to the inadequacies of Christian theologies that they feel are out of touch with the needs of the contemporary world. Their concern is with the necessity to create new theologies that are enlivened by a practical engagement with the issues and concerns of culture and society. Both positions, however, share a vision of creating vibrant communities of faith in the face of settled centers of power represented by dominant institutions.

The significance of the critical distance adopted by many intentional Christian communities from mainstream church life is highlighted in the general axiom, "the new belongs elsewhere."[31] In other words, the application of creative imagination and prophetic critique often takes place away from already established structures and mindsets. David Power notes how the marginal communities are providing a much needed "creative critique of the established ecclesiastical order, supported by a living proposal of alternative models."[32] They are exercising what Edward Schillebeeckx calls a "loyal opposition" or "provisional illegality" with respect to the institutional church's current disciplines and structures. Schillebeeckx cites the theological principle of the *non acceptatio legis* (the rejection of the law from above by opposition at the base) in his claim that renewal and revitalization within the church, as history clearly shows, comes from the bottom up rather than the top down. Schillebeeckx writes:

> It is clear from this that there is, in the history of the church, a way along which Christians can, working from below or from the base, develop a praxis in the Church that may be temporarily in competition with the praxis that is officially valid in the Church at that particular time. This new praxis from below may, however, in its

Christian opposition, ultimately even become the dominant praxis of the whole Church and in the long run be sanctioned by the official Church.[33]

Leonardo Boff links the ever-recurrent urge toward reform and renewal with the "spirit of community." Community is a free-blowing spirit, a vital force, ever renewing and always resistant of any efforts to capture it, order it, or control it. "The will to impregnate the institutional organizational aspect of the church with the spirit of community will never die in the church, and this is the wellspring of its vitality."[34] While it is true that the institutional has predominated over the communitarian in the church of modern times, Boff sees a "genuine renewal of the institutional framework of the church, springing from the impulses of the grassroots community."[35] The de-institutionalizing nature of these small communities is their strength and a life force for the church. For this reason, Boff feels that any efforts to reabsorb these communities into the institutional church will deaden their ferment for renewal. Rather, we should leave these communities their marginal character, perhaps even emphasize it, to allow for a freer reading of the Christian tradition.

Bernard Lee makes a similar point in discussing the "recovery of charism" among religious congregations.[36] Just as Boff sees community as a spirit that blows where it will, so too Lee argues that charism is not a property or an object that can be controlled or contained and thereby made stable and retrievable for every age. Rather, charism, like community, is a spirit that needs to be constantly recreated and reinvented in each present age which must grapple with the demands of new social situations. In other words, charism is an event or a happening more than it is a thing or a possession. This eventlike quality lends it a volatile, unstable nature: unpredictable, uncontrollable, never fulfilled and continually disrupting and transforming the established order of things.

The work of anthropologist Victor Turner also throws some light on the impetus of renewal that comes from spirit or community. Turner maintains that the experiences of community and marginality (or liminality) are more likely to revitalize and renew our social practices and institutions than the experiences of structure and institution. The sources of renewed life and vitality are not likely to be found in the structure equivalent to the institutional experience but rather in the antistructural experience of *communitas* or the quest for it.[37] As with Boff and Lee, *communitas* has a spontaneous quality of immediacy that interrupts and breaks through established patterns:

> Communitas breaks through the interstices of structure, in liminality; at the edges of structure, in marginality; and from beneath structure, in inferiority. It is almost everywhere held to be sacred or "holy," possibly because it transgresses or dissolves the norms that govern structured and institutionalized relationships and is accompanied by experiences of unprecedented potency.[38]

Commenting on Turner's work, Tom Driver notes that the liminal power of *communitas* is manifest most strongly among groups of people "who have little invested in the present social order." Marginal space becomes important because "it gives space for communitas to flow."[39] Turner reminds us, however, that the experience of *communitas* can never be maintained outside of its dialectical relationship with the experience of structure. We are set free from structure into *communitas* only to return to structure, yet a structure renewed by our experience of *communitas*. "Maximization of communitas provokes maximization of structure, which in turn produces revolutionary strivings for renewed communitas."[40] Turner argues that no society can function in a healthy and vibrant way without this ongoing dialectic.

Evelyn Whitehead, drawing on the work of sociologist Richard Schoenherr, also sees the two poles of community and institution in a dialectical tension with each other rather than in contradiction to each other.[41] Religious groups require both centralizing and decentralizing movements. The former is a structuring, ordering, conserving movement; the later a destructuring, renewing, transforming movement. Religious groups constantly live within the tensions generated by these two movements. It seems that "community" and "institution" — margin and center — will always live with some tensional suspicion of each other. No religious group can be sustainable over time without the ongoing interplay between these two renewing and centralizing activities of the Spirit.[42]

The problem, according to Boff, is not so much that we have the counterpoints of institution and community. We cannot escape these. The problem lies in the way these two poles relate to each other: "whether one pole seeks to absorb the other, cripple it, liquidate it, or each respects the other and opens itself to the other in constant willingness to be put to the question."[43] The institution needs to respect and value intentional Christian communities as a vital and dynamic force for renewal in the church and to rediscover its own "meaning and responsibility in the creation, support, and nurture of the communities."[44] For their part, intentional communities need to understand their need for institution: for the maintenance of their continuity, for preservation of their identity, and for the possibilities of networking over against the threat of fragmentation.

The hope, in other words, is for a mutual dialogue and interplay between grassroots initiatives and institutional structures. According to David Power, "it is not destruction, but growing complexity and diversity . . . a deliberate mixing of formal and informal structural elements, which seems to offer the greatest hopes for the future of the Church as a religious organization."[45] Yet the conversation between the formal and the informal, the centralizing and the decentralizing, is not an easy conversation to uphold. Rosemary Radford Ruether observes that rarely do we see an optimal interplay between spirit-filled community and institution. The relationship between the two is typically ill-conceived, particularly by the institution, but also by the renewal community.[46] On the part of the institution, it is usually the established power centers that label as *marginal* those who threaten prevailing structures and viewpoints. The tag *marginal* serves to displace these alternative communities as fringe dwellers of little or no account, who therefore need not be taken seriously nor engaged in dialogue.

On the part of the communities, they often delude themselves by imagining they can live without any institutional structure at all. As Radford Ruether notes, communities who claim to have rejected all institutional structure "fail to appreciate how much their ability to function is based on a constant use of institutions that they have neither created nor maintained."[47] Similarly, Robert Bellah and his team point out that there is nothing inherently wrong with institution; it simply means the way humans organize or pattern their lives together. Because our lives are lived in and through institutions, Bellah's team stresses the importance of renewing institutional life to allow for more active interaction in the way institutions form us and the way we form them.[48] In a similar vein, Radford Ruether writes:

> One must learn to make creative use of existing institutions without being stifled or controlled by them. In the process these institutions become more flexible and become vehicles for further creativity. This is precisely what is meant by the positive working of the dialectic of spiritual community and historical institution.[49]

It is not institutionalization as such that must be rejected, "but the myth that some particular form of historical institution is the only legitimate one."[50] In other words, the question is what type of institutionalizing we choose, how we decide to pattern our lives together: hierarchical or relational? exclusive or inclusive? a closed system or an open system? Radford Ruether cautions communities against taking the "institutionally defined options either of continuing on its terms or of cutting-off all connection with it and becoming sectarian and hostile to those who are working within established institutions."[51] Separatism, while it may appear the more radical stance, only serves the needs of the institutional order, demanding that communities either stay or leave on its terms.[52] Marginal communities have refused both the option to conform to the established limits and boundaries and the option to leave as disillusioned and isolated individuals. Rather, they have intentionally chosen to establish space in the margins, retaining a strong communal base for alternate readings of the Christian tradition in response to the questions and concerns of their contemporary situation.

We can see that the marginal space of intentional Christian communities is very much an in-between space, neither fully belonging yet neither fully cut off. As Mark C. Taylor notes, it is at "one and the same time inside and outside the network that it questions."[53] Turner calls it a "liminal" space that is "neither here nor there." He likens it to the "threshold," the place of crossing; the womb, where new life silently begins; the "wilderness," where nomads wander and the desert wind blows where it will.[54] Our discussion has raised other images: critical space, decentering space, illegal space, transgressing, de-institutionalizing, impulsive and spontaneous, unsettled and unsettling, loyal yet opposing, rending yet renewing, disruptive yet transforming. We have, then, a vital yet unstable border along which marginal communities edge their existence in "the interplay; in the interconnections; at the intersections, at the crossroads."[55] They live at the boundary that both joins and separates: inside and outside, belonging and non-belonging, fidelity and heresy.

The Hermeneutical Context
of Intentional Christian Communities

It was Friedrich Nietzsche who first asserted that "there are no facts . . . only interpretations."[56] Since then, hermeneutics has become a loose word encompassing many different historical, cultural, and intellectual contexts. Historians, theologians, sociologists, philosophers, literary critics, and artists are all interested in one way or another with hermeneutics. Broadly considered, hermeneutics is concerned with what it means to understand: be it a text, a symbol, another person, an event, a tradition, our own selves. Hans-Georg Gadamer tells us that "understanding is always interpretation"[57] and Thomas Groome reminds us that there is no uninterpreted experience: "We are always interpreting ourselves and the world around us; hermeneutics is ontological, that is, an aspect of our 'being' in the world. . . . We cannot be but hermeneutes in our world."[58] As David Tracy suggests, "whether we know it or not, to be human is to be a skilled interpreter."[59] However, while interpretation is a condition of human existence, we cannot simply take the interpretive process as an inevitability. "Whether we know it or not" has a lot to do with how skilled we can become in reading life: our own lives, the life of tradition, the life of society and culture, the life of other peoples who make up our world. The work that follows reflects a central educational commitment to bring the hermeneutical character of understanding into clearer view, so that members of small communities may become more intentional, more skilled, and thus more human in the ways they understand themselves, their tradition, and others.

"Reading," "writing," "text," and "book" are primary metaphors for hermeneutics; they remind us that we live and understand in and through language, and that every time we think and act (indeed, every time we experience), we are interpreting. We do not simply find reality *out there,* independent of our linguistic and contextual framework. Rather, it is our very participation in the traditions of historical, cultural, and linguistic communities that makes understanding possible.[60]

In speaking of tradition, I am aware that this word is laden with many different meanings for different people. I want to use the word "without yielding to the pressures of conservatism which, with a vice-like grip, lays claim to the very concept of tradition."[61] In focusing on the Christian tradition, I want to highlight its deeply textured complexity so as to avoid an all too easily grasped familiarity "when we utter that disclosive word ever in danger of becoming an empty label, 'Christianity'."[62] It is important to recognize that we can never really speak of simply one, pure, single tradition. As J. B. Metz suggests, "A Christianity that was preexistent to culture and history, or a culturally divested, culturally naked Christianity does not exist."[63] Attempts to securely possess a timeless essence or seamless core of Christianity must largely be given up in this age of historical consciousness.[64] Instead, we should acknowledge its numerous, shifting, interplaying "histories," what Gershom Scholem refers to as a tradition's "anarchistic plurality of sources."[65] In other words, although my focus is on Christian tradition, we must remember how many other traditions come into play when discussing Christianity.[66] For example, there are the Israelite traditions of biblical literature and the early Jewish Jesus-traditions that formed the basis of the Christian "Second Testament."[67] There are the nonbiblical traditions of the ancient Near East, sometimes referred to as pagan or goddess traditions. These traditions are important because historical Judaism and Christianity forged their identities by either rejecting or surreptitiously incorporating pagan religious beliefs into their own practices.[68] There are the dominant Western theological and philosophical traditions that have shaped our ways of thinking and being from Plato to Nietzsche, from Augustine and Aquinas to Luther and Rahner. There are the post-Enlightenment traditions of process philosophy, pragmatism, deconstruction, liberation and feminist theologies. There are all those traditions that stand as an other to Christianity: Asian, African, Hindu, Buddhist, and so on.[69] Particularly, there is Judaism, Christianity's own other, that which Christianity can neither exclude nor contain, that which "confronts Christianity all along its way as the irrepressible prophetic voice, not the voice of the precursor awaiting final interpretation but the voice of the outsider still awaiting acknowledgment."[70] Finally, there are those traditions that perhaps cannot be named, that confront the Christian West as those who do not belong, prophetic irritants who pull at the loose threads of all we have supposedly woven into a whole.

Amid these streams of history (and suppressed counterhistories), Christianity has woven its own distinctive text or way of interpreting the world. Throughout this work, I have chosen to use the metaphor of the "book" to speak of this Christian text of tradition. Yet it is a peculiarly Jewish metaphor, one that derives more from rabbinic Judaism than it does, for example, from the Christian Reformists' principle of *sola scriptura*. Whereas the latter were suspicious of interpretive tradition, the former grew out of a strong commitment to interpretive practice that generated the Talmudic spirals of commentary around commentary. Although Catholicism has also placed emphasis on the importance of tradition and commentary, it has tended, unlike rabbinic Judaism, to stress an adherence to formulated doctrines and dogmas in a way that is foreign to Jewish sensibilities.[71]

More specifically, the metaphor derives from my reading of the works of the Egyptian-born, French-speaking, Jewish poet Edmond Jabès (1912–1991). There was a time in Jabès's life when his Jewishness was no more than a cultural given, until he was forced from his homeland by the very fact of his Jewishness. Suddenly, he was starkly confronted with his own Jewish identity, and he spent the rest of his life grappling, in one way or another, with the question: what does it mean to be Jewish? Or rather, what does it mean to be an *exiled* Jew, a Jew who only becomes aware of *belonging* to the Jewish people and tradition through the experience of *nonbelonging?* "This may seem paradoxical," writes Jabès, "but is it is precisely in that break — in that non-belonging in search of its belonging — that I am without doubt most Jewish."[72]

In reflecting on my own Christian tradition, I find it helpful to speak of it as a "book" that provokes the question of our belonging — a book, however, that encompasses the whole effective history of Christian tradition: not only texts, but symbols, rituals, witnesses, events, images, and so on.[73] A book, also, that is immersed deeply in the play of many traditions and that cannot transcend the conflict of interpretations inscribed in its pages. We belong to this book not as the latest chapter added to an already long and dated text. Rather, we belong as those who continue the thread of questioning that runs through every page of the book in which we both write and are written. As Edmond Jabès says, "We always start out from a written text and come back to the text to be written."[74] In this sense, tradition is the conversation and writing that it generates, or as Gadamer says, it is "the conversation that we are."

The book, however, not only speaks of a tradition's effective history that continually claims our attention, it also speaks of the painful experience of alienation and exile, in which we can no longer find ourselves in the pages of the book. Yet even in this experience of absence we can and must still write. Indeed, this ongoing writing and commentary in the margins of the book is its very life. In other words, the book represents our radical belonging to tradition; absence and exile represent our alienation from the book, and the margins of the book represent the place where new interpretation and the writing of tradition occur. It is as if the aim of interpretation were to use what is already written as a launching pad for reading the writing of tradition to come. Interpretation is the keeper of tradition.

Yet it is only in and of tradition that interpretation both comes to life and dies.[75] "Where can the book blossom, except in the book?"

My contention is that marginal space is the gap in which hermeneutics begins, and ends — forms, and re-forms. It begins in the recognition that there is a gap between our tradition and our lives.[76] What is a gap, except perhaps a space — a blank space, a space like that of the margin? A blank space represents a lack or an absence, yet it also represents a hunger or a search. It is as much about what is missing and excluded as it is about the hope or vision for what could be, for new possibility.[77] My sense is that intentional Christian communities are living in this gap, this marginal space, along the edges of Christian tradition, a tradition in which they feel themselves both radically immersed and disturbingly alienated. They live both inside and outside of a religious tradition that both provokes their existence as possibility and haunts their existence as nonpossibility. They recognize the value of *belonging* — they recognize the provoking claim this tradition makes on their lives, both in its disclosive ability (telling us something about who we are) and its transformative potential (telling us something about who we might become), such that it demands our interpretive attention.[78] Yet they also experience a keen sense of *nonbelonging*. They recognize that the Christian tradition also contains many distortions, that it can tend to exclude and repress, that it has as much to do with power and domination as it does with truth and disclosure, and, as such, that it demands both critique and suspicion.

Marginal Christian communities live between these two worlds of *trust* and *suspicion*. Their experience lies suspended, we might say, on the edge of a tradition in which they feel both the need to belong and the impossibility of belonging. The issue before us is how this state of suspension between trust (belonging) and suspicion (nonbelonging) can be redeemed as a creative juncture for hermeneutical engagement. The following chapters explore ways in which this marginal space can be reclaimed as a creative, productive, vital site of receptive and critical engagement with a tradition's enriching and distorting effects and with our own contemporary questions and concerns.

In broader terms, this work is concerned with "giving a hermeneutic to a community,"[79] which means giving a community a way of understanding—themselves, their tradition, other people, and the world we live in. For marginal communities, this means giving them a hermeneutic that can help them understand what it means to *belong* to a religious tradition. In the first part of this work, I explore a *dialogical hermeneutic*. This hermeneutic highlights our radical belonging to the book and implies the need for a hermeneutic of retrieval. It leans toward a trusting hermeneutic for the sake of tradition's ongoing life and conversation in the course of history, fearing that too much suspicion would kill the conversation. The book constitutes who we are and makes a continually relevant claim on our lives, such that tradition always effectively shapes who we are even as we shape the ways tradition is becoming.

In terms of a community's educational praxis, I suggest that a dialogical hermeneutic is one that helps communities learn to creatively *engage* a tradition, to enter into fruitful conversation with a tradition, to become participants in shaping the future life of tradition in the context of changing historical situations. Conversation suggests that what is at stake here is not a critical distancing from tradition, but a critical engagement with tradition in both its positive and negative realities. It also suggests a to-and-fro dialogue in which neither partner in the conversation assumes dominance. It represents an open, questioning mode rather than a wary, critical mode that too often distances marginal communities from interpretive engagement.

Marginal communities also need a hermeneutic that can help them understand their experience of *nonbelonging*. In the second part of this work, I explore an *exilic hermeneutic*. This hermeneutic brings to the fore the disruptive experience of alienation from a tradition, where foundations tremble, distortions are brought to light, and the whole is ruptured by breaks, interruptions, and the experience of absence. The assumed normativity of tradition is put in question. Is it only a source of truth and disclosure — always meaningful and never distorted? What if we cannot find ourselves in tradition "as in dialogue"? Awareness of our alienation from the book implies the need for a hermeneutic of suspicion, one that can help communities deal with the distortions, ideologies, and inherent ambiguities present in any historical tradition, with those elements of tradition that create structures of exclusion and nonbelonging. It leans toward a suspicious hermeneutic for the sake of those voices that have been suppressed, silenced, or excluded from tradition, fearing that too much trust would lead us unwittingly into structures of power and domination.

In this interpretive moment, the key educational issue facing marginal communities is learning to invest their critique and suspicion with an emancipatory interest, as a means of *risking* tradition, not jettisoning it. Interpretive conversation must pass through moments of suspicion, not to impede the conversation but to develop it in such ways that fuller, more fruitful possibilities may emerge in front of us — shaping new, liberative futures. There is a sense that emancipation operates as a "critique from within," that "every exit from the book is made within the book."[80] In other words, the book is prolonged through its own subversion: "transgressing" the book in favor of another that will prolong it.[81]

In the third part of the work, I argue that it is between these two interpretive positions—between trust and suspicion, between belonging and non-belonging—that a marginal hermeneutic comes fully into play. Living in the twin moments of belonging and nonbelonging is living in the moment of marginality, in the moment of "the between." Marginal hermeneutics recognizes how much we belong to the book of tradition, how much we are written into existence by this tradition that has shaped us and claimed us. It also recognizes how much we are "outside" the book, that there is much in our experience that is not written into the book's pages, that there is much new writing and rewriting to be done. This rewriting happens in the margins of the book, between the text to which we belong, the text that does make a claim on our lives, and the place of nonbelonging, where we cannot find ourselves in the pages of tradition, where something of our own contemporary experience and questions and concerns has not been taken into account. This is where the *interpretive edge* of marginal Christian communities takes on most of its power and energy. We begin to see that these communities are reading their questions and writing their commentary in the margins of the book, between what is written and what has not been written, between the claims of tradition and the claims of new, contemporary situations. This interpretive space merges the language of trust with the language of suspicion and leans transformatively into the language of possibility, of new writing in the margins, which could also be called a hermeneutic of reconstruction.

With respect to a community's educational praxis, I suggest that a marginal hermeneutic is akin to a practical wisdom that "knows its way about, even and precisely when the way cannot be laid out beforehand."[82] It represents an interpretational activity that operates at its best when the way ahead is not established, but in the making: playing, discovering, transforming. It also suggests a profoundly communal activity in discerning the way forward through deliberation, conversation and decision making in specific, local, concrete situations among communities of interpreters. As Richard Bernstein suggests, and as this work also strongly argues, "it becomes all the more imperative to try again and again to foster and nurture those forms of communal life in which dialogue, conversation, practical discourse, and judgment are concretely embodied in our everyday practices."[83]

NOTES

The epigraphs are from the following works of Edmond Jabès: *The Book of Questions*, 2. 14. *The Book of Questions*, 1. 301; *The Book of Resemblances*, 1. 11; *The Book of Shares*, p. 75; *The Book of Questions*, 2. 36; *The Book of Shares*, p. 82.

1. Much has been written on the notable development and significance of basic Christian communities or basic ecclesial communities in Latin America. An authoritative treatise is Marcello deC. Azevedo, *Basic Ecclesial Communities in Brazil.* A Protestant perspective is provided by Guillermo Cook, *The Expectation of the Poor.* Leonardo Boff, *Ecclesiogenesis,* offers an analysis of basic communities from the perspective of liberation theology.

Attempts have been made to learn from and translate basic communities into First

World contexts: Margaret Hebblethwaite, *Basic is Beautiful: Basic Ecclesial Communities from Third World to First World;* and Jose Marins and team, *Basic Ecclesial Communities: The Church from the Roots.* Various authors have traced the origins of small communities in biblical times (Paul Hanson, *The People Called: The Growth of Community in the Bible;* Robert Banks, *Paul's Idea of Community: The Early House Churches in Their Historical Setting;* and Wayne Meeks, *The First Urban Christians*) and throughout Christian history (David Power, "Households of Faith in the Coming Church").

There is a burgeoning literature on contemporary expressions of intentional Christian community life in Western cultures. For example, Bernard Lee and Michael Cowan, *Dangerous Memories: House Churches and Our American Story;* Evelyn and James Whitehead, *Community of Faith: Crafting Christian Communities Today;* Arthur Baranowski, *Creating Small Faith Communities;* Robert and Julia Banks, *The Home Church;* David Prior, *The Church in the Home;* Peter Hodgson, *Revisioning the Church: Ecclesial Freedom in the New Paradigm;* Ian Fraser, *Living a Countersign: From Iona to BCCs;* James O'Halloran, *Signs of Hope: Developing Small Christian Communities;* Mary Britt, *In Search of New Wineskins: An Exploration of Models of Christian Community.*

A variety of small Christian community networks also offer analysis and information on a range of small-community initiatives: in Australia, *Communities Australia, Grapevine, The Paulian Association.* Melbourne, Adelaide, Parramatta, and Townsville dioceses also have active diocesan networks. In the United States: *Communitas, Sojourners, Voices, Buena Vista, National Alliance of Parishes Re-Structuring into Communities, North American Forum for Small Christian Communities.* In the United Kingdom: *National Association of Christian Communities and Networks.* Small communities are also an important part of the Women-church network.

2. Joseph Healey has compiled a list of thirty-five hundred names for small Christian community initiatives from six continents. He offers an analysis and interpretation of these names in "Evolving a World Church from the Bottom Up," *Background Paper for the International Consultation on Rediscovering Community — International Perspectives,"* University of Notre Dame, Indiana, U.S.A., December 8–12, 1991.

3. I will be focusing on Catholic expressions of intentional community life, although most intentional communities display a strong ecumenical spirit.

4. See Bernard Lee and Michael Cowan, *Dangerous Memories,* pp. 90–91.

5. Michael Cowan makes a similar distinction in his description of the life of a marginal house church, "Now You Are the Body of Christ," in Evelyn and James Whitehead, ed., *Community of Faith: Crafting Christian Communities Today,* pp. 113–23. In her study of small community life in Australia, Mary Britt notes that "two streams of development are clearly recognizable: renewal programs initiated by church leaders as a means to revitalise parishes, and grassroots initiatives in community building, undertaken independently of church structures." See *In Search of New Wineskins,* p. 20. See also my paper "Small Christian Communities: In the Mainstream and on the Margins," *Compass* 26/1 (Autumn 1992): 26–32.

6. Michael Mason, "Nurturing Small Faith Communities." Adapted from Workshop notes given at the *Gathering National Conference,* September 1989, Sydney.

7. Arthur Baranowski, *Creating Small Faith Communities,* p. 89.

8. Ibid., p. 23.

9. Leonardo Boff, *Ecclesiogenesis,* citing sociologist Pedro Demo, p. 6.

10. David Prior, *The Church in the Home*, p. 179.

11. Robert and Julia Banks, *The Home Church*, p. 111.

12. Cited by Prior in *The Church in the Home*, p. 60.

13. I sometimes refer to *intentional* Christian communities as *marginal* Christian communities to distinguish this expression of small community life from the parish-based, mainstream version.

14. Lee and Cowan, *Dangerous Memories*, pp. 1–2.

15. See Philip Berryman's and Pedro A. Ribeiro De Oliveira's reflections on the tension between base communities and the parochial system, in Eugene Bianchi and Rosemary Radford Ruether, eds. *A Democratic Catholic Church*, pp. 128–55.

16. Banks, *The Home Church*, p. 142.

17. Jim Cranswick, review of *Creating Small Faith Communities*, by Arthur Baranowski, in *Communities Australia* 2/1 (March 1989), p. 7. It is interesting to note that the Australian diocese of Townsville, which is attempting a restructuring of the diocese according to small Christian communities, has chosen to avoid using the word "parish" because it is too well identified with an established model it wants to break with. The report refers to smaller units of church as "Catholic communities" or "Ecclesial communities," not as parishes. See the report, *Never-Ending Story*, Task Force Final Report, September 13, 1991, pp. 59–65.

18. As Rosemary Haughton points out, we generally think of "church" as something scaled down, as something very big that has been divided up. Yet "church" is something we encounter in the localized experience, and each time we encounter that experience of church, in however small a situation, we are encountering church in the full sense. See "The Emerging Church" in *A New Heart for a New World*, pp. 138–39. Robert Banks, in analyzing Paul's understanding of church in New Testament times, makes a similar point; see *Paul's Idea of Community*, pp. 73–74. See also Bernard Lee and Michael Cowan, *Dangerous Memories*, pp. 19–28.

19. Peter C. Hodgson, *Revisioning the Church*, p. 87.

20. This eucharistic expression goes by many names among intentional Christian communities: Eucharist, agape meal, table fellowship, table ritual, sharing bread and wine, to name a few.

21. From the point of view of the current discipline of the Catholic church, there are obvious difficulties with intentional communities celebrating eucharist, especially those that are distinctively "lay-based" and grassroots. Yet, as Edward Schillebeeckx has shown, the strong connection between the ordained priest and the sacrament of the eucharist has not always been the case. In the early churches, eucharistic presidency was not tied to a sacramental power received in ordination, but with the pastoral leadership of community presidence. Ordination was to community leadership, and eucharistic presidency was derivative from community presidency. Moreover, in the early church communities the action of the eucharist was centered on the "we" of the *ecclesia*, not the "I" of the presider. For a brief account of Schillebeeckx's historico-theological study, see his chapter, "The Christian Community and its Office-Bearers," in *Concilium: The Right of a Community to a Priest*, pp. 95–133.

22. For further discussion, see my paper "Reclaiming Eucharist at the Heart of Small Community Life," *Compass* 27/4 (Summer 1993), pp. 18–23.

23. Rosemary Radford Ruether, *Women-Church*, p. 61.

24. These responses are taken from a survey I conducted of some fifty intentional

Christian communities. Responses came from communities meeting in Australia, the United States, and, to a lesser degree, the United Kingdom. I also spent some time visiting communities meeting in the Boston area of the United States.

25. Rebecca Chopp, *The Power to Speak*, p. 74.

26. Walter Brueggemann, *Interpretation and Obedience*, p. 128.

27. Ibid., p. 127.

28. Ibid., p. 134.

29. Chopp, *The Power to Speak*, p. 16.

30. Ibid., p. 128.

31. Gerald Arbuckle, *Out of Chaos*, p. 182.

32. David Power, "Households of Faith in the Coming Church," p. 238.

33. Edward Schillebeeckx, "The Christian Community and its Office-Bearers," p. 121. See also Edward Schillebeeckx, *The Church with a Human Face*, pp. 254–58.

34. Boff, *Ecclesiogenesis*, p. 7.

35. Ibid., p. 7.

36. Bernard Lee, "A Socio-Historical Theology of Charism."

37. Victor Turner, *The Ritual Process*, see esp. chap. 3.

38. Ibid., p. 128.

39. Tom Driver, *The Magic of Ritual*, p. 165. Driver provides further commentary and critique on Turner's work on pp. 227–38.

40. Turner, *The Ritual Process*, p. 129.

41. Evelyn Whitehead, "Leadership and Power: A View from the Social Sciences," in Michael Cowan, ed., *Alternative Futures for Worship: Leadership in Community*, pp. 42–46. See also Richard Schoenherr, "Power and Authority in Organized Religion: Disaggregating the Phenomenological Core." *Sociological Analysis* 47 (1987): 52–71.

42. Radford Ruether reveals the workings of this dynamic throughout Christian history; see *Women-Church*, pp. 11–40.

43. Boff, *Ecclesiogenesis*, p. 8.

44. Ibid., p. 8.

45. Power, "Households of Faith in the Coming Church," citing N. Luhmann, p. 240.

46. Radford Ruether, *Women-Church*, p. 32.

47. Ibid., p. 39.

48. Robert Bellah et al., *The Good Society*, see esp. pp. 3–18, 40.

49. Radford Ruether, *Women-Church*, p. 39.

50. Ibid., p. 33.

51. Ibid., p. 63.

52. Chopp makes this point also in *The Power to Speak*, p. 76.

53. Mark C. Taylor, *Erring*, p. 10.

54. Turner, *The Ritual Process*, see p. 95.

55. Taylor, *Erring*, citing Norman Brown, p. 173.

56. Friedrich Nietzsche, *The Will to Power*, section 481, as reprinted in "Interpretation," p. 53.

57. Hans-Georg Gadamer, *Truth and Method*, p. 307.

58. Thomas H. Groome, *Sharing Faith*, pp. 223–25.

59. David Tracy, *Plurality and Ambiguity*, p. 9.

60. See Gadamer, *Truth and Method*, pp. 276–84. See also David Tracy, *Plurality and Ambiguity*, pp. 47–50.

61. Andreas Huyssen, "Mapping the Postmodern," p. 12.

62. Tracy, *The Analogical Imagination*, p. 343.

63. J. B. Metz, "The 'One World': A Challenge to Western Christianity," p. 205.

64. Joseph O'Leary, *Questioning Back: The Overcoming of Metaphysics in the Christian Tradition*, see pp. 124, 203–25.

65. See David Biale's comment on Scholem's work in *Gershom Scholem: Kabbalah and Counter-History*, p. 80.

66. Rosemary Radford Ruether surveys some of these traditions in *Sexism and God-Talk*, pp. 20–46.

67. Many scholars have engaged in the important task of reclaiming the Jewish origins of Christianity. See, e.g., Bernard Lee, *The Galilean Jewishness of Jesus;* James Charlesworth, ed., *Jesus' Jewishness: Exploring the Place of Jesus in Early Judaism;* John Dominic Crossan, *The Historical Jesus: The Life of a Mediterranean Jewish Peasant;* J. Andrew Overman, *Matthew's Gospel and Formative Judaism;* Alan Segal, *Rebecca's Children: Judaism and Christianity in the Roman World;* Geza Vermes, *Jesus the Jew.*

68. See, e.g., Carol Christ, *Laughter of Aphrodite: Reflections on a Journey to the Goddess;* Merlin Stone, *When God Was a Woman;* Elinor Gadon, *The Once and Future Goddess;* Marija Gimbutas, *The Language of the Goddess.*

69. See, e.g., Leonard Swidler, *After the Absolute: The Dialogical Future of Religious Reflection;* John Hick and Paul Knitter, eds., *The Myth of Christian Uniqueness: Toward a Pluralistic Theology of Religions.*

70. Gerald Bruns, *Hermeneutics Ancient and Modern*, p. 208.

71. Leon Klenicki and Geoffrey Wigoder, eds., *A Dictionary of the Jewish-Christian Dialogue*, pp. 46–48.

72. Edmond Jabès, *From the Desert to the Book*, p. 64.

73. The notion of "effective history" is taken from Hans-Georg Gadamer, *Truth and Method*, see pp. 300–341. David Tracy speaks of it as the "Christian fact" in *Blessed Rage for Order*, p. 60 n. 33.

74. Edmond Jabès, *The Book of Margins*, p. 40.

75. Ibid., p. 10.

76. W. Dow Edgerton, *The Passion of Interpretation*, p. 12.

77. Ibid., see p. 41.

78. On the disclosive and transformative potential of a religious tradition's classic expressions, see David Tracy, *The Analogical Imagination*, pp. 99–153.

79. This phrase was suggested to me in a conversation with Mary Boys.

80. Jacques Derrida, *Writing and Difference*, p. 75.

81. Paul Auster, "Book of the Dead: An Interview with Edmond Jabès," in Eric Gould, ed., *The Sin of the Book*, p. 22. While I see the emancipatory interest of an exilic hermeneutics as a key educational issue for intentional communities, I believe it is equally important not to gloss over or too readily discharge the powerfully disturbing claim it makes. A related educational issue emerges here: learning how to live with ambiguity, indeterminacy, and endlessly ongoing interpretation that defers any possibility of sufficiency or closure.

82. John Caputo, *Radical Hermeneutics*, p. 213.

83. Richard Bernstein, *Beyond Objectivism and Relativism*, p. 229.

PART ONE:
IN THE BOOK

To trust what outlasts us.
To face the next inquiry.
Yesterday is an avid question.

To be in the book. To figure in the book of questions, to be a part of it. To be responsible for a word or a sentence, a stanza or a chapter.

To be able to say: "I am in the book. The book is my world, my country, my roof, and my riddle. The book is my breath and my rest."

I get up with the page that is turned. I lie down with the page put down. To be able to reply: "I belong to the race of words, which homes are built with" — when I know full well that this answer is still another question, that the home is constantly threatened.

I will evoke the book and provoke the questions.

"What is your lot?"
"To open the book."

"You try to be free through writing. How wrong. Every word unveils another tie." — Reb Léca.

[Yet Reb Elat says]: *"Love your ties to their last splendor, and you will be free."*

Freedom consists in going back to the sources.

("You show the book.
You make the walls come down." — Reb Kanah)

The open book occupies only a little space on the table, yet the space it engages is huge.

Only what continues to agitate our minds, to capture our thoughts, to appropriate our hearts from generation to generation, would be able to endure. . . .

What persists is what we stop at. . . . We give it duration. . . . We privilege it. . . . We live only in the event's reverberation. We cannot live in a frozen moment — we would be dead.

"Do not destroy the book. Two lives are sheltered there."
Edmond Jabès

Can link this to
place

CHAPTER ONE

DIALOGICAL HERMENEUTICS

An image often associated with hermeneutics is that of a text and a reader. Yet W. Dow Edgerton suggests that hermeneutics also speaks of a third "hidden presence." We see a reader and a text — we see only two — but "between the two, there is a third." According to Edgerton, the question hermeneutics asks is, "Who is the third?"[1] In other words, what happens between a text and a reader; what transpires between them? Hermeneutics is concerned with questions and possibilities "about the interpreter, about the text, about their relationship."[2]

David Linge, commenting on Hans-Georg Gadamer's work, notes that the relationship between a text and an interpreter is from the outset one of familiarity and alienation. The interpretive movement attempts to bridge the gap that exists between our familiar worlds of understanding and the strange, provoking worlds we encounter in texts. Hermeneutics "encompasses both the alien that we strive to understand and the familiar that we already understand."[3] Perhaps the mysterious "third" to which Edgerton refers represents this sense of a text's "otherness" that is both absent and yet present to us. When we think, for example, of a religious community's sacred texts, we can see that these texts are familiarly present to the community as the tradition that constitutes their identity. Yet such texts also generate continual dispute, dialogue, and reform within the community as it grapples with "a past that is not one with the present but an other to the present."[4] Hermeneutics, therefore, begins in acknowledging the gap that exists between our texts and our lives, yet proceeds by holding that gap open, in order for a new meaning, a new understanding, a "hidden third" to emerge: the wound of absence bleeding presence — tradition's life-blood.

The relationship between a text and an interpreter, between the past and the present, is the leading hermeneutical question in Hans-Georg Gadamer's work. As we shall see in this chapter, Gadamer's hermeneutics highlights the operative force of tradition in our lives. Our horizons are radically "prejudiced" and shaped by our belonging-to and participation-in history and tradition. However, Gadamer's hermeneutics also highlights the questions and concerns that the present brings to bear in the ongoing life of tradition. Tradition grows and changes in ways that constantly reconstruct what it considers to be paradigmatic, always norming itself anew. Here we face a key hermeneutical and educational question: how do we sustain a community's self-identity and at the same time allow for a community's freedom to reconstruct identity which is responsive to new and changing circumstances? Gadamer asks the question along these lines: How does the past in which we stand remain itself when we know it must become different to itself and thereby made relevant for the present, in order to survive as a living tradition?[5] Similarly, Gerald Bruns poses the hermeneutical question this way: "How do we stand with respect to all that comes down to us from the past?"[6] Because we encounter both our own and others' traditions as strange and familiar, Bruns considers this question the same as asking "How do we stand with respect to the world and others with whom we find ourselves?"[7]

We can see from the questions raised above that hermeneutics is concerned with a past (a text), a present (a reader), and the question about their relationship in shaping the future (writing). These are metaphors that need not be identified in all cases with written expression. *Text* can be understood metaphorically as whatever it is in the past that claims our interpretive attention: texts, symbols, events, beliefs, practices, and so on. *Reading* can be understood not only as a reading of texts but also a reading of our present reality. And *writing* can be understood as the act of construing something new through our present reading of what is given in the past. We interpret as much by looking for what might be the case as we do by asking what has been or is the case. As Edgerton suggests, hermeneutics is rooted in the *textual* nature of our experience, by which we gather our lives together through narrative patterns, symbols, and relationships to construct our worlds of belonging.[8] Because of its enduring and repeatable nature, this textual reality has a quality of the "past" to it. As such, hermeneutics always talks about the past, but only because it is concerned with the future; it dwells on what is repeatable but only to point away from it toward the unexpected. Why hermeneutics, why interpretation? "One *interprets* because of the unavoidable presence of the past; one *interprets* for the sake of the future; one *interprets* in order to shape the story of the future by reshaping the story of the past."[9]

The Effective Hold of Belonging

The past, as "all that comes down to us" and as "all that within which we stand" looms large in hermeneutics. This emphasis on our radical belongingness to the process of tradition and history is quite jarring to our modern sensibilities. We are profoundly shaped by the Enlightenment project's quest for freedom from all that constrains and limits us: our passions, our unconscious, our received beliefs, our cultural and religious heritage. Modernity represents a "ruthless forgetting" of the shared culture, beliefs, practices, and symbols that shape our human world.[10] We can trace a major source of this forgetting to the "doubting" philosophy of René Descartes, whose thought represents the beginnings of Enlightenment thinking. Descartes sought to find a secure and certain foundation for knowledge that was not influenced by presupposed beliefs. From a way of knowing too bound by tradition and its prejudices, Descartes found the certainty he was after in a way of knowing bound only to a thinking and reasoning subject. His famous "I think, therefore I am" meant that whatever else I may doubt, I cannot doubt my own ability to think, to reason. The prejudiced knowing of tradition and history was replaced by an ahistorical thinking self that generated its own certitude and became the ultimate point of reference for knowledge of the world.[11] This Enlightenment epistemology was later encapsulated in Immanuel Kant's motto: "Have courage to use your own reason!" — and free yourself from a blind obedience to tradition's imposing tutelage.[12]

The Enlightenment, therefore, turned its back on tradition and placed its trust in reason as the timeless and ultimate ground of knowledge and understanding. Modern consciousness represents a celebration of humanity's capacity for autonomous, critical, and rational thought, freed of the shackling prejudices and false prejudgments of the past. It is based on the conviction that once unburdened by tradition, humanity could achieve a "pure self-consciousness" that would generate a freedom from all that constrains us.[13] As Gadamer notes, for the enlightened thinker, "it is not tradition but reason that constitutes the ultimate source of authority."[14] In this age of reason, science soon came to assume the dominant role as the "gatekeeper" of truth.[15] Following the rule of Cartesian doubt, scientific rationality attempted to completely exclude prejudice to arrive at a disinterested, objective grasp of truth.[16] Reason, no longer embodied in communal traditions, became more and more the possession of a detached, knowing subject apprehending an idle, passive object. Knowledge came to be equated with a subject who is in control, and reason as a purely instrumental way to attain power and progress through technological mastery over the world. In short, as Richard Palmer notes, science and humanism became the watchwords in an age that placed the human subject as "the center and measure of all things."[17]

The Enlightenment left many positive legacies, including the rise of the modern state, advances in science and technology, and the development of a critical consciousness.[18] However, as Walter Brueggemann argues, it also left us with a

Gender

world constructed through the privilege of a white, male, Western, colonial hegemony.[19] The "project of objectivity" led to a "Cartesian masculinization of
thought" whereby certitude came to be linked with a rational, disinterested, and
disembodied mind, and objectivity with masculine power and domination: over
the earth (which was considered as bodily, material, and peculiarly "feminine")
and over non-Western cultures (which were considered inferior, primitive, and
"irrational," lacking Western culture's superior grasp of truth).[20]

Perhaps one of the most influential critiques of modernity's "Cartesianism" is
found in the philosophy of Martin Heidegger. According to Heidegger, modernity's "ruthless forgetting" represents a forgetfulness of our radical "being-in-
the-world." Understanding is not so much an epistemological question of how
we know the world. Rather, it is the ontological condition of being-in-the-world.
It is not an activity of consciousness by which we "know being." Rather, the way
we know, the way we understand, is the way we belong to the world, is our being.
As Gadamer notes, for Heidegger "the real question is not in what way being can
be understood but in what way understanding *is* being. . . ."[21] We never stand
over and above the world in order to know the world. We are not bare, thinking
subjects who reach out to know a world of objects. Rather, we are absorbed and
immersed in the world, never over against it as a subject to an object. Our situatedness in the world is not something we need to overcome; rather, it is our very
way of being — not a burden on knowledge, but the very condition of its possibility.[22] Commenting on Heidegger's work, Patricia Waugh writes as follows:

> Heidegger developed a critique of Cartesianism as the founding methodology of
> modernity: one which he saw as productive of the violences of the West and inade-
> quate as a ground for knowledge. . . . Instead of experiencing world as a texture
> through which we come to be, world is observed as an inert material body to be
> manipulated through a series of dualisms generated by the subject-object split
> (mind/body, spirit/matter, reason/emotion, masculinity/femininity). Modernity is
> thus a condition defined by a characteristic denial or disavowal of Being-in-the-
> world. A detached subjectivity has come to stand over an inert nature, speculating,
> observing, judging and manipulating it for its own ends. All relations become instru-
> mental. Behind each is an empty subjectivity swallowed up in calculative thinking,
> radically disembedded from world. . . . Heidegger advocates instead a return to a
> sense of situatedness in a world which pre-exists us and cannot be consciously
> manipulated or defined, but through which we come into being as it "worlds"
> through us. We can only come to be what we are within the world and through the
> textures of understanding which it provides. . . .[23]

Heidegger claims that all understanding is rooted in pre-understandings or
"fore-structures" that arise from our being located ("thrown") in a particular his-

torical time and place. Such fore-structures act as the horizon of meaning through which understanding becomes possible. In other words, all meanings are projected on the basis of our embeddedness in prior traditions and knowledge.[24] At work here is what Gadamer calls "effective-historical consciousness," by which he means the operative force of tradition in the lives of those who stand within it.[25] As "thrown" into this world — this language, this history, this tradition — our understanding is situated by a past that inevitably involves us in the "effective history" of a heritage of charged meanings.

The past looms large in hermeneutics because all interpretation is shaped by the historical, cultural, and religious traditions to which we belong. Gadamer claims that the Enlightenment's attempt to attain unprejudiced knowledge freed from the constraints of tradition is itself a "prejudice against prejudice."[26] To the Enlightenment thinker, Gadamer asks the following question:

> Does being situated within traditions really mean being subject to prejudices and limited in one's freedom? Is not, rather, all human existence, even the freest, limited and qualified in various ways? If this is true, the idea of an absolute reason is not a possibility for historical humanity. Reason exists for us only in concrete, historical terms — i.e., it is not its own master but remains constantly dependent on the given circumstances in which it operates.[27]

Prejudices constitute our very being-in-the-world.[28] In this sense, we cannot totally escape our prejudices, and this is part of what Heidegger means by our "thrownness" in the world, and what Gadamer means by our human finitude, and what Jabès hints at when he says: "Every word unveils another tie." This leads Gadamer to claim that "what before appeared as prejudicial to the concept of science and method, as only a 'subjective' approach to historical knowledge, today is placed in the foreground of fundamental inquiry."[29] Genuine understanding involves not the attempt to escape our belonging to tradition, but our participation in the event or happening of tradition: "Our usual relationship to the past is not characterized by distancing and freeing ourselves from tradition. Rather, we are always situated within traditions."[30] In other words, each of us belongs to tradition and history far more than they belong to us.[31] Moreover, it is this very belonging that makes understanding possible. Our historical situatedness in a particular language and culture is no barrier to understanding but the very condition of its possibility. As Gadamer says, "historical consciousness fails to understand its own nature if, in order to understand, it seeks to exclude what alone makes understanding possible."[32]

We may call this historical consciousness a move toward the postmodern, in the sense that it represents a shift beyond modernity's claims regarding the universality of reason.[33] A postmodern consciousness deeply suspects the optimism concealed in Western notions of reason. Even science, the supposed anchor of the modern age of reason, has not escaped the postmodern critique.[34] Our situation is now acknowledged to be far more historically conditioned, pluralistic, and ambiguous than reason's clear and distinct ideas would have us believe. To enter the postmodern world is, in effect, to re-enter the interpretive discourses of our cultural, religious, and social frameworks. If we find this passage unnerving, there is now little recourse open to us other than a recourse to a reality without language, without tradition, without history, without "place" or culture.[35] As Linell Cady notes, the textual character of hermeneutics has now replaced the rational character of science and modernity: "Not science, with its univocal access to reality, but literature, with its creation and exploration of multiple worlds, emerges as the paradigmatic postmodern genre."[36] The way in which all forms of knowledge are shaped by the force of prejudice and historical traditions has made hermeneutics a central concern in a variety of discourses, whether scientific, artistic, literary, religious, historical, or philosophical. Our conversations remain limited and fragile, partial and necessary exercises embedded within the living actualities of culture, society, and history.[37] This postmodern awareness is, according to Gerald Bruns, the "cold recognition, after years of radical aspiration, that there is no breaking free of the systems that contain us."[38] According to one of our most celebrated postmodernists, Jacques Derrida, we face a keen realization today that "we must begin *wherever we are* . . . in a text where we already believe ourselves to be."[39] As Bruns suggests, tradition is something that "cannot be done away with." It represents that "which must be faced . . . suffered or lived through."[40] "What is our lot?" asks Jabès. "To open the book."

The Circle of Belonging

If the past looms large in hermeneutics, we need to ask, What is our relationship to this past? If we cannot disengage ourselves from "all that within which we stand," what does it mean to belong? Gadamer stresses that interpretive understanding is always occurring through our participation in tradition that not only informs and shapes who we are but is also in the process of being reshaped and understood differently. This response stands in contrast to our usual tendency of reifying tradition as something given or determinate, something objective — a tendency we inherited from the Enlightenment. The Enlightenment viewed tradition as something that could be overthrown by replacing the authority of tradition with the authority of reason. The high claims of reason, however, spawned another response to the question of tradition: romanticism. With the growing dominance of an overconfident scientific rationality, romanticism reacted by seeking to reestablish the value of the past and tradition. Yet romanticism fell prey to the same Enlightenment ideals it sought to challenge. As Gadamer notes, its restoration project was itself influenced by the Enlightenment claims of objectivity, giving rise to the historical sciences of the nineteenth century: "the step to objective knowledge of the historical world, which stands on a par with the knowledge of nature achieved by science."[41]

The hermeneutical projects of Schleiermacher and Dilthey represent this thrust to restore the truth and relevance of the past by placing the meaning of a traditionary text in its past historical context. The aim of understanding a text became one of leaving behind our present situation and leaping back into the past to grasp the original intention of the author or the historical spirit and times in which a text was originally conceived. In other words, it was suggested that we could best understand a past text by reconstructing the original authorial intention along with the original historical context of which both the author and the text were products.[42]

Gadamer's work is influenced by the theological hermeneutics of Rudolf Bultmann, which offered a different response to the romantic and historicist approach to hermeneutics. As a student of Martin Heidegger, Bultmann shared Heidegger's conviction that it was not entirely possible for us to "leap" out of our situation to somehow recapture the intentions and meanings of a past situation. Rather, Bultmann was insistent that all our understandings are mediated to us through our participation in history. In this sense, it is not possible to interpret a text without already bringing to it the assumptions and pre-understandings that have shaped our historical horizons. "To understand history," writes Bultmann, "is possible only for one who does not stand over against it as a neutral, non-participating spectator but who stands within it and shares responsibility for it."[43] For Bultmann, it is our current questions and concerns that give fundamental shape to our belonging to history. We do not understand history by bracketing these questions to somehow reclaim a past understanding. Rather, we participate in historical knowing through the very "life relation" (our questions and concerns) with which we approach the subject matter presented to us in a text. The meaning of a past text is not "back there," given in the past, rather it is a "living concern," an event of understanding that occurs "only when the subject matter with which the text is concerned is also of concern to us."[44] We learn from Bultmann that if we do not stand over against historical tradition, neither does historical tradition stand over against us. The past is not something objective or given that stands over us and determines how we understand. Nor is it something external or bygone that we can stand over, as a subject standing over against an object. Rather, we ourselves participate in the process of tradition.

Gadamer reiterates Heidegger's insistence that our radical belonging to tradition cannot be set apart from the way this belonging is constantly projecting new possibilities for its future.[45] The twin moments of our *thrownness* in historical tradition and our *projection* of future possibilities "must always be thought together."[46] Shaun Gallagher notes that if we understand tradition as past, then, according to Heidegger, this does not mean that it is temporally removed from us. Rather, human existence *is* its past.

> We always find ourselves with a past that does not simply follow behind, but goes in advance, defining the contexts by which we come to interpret the world. Despite the fact that traditions operate for the most part "behind our backs," they are already there, ahead of us, conditioning our interpretations.[47]

It is from within this horizon of belonging that we project possibilities for our lives. In other words, although we are always conditioned by our particular social and historical location, it is this very facticity of our existence that enables us to project future possibilities and new understandings of ourselves and our world. Prejudices do not only effectively hold us, nor are they necessarily erroneous; they also open us to the world, as Gadamer says: "Prejudices are biases of our openness to the world."[48]

If interpretation theory reveals that our horizons are radically prejudiced and shaped by our belonging to tradition, it also reveals that this belonging opens us to new possibilities, to different understandings, to alternate ways of thinking, behaving, and belonging to tradition. What we are describing here is Gadamer's presentation of the hermeneutical circle.[49]

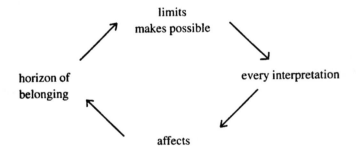

To say that our horizon makes possible every interpretation is to say that our historical situatedness presents no barrier to understanding but is rather the horizon from which understanding becomes possible. We always interpret as members of historical, cultural, symbolic communities. To say that our historically effected horizon limits every interpretation is to say that all pre-understandings are particular and perspectival, given in particular historical structures and social locations. We always dwell in the shadow and the light of our given assumptive worlds. To say that every interpretation, in turn, has its effect on the prior assumptions (horizon) that made it possible is to say that whenever an event of interpretation occurs, our pre-understandings are put at risk and modified to some degree. As Gadamer says, "we understand differently, if we understand at all."[50]

The hermeneutical circle suggests that we constantly shape tradition's becoming even as tradition effectively shapes us. As Gadamer tells us: "Tradition is not simply a permanent precondition; rather, *we produce it ourselves* inasmuch as we understand, participate in the evolution of tradition, and hence further determine it ourselves."[51] The past is never purely past, but the past as it addresses us in the present. Or as Jabès tells us: "Only what continues to agitate our minds, to capture our thoughts, to appropriate our hearts from generation to generation, would be able to endure."

This implies that historical tradition, if it is to be understood according to its address toward us, "must be understood at every moment, in every concrete situation, in a new and different way. Understanding here is always application."[52] "Does this not mean," asks Gadamer, that historical tradition "always needs to be restated? And does not this restatement always take place through its being related to the present?"[53] In other words, the past can only address us if its claim to truth provokes a question for us in the present. In this sense, both our own contemporary horizon and the horizon of tradition to which we belong are constantly in play with each other. The resulting dynamic is that interpretive activity stands between the past we belong to and our current questions and concerns that arise as we seek new possibilities and meanings for our future. As Georgia Warnke notes, "the past acquires its meaning in the light of present experiences and anticipations while the meaning of the present and anticipation of the future are conditioned by the way in which the past is understood."[54] Or, as Gadamer says, understanding is "participating in an event of tradition . . . in which past and present are constantly mediated."[55]

Hermeneutics, therefore, involves an encounter or dialogue between two sets of prejudices or historical horizons: that of the traditionary text or text analogue with its claims and concerns, and that of the interpreter's own historical situation with its questions and possibilities. "This between," writes Gadamer, "is the true locus of hermeneutics."[56] What emerges is an event of truth belonging neither to the past nor to the present, but something found only precariously and ambiguously in both. "Do not destroy the book," Jabès tells us, "Two lives are sheltered there."

Hermeneutical Dialogue

Given Gadamer's insight that all interpretation engages the expectations, questions, and concerns of our contemporary situation, we need to ask whether our interpretive activity leads us into a subjectivist position; that is, whether our interpretations are nothing more than we want them to be. Yet if our own experience is itself effected by the prejudice of the historical tradition in which we stand, we also need to ask, Are we simply locked into our prejudiced tradition with no way of attaining a critical distance from that tradition?[57] When Gadamer claims, for example, that our effective belonging to tradition illumines and makes possible our interpretation of tradition, marginal thinkers immediately raise the question of whether there is a difference between a situated perspective that illumines the meaning of tradition and one that simply legitimates it or even distorts it. Feminist thinkers, for example, are acutely aware that the effective history of Christian tradition has served to bury women's experience, keeping it silent and subservient to the authoritative norms of a patriarchal ordering. How can we be sure that the prejudices and assumptions we bring to bear in interpretive activity are not fundamentally distorted? Gadamer asks the question this way: "How can we break the spell of our own foremeanings?"[58] Or, as Georgia Warnke puts it, "We seem to be able to revise the prejudices we have inherited from tradition only by assuming the validity of other prejudices the tradition contains. . . . How can we ever learn to reject the truth we have assumed?"[59]

In responding to this question, Gadamer suggests that we do not primarily belong to a tradition in the sense of ideological support and maintenance of that tradition but in the sense that we are always already part of tradition and are provoked and shaped by it. Moreover, belonging to a tradition does not mean we simply adopt the views of tradition; rather, we continually and critically modify tradition according to changing historical circumstances that raise new questions and concerns. "It is a grave misunderstanding," writes Gadamer, "to assume that emphasis on the essential factor of tradition which enters into all understanding implies uncritical acceptance of tradition and sociopolitical conservatism." He goes on to say that "the confrontation of our historic tradition is *always a critical challenge of this tradition. . . . Every experience is such a confrontation.*"[60]

On the one hand, Gadamer affirms that the classic texts and symbols of tradition shape us and provoke us. Our prejudice is not set aside but properly "brought into play by being put at risk."[61] Just as our prejudices open us to the text, so too the text opens us to our prejudices. We need to be open to the text and allow its claim on us to risk our prejudices. This is Gadamer's response to the charge that our interpretations are nothing more than we want them to be. The claims of tradition are not just arbitrary claims.

On the other hand, our understanding of tradition is contingent upon our historical situatedness. Interpretation always involves "application" — not in the sense of applying a fixed, past meaning to a new situation, but in the sense that tradition only comes to realization in and through the happening of interpretation. In other words, contemporary understanding is "understanding differently" because it is understanding that is shaped by different historical concerns and questions in which tradition is coming to be in a new form, representing a new "happening" of tradition.[62] This is Gadamer's response to the charge that we are locked into our prejudiced tradition. At one point Gadamer will stress one position, at another point he will stress the other. His responses can sometimes appear contradictory. Yet he is not so much caught in a dilemma, as he is articulating an abiding tension: "Every encounter with tradition," writes Gadamer, "involves the experience of a tension between the text and the present. The hermeneutic task consists in not covering up this tension by attempting a naive assimilation of the two but in consciously bringing it out."[63] According to Georgia Warnke:

> Gadamer's hermeneutics attempts to move beyond both the conservatism of simply adopting the views of tradition and the subjectivism of interpreting it as a verification of one's own prejudices. Hermeneutic understanding rather participates in the self-formation of an interpretive tradition in which each new effort to understand reflects a new education and a new form of the tradition itself.[64]

The tension described above leads to the necessity for a hermeneutic dialogue. Whereas the hermeneutic circle gives the impression of going round and round endlessly, dialogue is an image of to-and-fro movement in which the truth of one's own horizon and that of the text's horizon "are both preserved in a new stage of the tradition and canceled as adequate positions on their own."[65] As Gary Aylesworth notes, this event of understanding "is both a fusion of horizons between epochs and an epochal event itself. The achievement of continuity among previously discontinuous moments is something 'new,' and thus presents a discontinuity on its own. In this way, the dialogical process remains open. . . ."[66]

Gerald Bruns reminds us that the notion of a fusion of horizons should not be read as a synthesis or integration of different perspectives into a new totality.[67] If this were the case, asks Gadamer, why "speak of the fusion of horizons and not simply of the formation of the one horizon, whose bounds are set in the depths of tradition?"[68] In other words, differences are not annulled or absorbed for the sake of maintaining a tradition's continuity; rather, the tension of differences generates the play of horizonal encounter. The fusion of horizons results from the encounter between different claims, never the effacing of differences into a unified or identical perspective. It is always, in David Tracy's words, an "identity-in-difference," which is not a bland acceptance or assimilation of different horizons, but a mutually critical appropriation between them.[69] The following sketch may help us capture something of the interpretive dynamic represented in Gadamer's hermeneutics:

Openness to subject-matter/provoking question

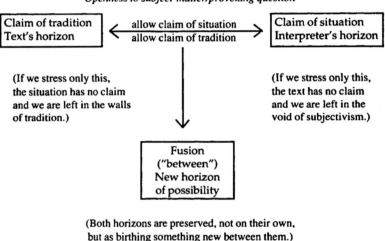

| Claim of tradition Text's horizon | ← allow claim of situation
← allow claim of tradition → | Claim of situation Interpreter's horizon |

(If we stress only this, the situation has no claim and we are left in the walls of tradition.)

(If we stress only this, the text has no claim and we are left in the void of subjectivism.)

Fusion
("between")
New horizon
of possibility

(Both horizons are preserved, not on their own, but as birthing something new between them.)

affects   affects

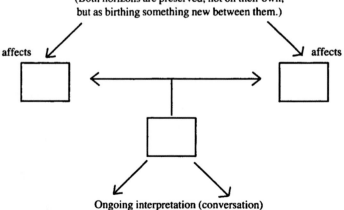

Ongoing interpretation (conversation)
in a historically effected tradition

Gadamer's hermeneutics is helpful in suggesting that tradition is not a static entity we consent to; rather, it is a living, dynamic activity we participate in — and through that participation, tradition is constantly "happening," "occurring," "coming to be." According to Gadamer,

> this occurrence means the coming into play, the playing out, of tradition in its constantly widening possibilities of significance and resonance . . . something comes into being that had not existed before and that exists from now on . . . something emerges that is contained in neither of the partners by themselves.[70]

"Historical tradition," writes Gadamer, "can be understood only as something always in the process of being defined by the course of events."[71] This is a celebration of the movement of meaning and tradition through history by means of continuing interpretations and their effects. In other words, it is in the event of interpretation that tradition itself happens. Tradition vanishes utterly when it is not interpreted. If we inquire into the life of tradition we would discover nothing more nor less than that which emerges in its continuing interpretations.[72] Tradition's way of being is to be different — only in this way does it remain itself. It is present only with each age in which it is understood.[73] Interpretation is not secondary; rather, tradition *is* its interpretation and lives in the multiple possibilities of its being. As Jabès suggests, "the space it engages is huge."

Between the Strange and the Familiar

It is important to note that Gadamer's understanding of tradition is closely tied to his understanding of language. Gadamer embraces the linguistic turn that is characteristic of twentieth-century thought, from Saussure and Wittgenstein to much contemporary literary theory. According to Gadamer, language does not just express but also constitutes experience. In other words, rather than simply *reflecting* meaning, language actually *produces* it. We cannot draw a distinction between language and the reality expressed in language, as though cultural expressions could change while the reality expressed in them remains the same. In a similar fashion, we cannot separate tradition from interpretive activity; rather, tradition lives in and through interpretive practice.[74] Gadamer speaks of tradition as "the conversation that we are" — tradition emerges and becomes what it is only in the conversation that it generates.[75]

There is little in Gadamer's writings to suggest that belonging to tradition — to "all that within which we stand" — implies a process either of exhaustion or inert imitation. Rather, there is always a vital element of freedom in tradition such that tradition never persists "because of the inertia of what once existed."[76] Gadamer highlights the participative and productive process of belonging, through which tradition is continually enlarging itself and growing in size. "By our participating in the things in which we are participating," Gadamer says, "we enrich them; they do not become smaller, but larger. The whole life of tradition consists exactly in this enrichment so that life is our culture and our past . . . always extending by participating."[77]

It is important to Gadamer (and Heidegger) that the German term for "belonging" (*gehören*) contains the root *hören*, which means to "listen to."[78] "We have heard [*gehört*]," Heidegger says, "when we belong to [*gehören*] what is said."[79] For Gadamer, belonging to tradition is like participating in a conversation, and central to the art of conversation is the process of listening: listening not just to each other, but a deeper listening that listens for "that to which we belong" in the to-and-fro of conversation.[80] This is a listening to what is being said between us, to what is leading our conversation and evoking its productive possibility. In this open mode of belonging and listening, we are no longer trying to dominate or control the conversation; rather, we willingly join with our conversation partner in a mutually participative process that brings out the nature of the subject matter (*Sache*) guiding us. We are listening for that which is emerging between us as a new, unthought possibility. In this sense, Bruns suggests that belonging to tradition means listening "for what remains unthought or unspoken in all that comes down to us from the past."[81] To belong to tradition, therefore, implies a "letting go" of tradition, listening to it so that we can release it, participating in it so that we can extend it, opening it up so that it can become more fully itself.[82]

The seeming paradox between "belonging" and "letting go" so that we can listen to what is emerging is likened by Gadamer to the way we are caught up in the play of a game. We belong to the game only when we let ourselves go and allow the game to play us, rather than we playing it.[83] Moreover, while we cannot play a game unless we have some familiarity with it, the game would never really be a game if it remained continually predictable. There is always an element of being played by the unexpected, the unfamiliar, the genuinely novel twists and turn of the game. The unfamiliar is never completely overcome by familiarity, but rather is that which enables play to happen. As Gallagher suggests, the hermeneutical situation is "not an imprisonment within a process of tradition which makes everything familiar." Rather, it provides "room to play" in which there is always an element of strangeness and unfamiliarity that requires some clearance to allow the play to happen.[84]

Whereas we are inclined to think of belonging to tradition in terms of its familiarity to us, as that which is "always the same," Gadamer suggests that if we truly listen to tradition we will hear it more according to its strange otherness than its familiar sameness. Though we are familiarly located in tradition, it is the alterity, strangeness, and unfamiliarity of tradition that "brings us up short" as an otherness that has something to say to us and that in the end refuses to fit our expectations and familiar understandings, thereby provoking us to revise or enlarge our initial horizon of understanding.[85] Commenting on this hermeneutical experience, Bruns writes as follows:

> In our encounter with a text that comes down to us from the past (or from another culture, or perhaps from our very midst), we always find that what the text says is not what we thought . . . but something else, something other that brings us up hard against the presuppositions or forestructures that we inhabit and that underwrite and make possible our efforts of understanding. The satirical effect of this encounter is to disrupt and fragment our self-possession. It is an event that alters our relation to the conceptual frameworks within which things are otherwise familiar and intelligible to us.[86]

Tradition becomes not a refuge of belonging nor a purely presupposed familiarity nor something that we can keep under control by making it fit our preconceptions or prevailing viewpoints; rather, it becomes something that refuses the "same" and impinges as "other."[87] Bruns reminds us that we must not "conflate and confuse tradition with the forms of cultural transmission that try to fix and control it." Instead of trying to "remove its strangeness," we need to enter its discourse to shake us free and release us from any presupposed familiarity.[88] As Gadamer says, openness to the otherness of tradition means "allowing tradition's claim . . . that it is has something to say to me . . . that I myself must accept that some things are against me."[89] In this sense, tradition is "that which says no to me,"[90] and hermeneutics is the "yes" to this "no." It is a recognition, along with Jabès, that while we belong to tradition — "to the race of words which homes are built with" — that this belonging is yet "still another question, that the home is constantly threatened."

The Priority of the Question

"Every experience worthy of its name," writes Gadamer, "thwarts an expectation."[91] In experience, there is a rupturing of expectations — something happens or we discover something that we did not expect, and our familiar world of understanding is put in question. For Gadamer, "experience is a process of disillusionment or disinvestiture that leaves us standing before the world without the protection of familiar concepts."[92] Experience, therefore, entails a certain negativity in which our plans and expectations break down, our purposes and desires are defeated. It is a painful process that teaches us the limitations and finitude of all our arrangements and expectations. The breakdown of expectation, however, is also a breakthrough into a new type of openness, a type of emancipation or releasement from some prior certainty or settled self-understanding. The experienced person, paradoxically, is someone who is open to new experience, because they are better disposed to expect the unexpected.[93]

According to Gadamer, experience places us in the realm of the question, which exposes us to the aporia of undecidability, the quandary that results when assurances and certainties no longer hold the way they used to. Yet hidden in a question's indeterminacy is its power to place things in the open, to break the fixity of dominant opinions, to keep things fluid and open to new possibilities.[94] "A question presses itself on us; we can no longer avoid it and persist in our accustomed opinion."[95] It is not so much we who raise questions; rather, questions arise or present themselves to us. We do not come to new understandings so much by coming to answers, as we do by questions that occur to us, "that break through into the open and thereby make an answer possible."[96]

Gadamer notes that although every writing of tradition appears as an assertion and hence a closure, it is in reality "the response to a prior question."[97] The interpreter's task, therefore, is to enter the world of this question, to ask, What is it (what question) provoked this text into being? "We can understand a text," Gadamer says, "only when we have understood the question to which it is an answer."[98] In entering the world of the text, we find that the text "is putting a question to us, the question that called it into being."[99] Yet we also find that this question — to which the text is an answer — "necessarily includes other possible answers."[100] We will inevitably bring into play our own questions as we listen for what the text has *not* said, as we seek answers it has not given to the questions we are raising today.[101] What emerges is a reciprocity of questioning whereby the text puts a question to us even as we raise questions of the text.

Gadamer gives a hermeneutical priority to the question because, in the to-and-fro of interpretive conversation, it is questioning that allows the subject matter to orient the conversation, rather than predetermined answers that push too hastily toward closure. "To conduct a conversation means to allow oneself to be conducted by the subject matter to which the partners in the dialogue are oriented."[102] Questioning keeps us open to where the conversation is leading in its emerging possibilities. Bernstein writes as follows:

> The conversation or dialogue that Gadamer takes to be the quintessence of hermeneutical understanding always evokes the memory of a living conversation or dialogue between persons. But Gadamer, in his analysis of dialogue and conversation, stresses not only the common bond and the genuine novelty that a turn in conversation may take but the mutuality, the respect required, the genuine seeking to listen to and understand what the other is saying, the openness to risk and test our opinions through such an encounter.[103]

Interpretive conversation becomes most productive where the conversation is uncertain, indeterminate — where the question comes into play and becomes a question, remains a question — where we realize that we do not know.[104] This is the very place where understanding begins. Gadamer tells us that "only the person who knows how to ask questions is able to persist in their questioning, which involves being able to preserve their orientation toward openness."[105] The same holds true in our conversation with tradition. The wandering question always has priority over the settled answer. Knowing that we do not know is to live within the openness of a question, of the still undetermined possibilities of both the situation and the tradition in which we find ourselves. In this clearing something new emerges and takes shape that did not exist before.

"To be in the book," Jabès says, is to belong to the "book of questions" — "I will evoke the book and provoke the questions." In a similar fashion, Gadamer claims that every encounter with the language of tradition "is an encounter with an unfinished event and is itself part of this event."[106] To belong to the "book of questions" means that our belonging to historical tradition is always a response to a question: the question posed by our belonging, and the becoming-something-other that every response elicits. "The new comes to be," writes Gadamer, "as the old is recollected in dissolution."[107] By granting a priority to the question, Gadamer is suggesting that whenever we engage our tradition, we are engaging a tradition that itself stands as an open question, and is thereby open to further conversation. Gadamer asserts that "the real and fundamental nature of a question is to make things indeterminate. Questions always bring out the undetermined possibilities of a thing."[108] This is the kind of open questioning that has not yet received a definitive answer, that brings both ourselves and the tradition out into the open. To come into conversation with tradition means, therefore, to understand that the questions to which the texts and symbols of tradition are a response are open ended and not closed. If the question remains open and not closed, then the response given by tradition is not definitive. Rather, it leads to further questions which merge with the interpreter's own questioning in the dialectical play between an interpreting community and the tradition.[109] What comes to expression in this conversation belongs between both partners; it is neither the horizon of the text, nor the horizon of the interpreter, but a new event of understanding that happens between them.

Perhaps we are in the realm here of Edgerton's hidden presence: "between the two, there is a third." A presence that hides itself — something that discloses meaning even as it conceals; something familiar even as it is strange; something that feels like home, yet distant as well; something old and yet new. Something that is always in-between — "this 'hermeneutical situation,' by which hermeneutics is always placed 'in the middle of things.'. . ."[110] The understanding we seek is never simply "there" to be discovered. Rather, it reveals itself only in and through the to-and-fro of interpretive conversation. It is an event, an event that we do not control (as a subject controlling an object); rather, it is an event of understanding that we get caught up in, an event that we belong to (rather than an object that belongs to us).[111] In this sense, hermeneutical experience has an ongoing and open character in which "meaning is always coming into being."[112] In the process of interpretive conversation, we "show the book," such that "the walls come down," revealing the hidden sources and questions of the book to which we belong.

Notes

The epigraphs introducing part 1 are from the following works of Edmond Jabès: *The Book of Resemblances*, 1. 99; *The Book of Questions*, 1. 31, 17, 37, 114–15, 387; *From the Desert to the Book*, pp. 27, 40–41; *The Book of Questions*, 1. 393.

1. W. Dow Edgerton, *The Passion of Interpretation*, p. 117.

2. Ibid., p. 12.

3. David Linge, introduction to Hans-Georg Gadamer's *Philosophical Hermeneutics*, p. xii.

4. Edgerton, *The Passion of Interpretation*, p. 125.

5. Hans-Georg Gadamer, "The Problem of Historical Consciousness," p. 135.

6. Gerald Bruns, *Hermeneutics Ancient and Modern*, p. 195.

7. Ibid., p. 249.

8. Edgerton, *The Passion of Interpretation*, p. 31. The "textual" metaphor of hermeneutics has its shortcomings that need to be recognized. As a metaphor, it speaks well of the linguisticality of human existence, yet it falls short as a metaphor for naming our earthly, bodily, physical, feeling-sensation existence. William Dean and John Cobb attempt to redress this shortcoming in their essays contained in Sheila Greeve Davaney, ed., *Theology at the End of Modernity*, pp. 41–60; 179–200.

9. Ibid., p. 32.

10. See Paul Rabinow and William Sullivan, "The Interpretive Turn: The Emergence of an Approach," in *Interpretive Social Science*, pp. 1–3. The phrase "ruthless forgetting" is Paul de Man's, as cited in Gerald Bruns, *Hermeneutics Ancient and Modern*, p. 199.

11. See Thomas Groome, *Sharing Faith*, pp. 59–61; Shaun Gallagher, *Hermeneutics and Education*, pp. 83–85; Walter Brueggemann, *Texts under Negotiation*, pp. 2–5.

12. Immanuel Kant, "What is Enlightenment?" in *Critique of Practical Reason*, p. 286.

13. See Jennifer Rike's introduction in her volume coedited with Werner Jeanrond, *Radical Pluralism and Truth*, p. xvi.

14. Gadamer, *Truth and Method*, p. 272.

15. Linell E. Cady, "Resisting the Postmodern Turn: Theology and Contextualization," p. 84.

16. Gadamer, *Truth and Method*, p. 271.

17. Richard Palmer, *Hermeneutics*, p. 145.

18. See Gordon Kaufman's foreword to Sheila Greve Davaney, ed., *Theology at the End of Modernity*, pp. ix–x.

19. Walter Brueggemann, *Texts under Negotiation*, p. 18.

20. Ibid., pp. 4–5. See also Linell Cady, "Resisting the Postmodern Turn," pp. 84–85.

21. Gadamer, *Philosophical Hermeneutics*, p. 49.

22. An introduction to Heidegger's major work, *Being and Time*, can be found in John Macquarrie's *Martin Heidegger*. Heidegger's influence on Gadamer's hermeneutical theory is noted by many authors, including Richard Palmer, *Hermeneutics*, pp. 124–39; Joel Weinsheimer, *Gadamer's Hermeneutics*, pp. 161–64; Anthony Thiselton, *The Two Horizons*, pp. 24–47, 143–204.

23. From Patricia Waugh's introduction to her reader, *Postmodernism*, p. 2. For representative writings from Heidegger, see "The Question Concerning Technology," 287–317; "On the Essence of Truth," 113–41; "The Origin of the Work of Art," 143–87 in *Basic Writings*.

24. See esp. sections 31–34 of Heidegger's *Being and Time*, translated by John Macquarrie and Edward Robinson, in Gayle Ormiston and Alan Schrift, eds., *The Hermeneutic Tradition*, pp.115–44.

25. Gadamer, *Truth and Method*, pp. 300–307. "Effective-historical consciousness" is a common English translation of Gadamer's key concept, *wirkungsgeschichtliches Bewusstsein*. However, the translators of the second revised edition of *Truth and Method* note that the term can also be translated as "historically effected consciousness." The difficulty in translation lies with trying to capture "Gadamer's delineation of a consciousness that is doubly related to tradition, at once 'affected' by history . . . and also itself brought into being—'effected'—by history, and consciousness that it is so" (Joel Weinsheimer and Donald G. Marshall, "Translators' Preface," p. xv).

26. Ibid., p. 270.

27. Ibid., p. 276.

28. It is important to note that Gadamer's "rehabilitation" of the word *prejudice* should not be read in the sense that we might speak, for example, of "racial prejudice." Rather, Gadamer is taking up Heidegger's insight that we are always projecting meaning on the basis of prior understandings. In this sense, "prejudice" for Gadamer means the "pre-understandings" we inevitably bring to all our interpretive activity.

29. Gadamer, "The Problem of Historical Consciousness," p. 132.

30. Gadamer, *Truth and Method*, p. 282.

31. Ibid., p. 276.

32. Ibid., p. 397.

33. Cady, "Resisting the Postmodern Turn," p. 86.

34. See, e.g., Paul Feyerabend, *Farewell to Reason;* Thomas Kuhn, *The Structure of Scientific Revolutions;* Sandra Harding, *The Science Question in Feminism;* Richard Bernstein, *Beyond Objectivism and Relativism* (esp. part 2, "Science, Rationality, and Incommensurability").

35. See David Tracy's reflections "The Question of History" in *Plurality and Ambiguity*, pp. 66–81.

36. Cady, "Resisting the Postmodern Turn," p. 87.

37. David Tracy, *Plurality and Ambiguity*, pp. 80–81.

38. Bruns, *Hermeneutics Ancient and Modern*, p. 196.

39. Jacques Derrida, *Of Grammatology*, p. 162.

40. Bruns, *Hermeneutics Ancient and Modern*, p. 205.

41. Gadamer, *Truth and Method*, p. 275.

42. Gadamer discusses Schleiermacher and Dilthey in *Truth and Method*, pp. 184–97; 218–42. See also Richard Palmer, *Hermeneutics*, pp. 84–123.
A romanticist hermeneutics reduces interpretation to authorial intention, equating the meaning of a text with what the author originally meant. A historicist hermeneutics reduces interpretation to the historical context of a text, locating the meaning of a text in the past. Gadamer is keen to insist that hermeneutical understanding is not found in the controls afforded by some critical or historical method that reconstructs the original past; rather, it is found in the to-and-fro of conversation between the interpreter and the classic text, event, or symbol.
Although the temptation to methodological control is real, Paul Ricoeur suggests that hermeneutical understanding and explanatory methods need not be enemies but wary allies. Methods drawn from the social sciences and from literary and historical criticism can help us know something of the world behind the text. However, Ricoeur reminds us that such explanatory methods function primarily as an initial step in the interpretive process. Their goal is to lead us into a fuller reception and participation in the world of new meaning and possibility that opens up in front of us. See *Hermeneutics and the Human Sciences*, pp. 145–64. Sandra Schneiders brings Gadamer and Ricoeur together in her work on New Testament hermeneutics, *The Revelatory Text*, as does David Tracy in his work on hermeneutical theology in *The Analogical Imagination*.

43. Rudolf Bultmann, *New Testament and Mythology and Other Basic Writings*, p. 150.

44. Ibid., p. 150.

45. Gadamer, *Truth and Method*, p. 262.

46. Gadamer, "The Problem of Historical Consciousness," p. 132.

47. Shaun Gallagher, *Hermeneutics and Education*, p. 85.

48. Gadamer, *Philosophical Hermeneutics*, p. 9.

49. Gadamer, *Truth and Method*, pp. 291–97. I am indebted to conversations with Michael Cowan at Loyola University, New Orleans, for this way of sketching the hermeneutical circle. See also my paper "The Interpretive Edge of Intentional Christian Communities: A Hermeneutical and Educational Exploration," *Compass* 27/3 (Spring 1993): 43–48.

50. Ibid., p. 297.

51. Ibid., p. 293 (italics mine).

52. Ibid., p. 309.

53. Ibid., p. 328.

54. Georgia Warnke, *Gadamer: Hermeneutics, Tradition and Reason*, p. 38.

55. Gadamer, *Truth and Method*, p. 290.

56. Ibid., p. 295.

57. This question is discussed by Georgia Warnke in *Gadamer: Hermeneutics, Tradition and Reason*, pp. 73–106.

58. Gadamer, *Truth and Method*, p. 268.

59. Warnke, *Gadamer: Hermeneutics, Tradition and Reason*, p. 91.

60. Gadamer, "The Problem of Historical Consciousness," p. 108.

61. Gadamer, *Truth and Method*, p. 299.

62. Ibid., see pp. 307–11 and 324–41. Gadamer reiterates that understanding is not a two-step process of first determining the past horizon of a text and then applying it to the present horizon. Rather, discerning a text's relevance for today is intrinsic to the one movement of interpretation which is also the one movement of understanding.

63. Ibid., p. 306.

64. Warnke, *Gadamer: Hermeneutics, Tradition and Reason*, p. 139.

65. Ibid., p. 103.

66. Gary Aylesworth, "Dialogue, Text, Narrative: Confronting Gadamer and Ricoeur," in Hugh Silverman, ed., *Gadamer and Hermeneutics*, p. 76.

67. Bruns, *Hermeneutics Ancient and Modern*, pp. 210, 237.

68. Gadamer, *Truth and Method*, p. 306.

69. David Tracy, *The Analogical Imagination*, p. 136.

70. Gadamer, *Truth and Method*, p. 462.

71. Ibid., p. 373.

72. See Joel Weinsheimer, *Gadamer's Hermeneutics*, pp. 250–51.

73. Ibid., pp. 114–15.

74. According to Gadamer, we live in the effective history of tradition because of language: "Language has no independent life apart from the world that comes to language within it. Not only is the world world only insofar as it comes into language, but language, too, has its real being only in the fact that the world is presented in it." Our "being-in-the-world is primordially linguistic" (*Truth and Method*, p. 443).

75. Gadamer, "Letter to Dallmayr," p. 95.

76. Gadamer, *Truth and Method*, p. 281.

77. Gadamer, "The Hermeneutics of Suspicion," p. 64.

78. Joel Weinsheimer and Donald Marshall note this in their "Translators' Preface" to Gadamer's *Truth and Method*, p. xvi.

79. Cited by Bruns, *Hermeneutics Ancient and Modern*, p. 157.

80. Gadamer, *Truth and Method*, pp. 367–68, 383–88.

81. Bruns, *Hermeneutics Ancient and Modern*, p. 158.

82. "Letting go," "releasement," and "openness" are terms central to Heidegger's notion of Gelassenheit. See Bruns, *Hermeneutics Ancient and Modern*, p. 158.

83. Gadamer, *Truth and Method*, pp. 101–10.

84. Gallagher, *Hermeneutics and Education*, p. 124.

85. In *Truth and Method*, Gadamer speaks of "being pulled up short by the text" (p. 268). According to Gadamer, hermeneutical experience does not approach tradition as an object whereby the Thou becomes an It. Nor does hermeneutical experience approach tradition through empathetic understanding of the Thou, i.e., we understand the other, but we do not allow that other to address us. This would stop short of true understanding — it would mean we understand the other in terms of its own world so that we do not have to let it into our world. Rather, true hermeneutical experience is experience of the other as an other that addresses me, that claims my attention, that puts at risk my present assumptions and pre-understandings (see pp. 358–62).

86. Bruns, *Hermeneutics Ancient and Modern*, p. 217.

87. This is a key theme in Bruns's chapter "What is Tradition?" in *Hermeneutics Ancient and Modern*, pp. 195–212.

88. Ibid., p. 202.

89. Gadamer, *Truth and Method*, p. 361.

90. Bruns, *Hermeneutics Ancient and Modern*, p. 210.

91. Gadamer, *Truth and Method*, p. 356.

92. Bruns, *Hermeneutics Ancient and Modern*, p. 155.

93. Gadamer, *Truth and Method*, pp. 355–57. See also Richard Palmer, *Hermeneutics*, p. 232; and Gerald Bruns, *Hermeneutics Ancient and Modern*, p. 184.

94. Gadamer, *Truth and Method*, p. 367.

95. Ibid., p. 366.

96. Ibid., p. 366.

97. Ibid., p. 370.

98. Ibid., p. 370.

99. Palmer, *Hermeneutics*, p. 168.

100. Gadamer, *Truth and Method*, p. 370.

101. Palmer, *Hermeneutics*, pp. 234–35.

102. Gadamer, *Truth and Method*, p. 367.

103. Bernstein, *Beyond Objectivism and Relativism*, p. 162.

104. However, Gadamer notes that "the openness of a question is not boundless. It is limited by the horizon of the question" (*Truth and Method*, p. 363). As Shaun Gallagher says, "every question is asked from a particular circumstance, within a specific hermeneutical situation." If a question were completely boundless, its meaning would disappear. See *Hermeneutics and Education*, p. 147.

105. Gadamer, *Truth and Method*, p. 367.

106. Ibid., p. 99.

107. Gadamer, cited in Gary Aylesworth, "Dialogue, Text, Narrative: Confronting Gadamer and Ricoeur," in Hugh Silverman, ed., *Gadamer and Hermeneutics*, p. 75.

108. Gadamer, *Truth and Method*, p. 375.

109. This reading of Gadamer's work follows closely that of Joel Weinsheimer, *Gadamer's Hermeneutics*, p. 210.

110. Gadamer, "The Problem of Historical Consciousness," p. 155.

111. Weinsheimer, *Gadamer's Hermeneutics*, p. 100.

112. Bernstein, *Beyond Objectivism and Relativism*, p. 139.

CHAPTER TWO

ENGAGING THE BOOK

? Look this to place ?

To be in the book, to be part of it, to be responsible for it, to be able to say "I am in the book" — this is a leading question for members of marginal Christian communities. In what sense can they find a place — a home — in the book of their belonging? The question is particularly acute for those communities whose relationship to their tradition is strained and tenuous yet still connected in a searching and questioning way. Such communities typically suffer a lack of meaningful equation between their experience of life and their experience of tradition. One intentional community described its beginnings in the following way:

> As we began, many of us — I would say especially among the Catholic members
> of the group — carried unresolved bitterness and resentment attached to experiences
> which we had had with our religious tradition. . . . Others of us were somewhere in
> between alienation and peace with our religious tradition. Everyone in the group had
> struggled about religious observance as adults and heads of families.
>
> All of this left us as a group ambivalent about our own Christian religious tradi-
> tion, as well as attracted to the alternative traditions of feminism, ecology, Native
> American culture, the Eastern religions, and existentialism. How could we begin to
> nurture a common spirituality?
>
> After fairly intense discussions, we opted somewhat ambivalently to start with the
> symbols and texts of the Christian tradition with which we were most familiar.[1]

It is a strange paradox, yet one worth highlighting, that even when people attempt to break with tradition because of the alienation they experience, the tradition nevertheless retains an effective hold. As we discussed in chap. 1, what is at work here is Gadamer's notion of "effective historical consciousness" — the operative force of tradition in people's lives, so that even in reacting against it they remain conditioned by it. However, this does not imply that tradition has a dominating hold that constrains all our possibilities. As we also noted in the first

? Feminist thinking ?

chapter, it is our very belonging to tradition that makes new understanding possible. Marginal communities, whose tendency is to decry the authority and claims of tradition, are reminded by Gadamer that we always interpret our world and our experience as members of historical, cultural, "traditioned" communities. As Rosemary Radford Ruether suggests, our need to situate ourselves meaningfully within a tradition — to find our home in the book — can never be realized in a cultural or historical vacuum:

> The effort to express contemporary experience in a cultural and historical vacuum is both self-deluding and unsatisfying. It is self-deluding because to communicate at all to oneself and others, one makes use of patterns of thought, however transformed by new experience, that have a history. It is unsatisfying because, however much one disregards large historical periods of dominant traditions, one still seeks to encompass this 'fallen history' within a larger context of authentic and truthful life.[2]

The community described above wondered where they should start, how they could find again their "belonging." Should they start with their contemporary experience? With alternative traditions? Or with their own tradition with which they were most familiar? I think their decision to begin with the symbols and texts of their Christian tradition reflects a deep-seated awareness of the effective hold this tradition has upon their lives. Yet I do not see their decision, taken after "intense discussions," as merely conceding to tradition. Rather, I see it as an act of intentionality or, as Joyce Quiring Erickson says, as the ability to "choose one's home — to understand and change the conditions that allow one to be 'at home'. . . ." Erickson reminds us that such a choice is circumscribed neither by complete freedom nor complete determinism. " 'Working it out' is required in order to be 'at home'. . . ." What is required is an intentionality that "calls forth attentiveness and effort."[3]

What does this imply for marginal communities who are struggling on the edges of their tradition? It suggests that the route to liberation from the negative and alienating realities of a tradition is not to step outside of tradition and declare an autonomy that is virtually impossible. Rather, the educative task is to help communities realize that the "way out" — the "exodus" — from alienation to freedom is to enter into a vigorous, honest, and searching conversation with their tradition in both its enriching and distorting effects.[4]

Moving From Critical Distance to Hermeneutical Openness

Conversation suggests that what is at stake for the educational life of intentional Christian communities is not a critical distancing from tradition but a critical engagement with tradition. It also suggests a two-way process, a to-and-fro, a dialogue in which neither partner in the conversation assumes dominance, and neither can come away from the conversation unchanged. As we noted in chap. 1, the idea of being able to achieve a freedom from tradition via a critical distance is a result of an Enlightenment hermeneutic. The Enlightenment sought to free itself from the prejudiced knowledge of tradition to arrive at a more reasoned, objective, and autonomous knowing. Shaun Gallagher sees this type of critical, disengaged thinking as a plague of modern educational theories and practices. Problem solving and critical thinking became the dominant hallmarks of education "under the control of an autonomous, prejudice-free, pure subjectivity which, by means of an idealized scientific method, approaches a problem in an absolutely disconnected and objective way."[5] Education was placed at the service of a narrow, technological understanding under the spell of an overconfident Enlightenment rationality.

> By reducing everything to a solvable problem, and by denying the permanency of certain fundamental ambiguities, the modern individual's own self-understanding is endangered. Our modern understanding falls prey to the illusion that our control is complete, that we are independent and self-empowered subjects who order the objective world. This illusory understanding is what closes off the possibilities of human self-understanding.[6]

In his work *Higher Education and the Human Spirit*, Bernard Meland argues that rational ways of knowing have tended to neglect deeper, intuitive ways of knowing, what he calls an "appreciative consciousness" or a felt "wisdom of the body."[7] "Feeling" the sense of life's "unsayableness" has given way to the rationalist's quest for what is distinctly clear and "sayable." Yet according to Meland, "we live more deeply than we think." If we are to be faithful to lived experience, this "more deeply" should be reflected in our ways of knowing. The deep, rich, intuitive realm of the "unsayable" requires a perceptive, intuitive grasp of experience that is inaccessible to rational analysis and conceptual thinking. Meland argues for a knowing that is appreciative and intuitive of this deeper sense. Unlike the Enlightenment's appeal to rational consciousness with its concern for clear and distinct ideas, he appeals to an appreciative consciousness that is attuned to humanity's way of apprehending the world through a sense of value, a sense of beauty, of feeling, affection, intuition—through moral, religious, and aesthetic experience. "A sense of the-more-than-the-mind-can-grasp," writes Meland," attends every act of cognition where the appreciative consciousness is operative."[8]

Parker Palmer also believes that our approaches to education have too long been held under sway by an Enlightenment concern with facts, theories, objectiv-

ity, and a "reality out there."[9] Palmer contrasts the world of Enlightenment epistemology, which is about "knowing truth" (as factual, theoretical, objective, controlling), with the world of hermeneutical understanding, which is about "truthful
knowing" (as receptive, participative, relational, engaging). The following table
highlights some of the contrasts drawn by Palmer.[10]

KNOWING TRUTH	TRUTHFUL KNOWING
Factual Knowing "Fact" (Latin *facere*, "to make") We see ourselves as makers of the world, as "master builders" who take pride in what we have built with "our facts."	**Receptive Knowing** We see ourselves as recipients of the world as gift; knowing is receptive; it is a way of fruitfully receiving and celebrating life's gift (p. 22).
Theoretical Knowing "Theory" (Greek *theoros*, "spectator") We regard what we know as "out there" and we relate to it at a distance, as de- tached spectators, rather than engaged players.	**Participative Knowing** We do not reduce the world to lifeless "things." Rather, we fill all things with vital, pulsating life. We engage the world as an "organic whole" of which we are an integral part (p. 25).
Objective Knowing "Objective" (Latin root, "to put against, to oppose") We stand over-against the world and place ourselves in an adversarial relationship with the world and each other.	**Relational Knowing** We see truth as between us, in rela- tionship, to be found in a dialogue of knowers. Reality is structured as a relational, mutually responsive community of being. As we enter those relationships, knowledge of reality is unlocked (p. 53).
Knowing that Controls "Reality" (Latin root *res*, meaning a "thing," "property" or a "possession") We seek to know reality in order to lay claim to things, to own and control them. Knowledge becomes a quest for power and domination.	**Knowing that Belongs** We allow our knowing to draw us into relationship with the known, not as a separate object to be manipulated but as something we belong to be- cause it is part of who we are (p. 57). Knowing is not about owning and controlling but about belonging to what is known. Truthful knowing "weds" knower and known (p. 31).

Palmer concludes that "to know truth is to enter into the life of that which we
know and to allow it to enter into ours." It is not about manufacturing a world, or
manipulating it, or keeping it at a distance, or trying to control it. Rather, "truth
involves entering a relationship with someone or something genuinely other than
us, but with whom we are intimately bound."[11] Truth is not so much something

"over which" we stand; rather, it is something "under which" we stand. We "under-stand" truth to the extent that we "stand-under" its "spell."[12]

In a fashion similar to Palmer, Peter Elbow believes we have been so schooled into an Enlightenment thinking that proceeds via "methodological doubt" that it takes an enormous shift for us to enter the world of "belief."[13] Belief, however, does not imply unquestioning assent, but joining oneself to what is being said. It is a profoundly open mode of receptive listening rather than our usual tendency to critique, to doubt, to interject with our "yes, but. . . ." Methodological doubt too quickly distances us from the conversation at hand and stifles whatever productivity may emerge between open, engaged conversation partners. For Elbow, doubt implies disinterested detachment, whereas belief implies a merging with an other and participation in community. Doubting interrupts and makes a lot of noise, whereas believing allows for deep silence and listening. Doubting tends more toward refusal, "saying no," and pushing away; whereas believing is more akin to accepting, "saying yes," and entering the worldview of the other.[14] Methodological doubt not only keeps us distanced and disengaged; it also "caters too comfortably to our natural impulse to protect and retain the views we already hold." Belief, however, asks us to genuinely enter the realm of "unfamiliar or threatening ideas instead of just arguing against them without experiencing them or feeling their forces."[15]

Members of marginal Christian communities are typically strong critics of their tradition. They are great doubters and reluctant believers. In this sense, their educational experience with respect to tradition is deeply shaped by the critical thinking of an Enlightenment rationality. Gallagher, however, reminds such critical communities that to question a tradition requires an active participation in the hermeneutical process of tradition, rather than a "pretentious disconnection" from that process.[16] What this implies for marginal Christian communities is that tradition is reformed *within* the tradition. There is a twofold recognition here. On the one hand, as was argued in chap. 1, the process of tradition is a living force that enters into all understanding. Emancipation can never achieve total escape from the process of tradition. As Gallagher notes, it must be worked on from the inside — "it can never be accomplished outside the hermeneutical constraints of the process of tradition and language."[17] On the other hand, tradition is not simply an external force that determines how we understand. Nor is it "a bygone past, or a finished, lifeless mass. Rather, we ourselves live through the process of tradition and provide it with its force."[18] Both these insights can be profoundly freeing for the educational life of marginal Christian communities. As Gallagher suggests, "education is not the mere reproduction of tradition any more than it is an escape from tradition. The truth lies somewhere between these two extremes in the notion of a 'transformation' of tradition."[19] Many marginal communities expend much frustrated energy in trying to escape rather than engage that to which they belong. They see their suspicions, their critiques, their doubts leading them further and further away from tradition, rather than recognize that their critical reading is part of the ongoing process of interpretation and a vital sign that they are indispensable participants in transforming and remaking tradition into a new happening, a new event, a new mode of being.

If marginal Christian communities are characteristically critical, suspicious, rebellious communities, then interpretation represents a way of "redeeming rebellion."[20] The educational task becomes one of facilitating this redemptive process so that suspicion, critique, and radical questioning are not left in an unredeemable state, lost somewhere off the pages of tradition, but are rather brought into fruitful and engaging play with tradition. Marginal communities will never lose their critical edge, but how does their critical edge become just that, an *edge* rather than a *wedge* that constantly splits them off from tradition? One way to redeem rebellion is to lead marginal communities out of a paralyzing critical mode into the hermeneutical openness of the question, from the driving wedge of constant criticism into the cutting edge of ongoing questioning. The following table represents my reading of Gadamer's preference for giving a priority to the mode of open questioning over against the dominance of a critical thinking that too often distances the interpreter from the subject matter at hand.

QUESTIONING	CRITIQUING
Risking	Doubting
Provoking	Fending
Open Space	Guarded Space
Guided by subject matter	Governed by technique
Conversational (to-and-fro)	Methodological (step-by-step)
Deepening	Distancing
Invested	Detached
Plumbs	Dissects
Explorational	Analytical
Leading	Controlling
Summonses	Directs
Creates indeterminacy	Creates a measure of truth
Knows it does not know	Claims a more definitive knowing
Sustains energy	Drains energy
(ongoing questioning is more sustainable, more likely to lead to new possibility)	(ongoing critique wears itself out, more likely to lead to paralysis)

Marginal Christian communities, in their willingness to let questions of suspicion and critique arise, are claiming a space where there is freedom to explore alternate readings of tradition that counter many of its ingrained distortions. However, the danger of such a strongly critical hand is that it can be overplayed to the detriment of conversation and transformative participation within tradition. The critical distance adopted by marginal communities can all too easily lead to being cut off, in which case their prophetic critique loses its power to truly function as a reforming/transforming voice. Such communities are no longer suspicious, but rebellious; no longer risking a trust in tradition, but denying tradition's claim; no longer marginal and prophetic, but hardened and cynical. A key educative task for marginal communities is to find ways that can lead them back into a vital and vigorous conversation with tradition. Such communities are typically very good at exercising critique, but they are often worn down by it. They need to learn how to transform their distancing, wary, critical sensibilities into open, conversational, questioning sensibilities. This would in no way minimize the efforts of marginal communities to explore alternatives to dominant orderings of social and ecclesial expression. Rather, it would support their questions, visions, and interpretive voices so that the emancipatory process can be more fully effected "through discourse, communication and educational conversation."[21]

Erickson said that to "be at home" requires a continual process of "working it out." It represents a measure of intentionality that continually stays with the question "What is home?" In a similar fashion, we might wonder why Edmond Jabès speaks of belonging to the "Book of Questions." Might it be, as he suggests, that the deepest and most profound way to belong to the book is to continually engage the question, What does it mean to belong to this people, this history, this tradition? "What does it mean to be Jewish?" asks Jabès. "I for one am tempted to reply it means being the person this question addresses, who quietly keeps asking it of themselves."[22] What does it mean to be Jewish, or to be Catholic, or Christian? It means to engage one's tradition rather than distance or remove ourselves from it, to open ourselves to the claim and address this question continually makes upon us.

Learning to Engage Tradition

According to Shaun Gallagher, our proper relationship to tradition is neither a "blind acceptance or reproduction" nor a "Cartesian denial or escape."[23] Rather, our relationship to tradition is most effective when we learn to engage and participate in tradition and, through that engagement, transform both ourselves and tradition toward ever-widening possibilities. Gallagher writes:

In educational experience the participants neither escape nor repeat traditions, they transform them. The productivity of education involves the transformation of traditions, subject matters, and, most importantly, individuals and societies. . . .

In the learning process we are involved in a transformation which takes us beyond what our relationship to tradition has already supplied.

In educational experience, traditions are continued, not as reproduced past, but as transformed past, insofar as they are challenged and questioned, and insofar as they take on new meanings in our present interpretations.[24]

Learning to engage a tradition is important because it makes a claim on us, because it is part of who we have been and who we are (its effective hold), yet also because it is part of who we may become (its productive possibility). According to David Tracy, a theologian who draws significantly on the hermeneutical work of Gadamer and Ricoeur, engaging a tradition means we need to become *intentional* about the ways in which we interpret our tradition and the ways in which we interpret our present situation, and the ways in which these two interpretations engage each other as "mutually critical correlations." In other words, we need to pay attention to the claims that tradition makes upon us, and we need to pay attention to our experience and the claims that it makes. Interpretive understanding happens in the critical correlation between these two poles, in which new interpretations of both past and present are risked for envisioning a Christian future.[25] Tracy proposes five "moments" of the interpretive process that can help communities of interpretation pay attention to the dynamics of what it means to engage a religious tradition from a hermeneutical position.[26]

(i) The Claims of the Situation

We always bring to the interpretive task our own assumptions, expectations, questions, and concerns arising from the historical circumstances in which we find ourselves. These pre-understandings bear the marks of our personal histories, our social location, our cultural symbols, our religious traditions — in short, our social, symbolic, and linguistic world. This is quite a tangle, one from which we can never quite free ourselves to analyze all the presuppositions that inescapably condition our understanding. However, we can watch what happens when we interpret. When we read a text, for example, we can notice what stands out for us and what remains in the background. This will be different for different people because of the different situations that people find themselves in and, hence, the different questions and concerns they bring to the text. Tracy asks us to consider, for example, "the different kinds of theology that emerge when a profound sense of oppression and/or alienation as distinct from a profound sense of fundamental trust is explicated as *the* hermeneutical key to contemporary

There can never be one interpretation

experience."[27] Feminist readers will engage a text differently than nonfeminists, readers of indigenous cultures differently than readers of Eurocentric cultures, marginal communities differently than mainstream communities, and so on. The text, therefore, is open to a plurality of interpretations, and this plurality derives not simply from the text itself but from the very claims of the situation that subject the text to the interrogation of contemporary questions and concerns.[28]

This suggests that interpretation always involves some free construction on our part, that we are always constructing the meaning of a text according to the issues and demands of our situation.[29] Rather than attempt to escape or bracket the questions of our situation, intentional communities need to bring them fully into play, to attend to the fundamental questions that the situation elicits, provokes, and discloses in front of them.

Sallie McFague believes that what we need today is a new naming of ourselves that is "commensurate *with our own times.*" We cannot continue using "names from a bygone era" that may have once been helpful but now need to be risked to ensure a more contemporary faith resonant with today's questions and sensibilities.[30] "In order to do theology," writes McFague, "one must in each age do it differently. To refuse this task is to settle for a theology appropriate for some other time than one's own."[31] Both McFague and Tracy argue that theological reflection must attend to the questions of our contemporary horizon, and this means paying attention to our experience, to our cultural symbols, to our political and economic social systems, to contemporary thinkers, writers, and artists, to all that shapes our horizon of understanding in both its positive and negative realities.[32] Our theologies will be sorely inadequate unless we take seriously the task "to identify primary metaphors and models from contemporary experience and elucidate their conceptual implications in order to express Christian faith for our day in powerful, persuasive ways."[33]

(ii) The Claims of Tradition

We can understand best how Tracy speaks of the claims of tradition through his notion of the "classic."[34] Tracy suggests that the classic serves as a paradigm for the normative hold of tradition: "The classic is important hermeneutically because it represents the best exemplar of what we seek: an example of both radical stability become permanence and radical instability become excess of meaning through ever-changing receptions."[35] We recognize in our classic expressions (our texts, symbols, rituals) a disclosive and transformative truth about our lives which is so compelling that "we cannot deny them some kind of normative status."[36] Their "excess" is such that they continually yield new meaning in different ages, always resisting definitive interpretation. Their "permanence" is such that they continually claim our attention — not as timeless, abstract truths, but in the concrete, continually relevant claims they make upon our lives. The classics endure, awaiting ever-new appropriations of meaning, binding together past and present. As such, a classic is "always retrievable, always in need of appropriation and critical evaluation, always disclosive and transformative with its truth of importance, always open to new application and thereby new interpretation."[37]

Tracy is convinced that the classics are worth our attention. In other words, the past is worth our attention. Why? Not simply as a cultural legacy, nor simply for aesthetic appreciation, but because the past has something to teach us. In a sense, Tracy gives this past and the classics of tradition a normative status. They are normative not only because they are who we are but because they continue to shape who we may become. Hermeneutics and the need for interpretation comes into effect only if we assign some normativity to the past and to the classics. If the past exerts no truth claims, makes no claim to attention, then hermeneutics need not be undertaken at all. There can be no classics unless there are people willing to interpret them, and there is no need for interpretation unless there are classics that serve to provoke our interpretive attention.[38]

Tracy recognizes that there is also a dark side to the classics. Many of our classics have exerted distortive as well as disclosive influence in their effective histories. Yet he nevertheless stands firm in his conviction that the classics of our tradition are very much present to us, claiming our attention. They are present not simply as past but as mediated by interpretive conversation:

> If the text is a genuinely classic one, my present horizon of understanding should always be provoked, challenged, transformed. In encountering a classic we are compelled to believe . . . "that something else might be the case than is the case." I will understand not merely something that was of interest back then, as a period piece, whose use, although valid then, is now spent. Rather I will grasp something of genuine interest here and now, in this time and place.[39]

We have access to the past only as mediated by its truth claim, that is, a claim to truth that is provoking for us in the present. Our only access to the past is through what the present shares or can share with it. Hence, the importance of conversation and interpretation. "The heart of the hermeneutical position is the recognition that all interpretation is a mediation of past and present, a translation carried on within the effective history of a tradition to retrieve its sometimes strange, sometimes familiar meanings."[40]

(iii) The Game of Conversation

What happens when intentional communities engage a conversation between the horizon of their contemporary situation and the horizon of tradition? Following Gadamer, Tracy suggests that what happens is a to-and-fro movement that is similar to the way we play a game, or rather, the way a game plays us. We never play a game well if we are constantly thinking about the rules and conditions of the game. Rather, at some point we must "lose" ourselves in the game and allow it to play us, rather than we playing it. The movement of the game must take over if there is to be any game at all.[41] Tracy suggests that what we "give ourselves over to" in any interpretive conversation is the "play of the question."[42] It is the question that becomes the common subject matter between the text and the interpreter. Every text is a response to a provoking question, and every community interprets a text according to its own contemporary questions and responses. What comes to the fore is a new horizon of possibility as both the text and the community engage the question which has now become the common subject matter between them. It is as if the subject matter is released in the back-and-forth movement between the text and the interpretive community.[43] Tracy explains as follows:

> The movement in conversation is questioning itself. Neither my present opinions on the question nor the text's original response to the question, but the question itself, must control every conversation. . . . We learn to play the game of conversation when we allow the questioning to take over.[44]

Any genuine encounter with tradition is an encounter with something that is other, something that is different. Belonging to the book involves, in a paradoxical fashion, allowing the book to provoke our nonbelonging — the place where the book becomes strangely unfamiliar, rather than simply the same. It means to provoke the familiar into unfamiliarity, to allow the book to lure us by its "power of strangeness."[45] It is to enter the realm of the question, to recognize that we do not know, to expect the unexpected. "The heart of dialogue," writes Jabès, "beats with questions."[46]

Exposure to this otherness and difference is essential for any authentic conversation. When we allow the common subject matter — the question in play — to assume primacy, we are moving out of a secure and familiar world into a provoking world of difference and strangeness. Yet, paradoxically, it is only in allowing the different to be different, that we also begin to see "the different *as* possible."[47] It is only in allowing our world to be provoked by a questioning that risks the familiar that our world can be enlarged into a new possibility. Otherness and difference can become genuine possibility if we are willing to risk ourselves by allowing the to-and-fro of questioning and conversation to play us into new ways of belonging to the book. "We must follow those questions — however initially different, other, or even strange — until the unique result of this kind of interaction occurs: the exploration of possibility as possible and thus as similarity-in-difference."[48] The constantly shifting horizons between both text and community in conversation leads toward a new "fusion of horizons," what Tracy calls an "identity-in-difference: an interpretation that will recognise itself as 'understanding differently' insofar as it understands at all."[49]

In following the track of the question, the familiar is put at risk and is never felt the same way again. All that we took as "home" becomes indeterminate, different, provocatively mysterious again, evocative once more of new, unthought possibilities. From a radical belonging to tradition, through a venturing out into the open and unknown spaces of the question, we return to rewrite ourselves anew, as if to another self, another tradition. We realize we have not left the book to which we belong — the book, however, different to itself for having been reshaped through its own reading.

(iv) Argument and Suspicion

Tracy notes that as we engage the classics of our tradition in the light of our contemporary situation, a variety of responses is possible, ranging from "a tentative sense of resonance with the question posed by the text through senses of import or even shock of recognition or repugnance elicited by the classic text."[50] Sometimes we will find ourselves in strong disagreement with a classic, even to the point where some aspect of our tradition is placed permanently under suspicion. As we shall discuss further in part 2, there will be times when the conversational model of interpretation needs to be interrupted by a hermeneutic of suspicion.

At this point, however, it seems important to note that when a marginal community adopts a critical stance in relation to their religious tradition, it can be difficult for them to hear again the transformative, provocative claims that are present in the tradition. Particularly when a critical stance becomes habitual, encrusted, or hardened over time, communities can find the life-giving potential of tradition quickly draining away. Preoccupation with (or a long, hard look at) the systematically distorted patterns present within the Christian tradition — such as patriarchy, hierarchical structuring, and dominating relations over earth and indigenous cultures — can lead critical communities into a deathly and paralyzing view of tradition. Of course, many people elect to leave the Christian tradition, yet we may wonder whether there is any other tradition or alternate space to be found that is *not* affected by the distorted strains of the collective Western cultural heritage that have effectively shaped us all. In this regard, the critical feminist theologian Rosemary Radford Ruether writes as follows:

Classical Western cultural traditions, which were codified between 500 B.C.E. and 800 C.E., and of which Christianity is a major expression, have justified and sacralized relationships of domination....

But these classical traditions did not only sacralize patriarchal hierarchy over women, workers, and the earth. They also struggled with what they perceived to be injustice and sin and sought to create just and loving relations between people in their relation to the earth and to the divine....

These glimpses are a precious legacy that need to be separated from the toxic waste of sacralized domination. We do not need to and should not totalize negative judgment against past biblical and Christian cultures. It would be surprising indeed if there were no positive insights that could be reclaimed from three thousand years of collective human struggle about the meaning of life and the way to live justly and well.[51]

Ruether is suggesting that we can find much of value in the biblical and Christian traditions that needs to be remembered and retrieved, that the same tradition we might regard with a measure of suspicion can also be used to reconstruct our cultural and religious histories. To engage a tradition is to engage its darkness as well as its light, but more importantly, it is to engage it as something we are responsible for, both in what it has been and what it may productively become. According to Gordon Kaufman, we must take full responsibility for the symbolic contexts that shape all our experiencing and knowing, the "overarching patterns of symbolism (religious and secular) which humankind has created during its long history."[52] Hermeneutical engagement takes up the primary symbols and practices of our religious tradition and cultural life in order to contribute to their evaluation, interpretation, and reconstruction for the possibility of a better world.[53]

We should also remember that Tracy is proposing a *mutually critical* conversation between a community's tradition and its contemporary situation. "Mutually critical" suggests that, on the one hand, there will be times when our religious tradition puts many of our current pre-understandings at risk, challenging us to think and act differently. On the other hand, there will be times when our tradition's former receptions and claims to truth will be challenged and put at risk by the emerging questions and concerns of our contemporary situation. As in any genuine conversation, neither partner can come away unchanged. Every true and responsible conversation puts all its participants at risk.[54]

(v) New Possibilities in Front of Us

The final moment of Tracy's interpretive process follows Gadamer's notion that whenever interpretive understanding happens, it happens differently because it is understanding that is shaped by different historical concerns and questions in which the tradition is coming to be in a new form. Tracy also follows Paul Ricoeur in suggesting that understanding does not just reflect the world that has already been, but leans transformatively into the world that is becoming.

According to Ricoeur, a text is distanced from its original author, situation, and audience because its meaning is no longer dependent on them — but on us, the readers, who are now present to it.[55] Because the meaning of a text is no longer dependent on its originating world, it is free to enter into our world, and this gives classic texts an interpretive productivity that goes beyond original intentions. The distance we experience between ourselves and a past text becomes a productive distance when we "include the otherness within the ownness."[56] It is in allowing the provoking otherness and strangeness of a text to speak that a new and possible world is brought into being between text and reader. The text has a unique ability to continuously unfold, reveal, disclose a world in front of it. Its otherness continuously provokes new forms of ownness, new appropriations, new ways of being. This is the gift of classic texts — their meaning, their reference, their subject matter, can continuously stand out in front of the text (not behind it) to awaken interpretive possibilities. Interpretation is always potentially creative.

> The meaning of the text does not lie "behind" it (in the mind of the author, the original social setting, the original audience) nor even "in" the text itself. Rather the meaning of the text lies in front of the text — in the now common question, the now common subject matter, of both text and interpreter.[57]

Interpretive understanding lies out in front of both our tradition and our contemporary situation as the two are in conversation, continuously evoking new horizons of meaning.

Educational Approaches Toward Hermeneutical Engagement

Hermeneutical theory is typically wary of proposing interpretive methods that can be applied to a tradition's texts, symbols, or events. The danger is that a reliance on method could lead us into a false security that presumes we can control the interpretive process. However, while the temptation to methodological control is real, various theologians and educators have proposed approaches for hermeneutical engagement that offer practical guidance for the interpretive life of intentional communities. Most of these approaches share a kinship with the conversational model of dialogical hermeneutics. I have already explored Tracy's five moments at some length, so I shall simply sketch the following approaches in a table format to highlight some of their main points.

Conversation with a Text (Michael Cowan & Bernard Lee)[58]	The Cycle of Interpretation (John Vogelsang)[59]	Practical Biblical Interpretation (Ernest Hess)[60]	Shared Christian Praxis (Thomas Groome)[61]
1. Community members *attend to their initial responses to the text.* In what ways did we find ourselves agreeing or disagreeing with the text? What surprises occurred? What didn't we understand? The first movement focuses on the horizon of the interpretive community.	**1.** *Our Story.* Hearing a text brings our pre-understandings to the fore, because we always hear the text through these pre-understandings. Community members name their different values, beliefs, concerns, agendas, and experiences that influence the way they are hearing the text.	**1.** *Engaging our Prejudices: starting from where we are.* The community draws upon, makes use of, or otherwise engages the pre-understandings that lead persons to attend to the text itself.	**1.** *Naming Present Praxis.* Community members express their own understanding, reaction, feeling, valuing, activity, belief, truth, etc., around the particular text or subject matter at hand.
			2. *Critical Reflection on Present Praxis.* The community engages in a critical reflection on our interpretations, beliefs, and actions and on the likely or intended consequence of these. This is an attempt to become critically aware of the social conditioning, norms, assumptions, etc. that are embodied in the community's present praxis.
2. The community seeks a *deeper understanding of the text on its own grounds.* What provoked this text into being? What question is it seeking to answer? A better understanding of the world of the text is facilitated through the use of tools drawn from the social sciences or literary or historical criticism. The second movement focuses on the horizon of the text.	**2.** *The Story.* The text claims our attention as both similar to and different from our initial pre-understandings. The community asks the text what it is saying and what its context is (historical, literary, traditional, ideological), in order to recognize its otherness and difference from us (and hence its provoking claim).	**2.** *Widening our horizon through encounter with the text — letting the text speak.* We let the text speak in its own voice through a disciplined reading of the text in its context. We allow the "otherness" of the text to question and challenge us.	**3.** *Encounter with the Christian Story and Vision.* The community makes accessible the story (scriptures, symbols, rituals, etc.) and the vision (the response the story invites, its possibility for our lives) of the Christian tradition as it pertains to the theme or subject matter at hand.

		3.*Widening our horizon through encounter with others.* Our conversation with the text's subject matter is fostered through encounter with the interpretations of others — both from within and "outside" our tradition.	
3. The community *"talks back" to the text.* Does the text's view of reality resonate with our understanding of life? Is it at odds with our understanding of life? In what ways? The third movement focuses on the to-and-fro conversation between the horizon of the text and the horizon of the interpretive community.	**3.** *The Story Unfolding in History.* Our story and "the story" come into conversation. We recognize and challenge the text and then critically assess what we discover. We respond to and act upon what is revealed in the conversation in order to participate in the reconstruction of society and tradition.	**4.** *Risking our Prejudices in the Play of Conversation.* We engage the questions that have arisen from previous steps: the questions we bring from our present situation; the questions the text directs to us; the questions raised by others from within and outside our tradition. These various questions, perspectives and stories are intentionally "put into play" with one another as the community engages in a to-and-fro process of mutual questions and answers.	**4.** *Dialectical Hermeneutic Between the Christian Story and the Community's Story.* What does the Christian story mean for (affirm, call into question, invite beyond) our stories, and how do our stories respond to (affirm, recognize limits of, push beyond) the Christian story?
4. The community *seeks possibilities for life emerging from their conversation with the text.* How has our conversation with the text and among each other transformed our way of understanding? What new possibilities can we envisage for our lives? The fourth movement focuses on what lies "in front of" our conversation with the text.		**5.** *"Fusing of Horizons," Pushing Toward Present Application.* The community expresses and celebrates the new possibilities and insights that have emerged and seek to live out their practical implications.	**5.** *Invitation to a New or Renewed Praxis.* In the light of all that has gone before, the community is invited to a decision/ response that represents a new or renewed Christian praxis.

Belonging to a Dialogical Community

Gadamer's dialogical hermeneutics speaks to us not only of belonging to tradition but also of belonging to communities of interpreters. In chap. 1, we noted Gadamer's critique of the Enlightenment project that sought to free itself from the shaping influence of our cultural, religious, and social frameworks. Throughout the modern era, freedom became powerfully identified with autonomy, the autonomy of the self. Descartes's absolute certainty of the self ("that thinks and therefore is") meant that "man" became the decisive *subject* turning everything else into *objects.* Objects, in other words, that are not intimately related to the self; rather, objects that exist only in service of an autonomous, knowing subject that orders, controls, and masters the world.[62] This is the "I" who claims independence and the self's own certainty, an "I" in control, neither dependent nor receptive.

However, in the same way Gadamer reminds us that we do not reach knowledge or understanding by escaping our traditions, so too we do not exist as selves without the presence of others, without the web of relationships within which every "I" emerges. As Mark C. Taylor notes, our identities do not exist independently prior to our relationships but continuously emerge from them:

> In the very struggle to achieve distinction by standing apart from other selves, the individual eventually comes to realize an unavoidable commonality, which grows out of inevitable relationships with others. . . . There is no such thing as an original individual who initially stands outside a field of interaction and subsequently enters a matrix of relations that remains contingent and accidental. . . . In contrast to the substantial individual, the deindividualized subject is *co-relative* and *codependent.*[63]

According to Sandra Harding, the West typically views the self as "autonomous, individualistic, self-interested, fundamentally isolated from other people and from nature, and threatened by these others unless the others are dominated by the self."[64] She notes how this Western understanding is completely alien to many indigenous cultures and to many women, who view the self as radically constituted by relationships. To be a self in the presence of others is not a derivative experience but primordial: "Community is not a collection of fundamentally isolated individuals but ontologically primary." The individual receives their sense of self "only through their relationships within a community."[65] This contrasting ontology (way of being) leads to a contrasting epistemology (way of knowing) that places truth in the realm of relationality and a community of inquirers.[66]

"It is no accident," writes Parker Palmer, "that communal images of pedagogy are being recovered even as communal images of epistemology are being reclaimed."[67] Palmer sees education as a process of creating communal meaning that draws us out of our isolated knowing into a knowing that interacts with each other and with the subject matter at hand. We do not learn by knowing a subject in an isolated fashion; rather, we learn by looking at the world *through* the subject matter in interaction with each other.[68] Communities of intentional learners

> are learning by listening and responding faithfully to each other and to the subject at hand. They are using an educational process that is not individualized and competitive but communal and cooperative, one that reflects the communal nature of reality itself.[69]

Stephen Brookfield, a leading theorist and practitioner of adult education, sees small, "educative" communities as highly appropriate settings for developing interactive, intentional learning among adult learners. They provide "a powerful support for adults who wish to experiment with ideas, opinions, and alternative interpretations and to test these out in the company of others engaged in a similar quest."[70] One can sense the quality of interpretive play and community conversation in the dynamic Brookfield is naming. His appraisal of the highly valued pedagogic setting of small communities is relevant to the life of intentional Christian communities. Members of such communities are often engaged in a redefinition of themselves and in a reinterpretation of their religious tradition from a newly realized vantage point, that of collaborative interpretation.

> The adults in these groups are attempting to create new meaning systems. They are reinforcing each other's dormant, half-perceived feeling that there is some massive disjunction between their present ways of living and thinking, on the one hand, and the kind of existence they ideally envisage for themselves, on the other.[71]

Brookfield sees intentional, self-directed learning as central to the practice of adult education. Some of the key words he uses to describe a small community of adult learners are the following: purposeful or intentional conversation, mutual interest, deliberation, participation, respect, a skepticism of authoritativeness, openness to divergent perspectives, truthfulness, freedom, equality.[72] Brookfield is keen to insist that the importance of self-directed learning should by no means be equated with an autonomous, independent learning. Rather, self-directed learning is premised on the need for a community of learners, on conversation, on communal deliberation, and on engagement with our social and cultural contexts as actors-reflectors.[73] Indeed, Brookfield names the hallmarks of self-directed learning that are very similar to the hallmarks of an intentional Christian community: intentional, mutual, collaborative, praxis-centered, critically engaged, and empowering.[74]

Relational Power

One of the great gifts of intentional Christian communities is their commitment to mutuality, inclusiveness, and open and honest dialogue among equals.

Intentional communities are places of relational power. Martin Buber describes the power of relationship as "Spirit" when he says: "Spirit is not in the *I*, but between *I* and *Thou*."[75] Human beings find authentic existence in and through deep and mutual relating. We become ourselves only in and through each other. "Through the *Thou* a man [*sic*] becomes *I*."[76] I am not actually "I" until I encounter You. In other words, who I am does not exist prior to my relating, but emerges from it. According to Buber, there is power in relationship because life is about relationship: "All real living is meeting."[77]

A Meeting[78]

a community of friends
all their antennae out
weaving together a fabric of agreement
how much listening can a room hold?
in a sea of ambiguity
        each one takes a turn
        catching a thread of clarity
and offering it to the rest
caring sensitive fingers
probing the tangle of ideas
sorting the threads
tying loose ends
thoughtfully
holding the pattern-that-might-be
        in the mind's eye
the skill and the patience
        intelligence and creativity
        of a dozen lovers
feeling
thinking
building with fine familiar tools
in an uncharted land

John Stewart believes that a dialogical hermeneutic is not only helpful for communities learning to engage their religious tradition's texts and symbols; it is also helpful for learning the art of mutual engagement and conversation *between* members of intentional communities. Stewart contrasts two approaches to hermeneutics: the reproductive and the productive.[79] The reproductive approach claims that in order for us to understand a text, we need to *reproduce* the author's original intent. In other words, *meaning* is viewed as synonymous with the author's *intent*. This type of hermeneutic lies behind much contemporary theory concerning effective communication, which usually goes something like this: "If we want to reach some form of meaning or understanding between us, then I need to grasp as best I can what you are saying to me (the intention behind your words), and you need to grasp as best as you can what I am saying to you (the intention behind my words)."

However, there is something limiting in this approach to mutual conversation. The focus of understanding rests simply on reproducing the intent of what the other is saying. While we must make an effort to understand an other (be it text or person) within the context of their own horizon, this is only a means toward, not an end, of understanding. If we treat it as an end, we have turned the other into an object over which we have control, and which need not have a claim on our lives. In this sense, we have stopped short of true understanding, which involves letting the other affect us.[80]

This leads Stewart to the alternate approach to hermeneutics: the *productive*. According to this approach, a full understanding is not reached by simply trying to reproduce our conversation partner's intent or meaning. Rather, the focus is more one of *producing* with the other person mutual meanings between us. Meaning resides not simply in my understanding of what you are saying (though it certainly includes this); it resides more fully in the to-and-fro of conversation between us. Such a process is productive of insight, not merely reproductive of intent. We are producing a full response to the issues we face that often leads to insights and ideas that neither one of us could have generated alone. As Stewart says, "the listener is not simply 'open to what the other means' so that he or she can reproduce it; instead, the listener is open to meanings that are being developed *between* oneself and one's partner."[81] This is *interpretive* listening, which has a broader focus than *empathic* or *reproductive* listening. Stewart and his colleague Milt Thomas suggest a concrete and graphic image of productive conversation:

> Picture yourself sitting on one side of a potter's wheel with your conversation partner across from you. As you work (talk) together, each of you adds clay to the form on the wheel, and each uses wet fingers, thumbs and palms to shape the finished product. Like clay, talk is tangible and malleable; it's out there to hear, to record, and to shape. If I am unclear or uncertain about what I am thinking about or what I want to say, I can put something out there and you can modify its shape, ask me to add more clay, or add some of your own. Your specific shaping, which you could only have done in response to the shape I formed, may move in a direction I would

never have envisioned. The clay you add may be an idea I've thought of before — though not here in this form — or it may be completely new to me.[82]

This image helps us to see conversation as a mutual, playful, open-ended, productive enterprise. The focus is on the creative interplay between us. What we fashion together is not mine or yours, but *ours,* the result of both our active shapings.

Many intentional communities are keen advocates of the need for respectful listening to enable a deeper meeting between persons. However, Stewart believes we need to move beyond the already difficult process of listening to an other's story or experience to a broader approach that focuses on those meanings that are being co-produced between us in the mutual to-and-fro of honest conversation. Such conversation is demanding in its claims on us and much more difficult to accomplish than the simple (yet difficult) telling-and-listening process of empathic communication.[83] As David Tracy notes, we need to be willing to risk that form of conversation that brings with it some even "harder" rules than empathic listening:

> Conversation is a game with some hard rules: say only what you mean; say it as accurately as you can; listen to and respect what the other says, however different or other; be willing to correct or defend your opinions if challenged by the conversation partner; be willing to argue if necessary, to confront if demanded, to endure necessary conflict, to change your mind if the evidence suggests it.[84]

Tracy is suggesting that mutually productive conversation involves the ability to both influence and be influenced. This conception of mutuality is relevant to the ways leadership and power are exercised within intentional Christian communities. We typically see power as the strength to be able to control or influence others; we forget that power is also the capacity to be receptive to the other. Bernard Loomer describes "relational power" as the "ability both to produce and to undergo an effect," "to influence others and to be influenced by others."[85] Loomer is keen to reclaim the receptive dimension of power. "Our openness to be influenced by another," he writes, "is a measure of our own strength and size, even and especially when this influence of the other helps to effect a creative transformation of ourselves and our world."[86] Power is not about exerting control and resisting influence; to be powerful is to be able to participate in the flow of reciprocal relationship.

Evelyn and James Whitehead remind us that power is not an entity someone possesses (as in the phrase, "that person has power"). Rather, power resides in the community as a whole, in the flow of interaction between people:

We are beginning to recognize power as a *relationship* rather than as an individual possession. Power refers to interactions that go on among us. It describes the energy with which we attract each other and bind ourselves in mutual commitment. . . . Power, then, is essentially social. To understand social power we must look at relationships — at what goes on among people rather than at individuals alone. As members of the community interact, power flows in many directions. As power stirs in the group, its members begin to shape this energy into patterns that give order and meaning to their common life.[87]

Power and leadership happen in the give-and-take of the whole group, as people interact with one another in ways that *lead to* the community's ongoing life and growth. In a world where the practice of power is so often equated with the exercise of unilateral control and authority over others, as a one-way transaction flowing downward, intentional communities can speak strongly about a more fundamental power that belongs to the "we" of community. Leadership is returned to the heart of community and mutuality to the heart of what it means to be communities of power.

Notes

1. Michael A. Cowan, "The Practical Challenges of Beginning and Sustaining a Small Community of Faith." Excerpt from the keynote address presented at the *Gathering National Conference*, 1989, Sydney. Excerpt published in *The Catholic Weekly*, October 25, 19⁸⁰, Sydney, p. 18.

2. Rosemary Radford Ruether, *Sexism and God-Talk*, p. 18.

3. Joyce Quiring Erickson, "On Being at Home," p. 244.

4. See David Tracy, *The Analogical Imagination*, p. 100.

5. Shaun Gallagher, *Hermeneutics and Education*, p. 186.

6. Ibid., p. 177. See also Susan Handelman's very fine article "Emunah: the Craft of Faith," where she grapples with the issue of educational practices that are too constrained by an overemphasis on "critical thinking," neglecting the craft of "religious" thinking that engages our deepest questions about life and seeks to find meaningful connections between our learning and our living.

7. Bernard Meland, "The Appreciative Consciousness," in *Higher Education and the Human Spirit*, pp. 48–78.

8. Ibid., p. 64.

9. Parker Palmer, *To Know As We Are Known*, pp. 20–32.

10. The references in the chart to page numbers are from Palmer's book *To Know As We Are Known*.

11. Ibid., p. 31.

12. This difference between "over-standing" and "under-standing" is an insight drawn from Raimon Panikkar. See Gerard Hall, "Raimon Panikkar's Hermeneutics of Religious Pluralism," p. 214.

13. Peter Elbow, "Methodological Doubting and Believing: Contraries in Inquiry," in *Embracing Contraries: Explorations in Learning and Teaching*, pp. 253–300.

14. Ibid., p. 266.

15. Ibid., p. 263.

16. Gallagher, *Hermeneutics and Education,* p. 237.

17. Ibid., p. 273.

18. Ibid., p. 86.

19. Ibid., p. 182.

20. I have borrowed this phrase from Susan Handelman, *The Slayers of Moses: The Emergence of Rabbinic Interpretation in Modern Literary Theory,* p. 195.

21. Gallagher, *Hermeneutics and Education,* p. 273.

22. Edmond Jabès, *The Book of Resemblances,* 3. 31 (adapted for inclusive language).

23. Gallagher, *Hermeneutics and Education,* p. 193.

24. Ibid., pp. 189, 99.

25. David Tracy, *Blessed Rage for Order,* pp. 43–63. It is important to note that we can distinguish, but we can never entirely separate, our interpretation of the situation and our interpretation of the tradition. The two are always influencing one another. For further comment and critique on the correlational model, see Francis Schüssler Fiorenza, "The Crisis of Hermeneutics and Christian Theology," pp. 128–40, and "Systematic Theology: Tasks and Methods," pp. 55–61. See also Elisabeth Schüssler Fiorenza, *But She Said,* pp. 142–43. Tracy defends the correlational model in "The Uneasy Alliance Reconceived: Catholic Theological Method, Modernity and Postmodernity." For an overview of Tracy's theological hermeneutics, see Werner Jeanrond, *Text and Interpretation,* pp. 129–53; T. Howland Sanks, "David Tracy's Theological Project: An Overview and Some Implications." For a lively conversation between contemporary thinkers and Tracy's work, see Werner Jeanrond and Jennifer Rike, eds., *Radical Pluralism and Truth: David Tracy and the Hermeneutics of Religion.*

26. Tracy summarizes these five interpretive moments in *The Analogical Imagination,* pp. 118–20, 130–31, 152. The following review of his work follows closely my paper "Theological Hermeneutics in the Works of David Tracy," *Compass* 27/4 (Summer 1993): 18–23.

27. Tracy, "Theological Method," p. 54.

28. Tracy offers his own analysis of our contemporary situation in *The Analogical Imagination,* chaps. 8 and 9, and in his articles, "Practical Theology in the Situation of Global Pluralism," and "On Naming the Present." Sally McFague also offers her interpretation of the contemporary situation in *Models of God,* chap. 1.

29. Bernard Lee makes this point in his article "Practical Theology: Its Character and Possible Implications for Higher Education," p. 30.

30. Sallie McFague, *Models of God,* p. 3.

31. Ibid., p. 30.

32. On this reading, theology should not limit itself to interpreting the tradition's classic expressions but must also draw upon other sources for theological reflection.

33. McFague, *Models of God,* p. 35.

34. Tracy typically speaks of the classic text, though classics can be persons, events, symbols, rituals, texts: those realities that have effectively created and recreated meaning for a particular culture or religious tradition. See *The Analogical Imagination,* pp. 99–153.

35. Tracy, *Plurality and Ambiguity,* p. 14.

36. Tracy, *The Analogical Imagination,* p. 109.

37. Ibid., p. 115.

38. Tracy notes that "some classics will disappear from the canon while others, once forgotten or even repressed, will reappear" (*Plurality and Ambiguity*, p. 12). Similarly, the constantly shifting horizons of both traditionary texts and interpretive readers will evoke new emerging classics and, hopefully, expand our notion of the classic so that it can become more inclusive than has been the case up until now.

39. Tracy, *The Analogical Imagination*, p. 102.

40. Ibid., p. 99.

41. Tracy, "Theological Method," p. 41.

42. Tracy, *The Analogical Imagination*, p. 101; and *Plurality and Ambiguity*, p. 18.

43. David Tracy (with Robert Grant), *A Short History of the Interpretation of the Bible*, pp. 158–60.

44. Tracy, *Plurality and Ambiguity*, p. 18.

45. This phrase is taken from Richard Rorty, *Philosophy and the Mirror of Nature*, p. 360.

46. Edmond Jabès, *The Book of Dialogue*, p. 21.

47. Tracy, *Plurality and Ambiguity*, p. 20.

48. Ibid., p. 20.

49. Tracy, *The Analogical Imagination*, p. 136.

50. Tracy, "Theological Method," p. 41.

51. Rosemary Radford Ruether, *Gaia and God*, pp. 3–4.

52. Gordon Kaufman, "Foreword" to Sheila Greeve Davaney, ed., *Theology at the End of Modernity*, p. xi.

53. Linell Cady, "Resisting the Postmodern Turn," p. 95.

54. Tracy, *Plurality and Ambiguity*, see p. 99. At the close of *Blessed Rage for Order*, Tracy poses the challenge daringly and unreservedly: "For anyone who accepts this model for doing theology, no one of the traditional Christian answers . . . can simply be assumed. Rather, all must be reinvestigated. . . . In some cases, the symbols and doctrines may well find an appropriate contemporary expression by means of a hermeneutics of restoration. In still other cases, those symbols and doctrines may not bear the power of meaningfulness, meaning or truth any longer — either to our common human experience or to the central meanings disclosed by Christian texts and tradition. In these later cases, those negative conclusions exemplified by various hermeneutics of suspicion upon Christian meanings must be honestly and candidly stated with a methodological rigor appropriate to the seriousness of the subject matter" (pp. 238–39).

55. Paul Ricoeur, *Hermeneutics and the Human Sciences*, see esp. "The Hermeneutical Function of Distanciation," pp. 131–44.

56. Ricoeur, *Interpretation Theory: Discourse and the Surplus of Meaning*, p. 43.

57. Tracy, "Theological Method," p. 42. See also Ricoeur, *Hermeneutics and the Human Sciences*, p. 177.

58. Michael A. Cowan, "Conversation with a Text," unpublished paper, Institute for Ministry, Loyola University, New Orleans. A similar approach is presented by Bernard Lee, "Shared Homily: Conversation That Puts Communities at Risk," in Bernard Lee, ed., *Alternative Futures for Worship*, Volume 3, *The Eucharist*, pp. 157–74.

59. John Vogelsang, "A Hermeneutics of Reconstruction," pp. 172–77.

60. Ernest Hess, "Practical Biblical Interpretation," pp. 195–210.

61. Thomas Groome, *Christian Religious Education,* pp. 207–23; and *Sharing Faith,* pp. 146–48.

62. Mark C. Taylor, *Erring,* pp. 22–27.

63. Ibid., pp. 132, 135.

64. Sandra Harding, *The Science Question in Feminism,* p. 171.

65. Ibid., p. 170.

66. Elaine Atkins redescribes education as a social process that aims at creating communal meaning among communities of learners. See her article, "Reframing Curriculum Theory in Terms of Interpretation and Practice: A Hermeneutical Approach," esp. pp. 443–47.

67. Palmer, *To Know As We Are Known,* p. xvii.

68. Ibid., p. 99.

69. Ibid., p. 94.

70. Stephen Brookfield, *Understanding and Facilitating Adult Learning,* p. 247.

71. Ibid., p. 142.

72. Ibid., pp. 138–39.

73. Ibid., pp. 56–59.

74. Ibid., pp. 9–11, 113–14.

75. Martin Buber, *I and Thou,* p. 39.

76. Ibid., p. 28.

77. Ibid., p. 11.

78. This poem by Pamela Haines is taken from *Building United Judgment,* Center for Conflict Resolution, Wisconsin, 1981.

79. John Stewart, "Interpretive Listening: An Alternative to Empathy," pp. 381–82.

80. Gadamer makes this point in *Truth and Method,* pp. 303, 358–61.

81. Stewart, "Interpretive Listening," p. 384.

82. John Stewart and Milt Thomas, "Dialogic Listening: Sculpting Mutual Meanings," p. 196.

83. Bernard Lee and Michael Cowan offer some practical guidelines for coproductive mutuality among members of intentional communities in *Dangerous Memories,* pp. 123–35.

84. Tracy, *Plurality and Ambiguity,* p. 19.

85. Bernard Loomer, "Two Kinds of Power," p. 20.

86. Ibid., p. 21. Loomer's understanding of relational power is discussed further in Evelyn Whitehead, "Leadership and Power: A View From the Social Sciences," in Michael Cowan, ed., *Alternative Futures for Worship: Leadership Ministry in Community,* pp. 49–51; Bernard Lee and Michael Cowan, *Dangerous Memories,* pp. 187–89; Denis Edwards, *Called to be Church in Australia,* pp. 94–95.

87. James and Evelyn Whitehead, *The Emerging Laity,* pp. 36, 39.

PART TWO:
OUTSIDE THE BOOK

Where others would find certainty, we risk moving on an immense field in motion.

Where others find occasion to affirm, we find doubt, fear, anxiety, infinite questioning. Subversive words, breeding polemics because strife-ridden and molded from misgivings. . . .

Roving across a negative explanation . . . we come into the power to name; power which undermines any manifestation of any presence, any stray impulse toward the idea of force, and of course denounces as absurd any will to dominate.

"Exile, too, is an option." — Reb Assira

"Where are you, Yukel?"
"Outside the book, where words without sound or sense wander, dispersed by the winds like pollen of the last flowers."

The book is a labyrinth. You think you are leaving and you only get in deeper. You have no chance of running off. For that, you must destroy the work. You cannot make up your mind to do that. I notice your anxiety mounting.

Yukel, how many pages to live, to die, are . . . between the book and leaving the book?

(*"Grant me my bright birth. I am the rebellious, the absent."* — Reb Vérid)

("Revolt is a crumpled page in the waste basket," wrote Reb Tislit. "But often a masterpiece is born from this sacrificed page.")

A good day lets darkness have its share.

"You shall not break the book in anger," wrote Reb Chemoul, "but in love. For it is in its breaking that it opens to the divine Word."
"No need to break the book," replied Reb Haggaï.
"It is already broken. Writing only confirms the cracks, explains and interprets them for you."

"Book rejected and reclaimed by the book."

["Every exit from the book is made within the book." — "Reb" Derrida.]

(Thus the exile does not leave the land from which he was chased; land, however, foreign to itself for being reshaped in exile.)

Book written twice: in the book and outside it.

Edmond Jabès

CHAPTER THREE

EXILIC HERMENEUTICS

To speak of an exilic hermeneutic is to speak of the experience of finding ourselves "outside the book." Exilic hermeneutics is profoundly and acutely aware of the stark contradictions that exist between the claims of the book of our belonging and the jarring, interruptive realities of our contemporary situation. These "interruptions" have taken the form of the radical questioning of Enlightenment modes of confident certitude; the recognition of the contextuality and multiple narratives of history; the feminist critique of a patriarchal, Eurocentric, colonial hegemony; the tormenting discontinuities of historical "progress" represented by the Holocaust, Hiroshima, and the genocide of indigenous cultures; the "irruption of the poor";[1] the critique of scientific and technological rationality and its arrogant disregard for earth and ecology; the recognition that hidden within our claims to truth are also claims to power and domination. We should not place these interruptive critiques in the realm of some remote, intellectual curiosity. Rather, these are strong issues that touch on the lives of many members of intentional Christian communities who are concerned both with the claims and promises of the book to which they belong, and the questions and interruptions raised by contemporary historical experience.

These interruptions place us in the realm of the postmodern age, an age whose description is still being written.[2] According to David Tracy, it is an age that now recognizes the difference between "errors" that can be "corrected," and systematic distortions which are so deep that we cannot but sense our exilic condition with respect to "all that within which we stand." It is an age that leads us into a profound sense of alienation and suspicion toward our traditions of belonging and our confident hopes of progress and freedom:

Should these interruptions lead us to believe that something is fundamentally and systematically awry in our history and our society? We can trust ourselves to conversation and argument when our only problem is error. But if we face something more elusive and profound than error, if we face systematic distortion, then another intellectual strategy is called for. That other strategy we name a hermeneutics of suspicion."[3]

A hermeneutics of suspicion — perhaps this phrase throws some light on that strange remark made by one of Jabès's imaginary rabbis: "exile, too, is an option." Can we break with our past — with all that comes down to us — to find a place from which to critique that to which we belong? This is where the metaphor of "exile" becomes important; it brings to mind the haunting proximity of home. The experience of finding ourselves exiled from the book's pages is the experience of living in a strange, foreign land that nevertheless calls out to the land of our belonging. According to Tracy, we experience the reality of our homelessness as we sense the uncanny presence of the "no-longer," of that which is absent to us: "the no-longer of the presence of the liberating classics of our heritage, the no-longer of real community and non-authoritarian authority, the no-longer recognizability of mystery . . . the no-longer of a conversation which should not have been broken. . . ."[4] In other words, it is only by recognizing the claim of that to which we belong that we can even begin to raise the question of nonbelonging. The experience of finding ourselves exiled from the pages of the book (where something of our own contemporary situation is not taken into account), or the question of leaving (exiting) the book to engage in its critique, can only be taken up in a context of recognized belonging. Even Derrida says as much when he writes: "I cannot conceive of a radical critique which would not be ultimately motivated by some sort of affirmation, acknowledged or not."[5]

In what way is exile an option, something chosen? Generally speaking, I think it is true that we are more inclined to stay close to all that has gone before us because it is not an easy thing to depart — to take leave of "all that to which we belong." It is not easy to think a new thing; harder still to live in a condition of exile. Yet sometimes that is what it takes to escape the binding of a book that no longer holds as it used to. Particularly in the face of dominant institutions and orderings of reality that cling to the safety of the same, there are times that urge us to depart, times when we feel we must take up the nomadic existence of an exiled wanderer, in order to enlarge and set free the home to which we belong — the place we never really leave. Maybe this is why it is such an unexpected and alarming freedom — to realize that exile is an option for those who are willing to recognize and live with the ambiguity that "we leave the book only in order to really enter it, and once inside, there is no exit."[6] When we think we are leaving, we only "get in deeper"; yet we bring with us the "pollen of the last flowers" taken from our wanderings outside the book, and the book blooms again.

In this chapter, I will look at two different perspectives from those who have critiqued the book of belonging, those who believe that in some sense "exile, too, is an option." The first perspective draws upon the thinking of the critical theorists, represented best by the work of Jürgen Habermas.[7] Habermas critiques the dialogical hermeneutics of Gadamer, claiming that Gadamer allows us no freedom to leave the book in order to gain a critical perspective on the ways of our belonging. Whereas Gadamer highlights the way all interpretation is held by the process of tradition, Habermas believes that the hold of tradition can be loosened or set free by critical reflection. Whereas Gadamer is concerned with "understanding" and allowing the book to "disclose" itself, Habermas is concerned with "emancipation" and freeing ourselves from all that is "distorted" within the book.

The second perspective takes up that line of thinking that could be loosely described as deconstructionist (or poststructuralist). The most notable scholar in this field is, of course, Jacques Derrida. I cannot pretend to be an adept or well-practiced reader of Derrida, whose work is, as many will acknowledge, demanding and difficult to read. Moreover, the literature of deconstruction represents a vast field — there are many variant and divergent readings. My concern lies more with the general direction of deconstructionist strategy: its ability to reveal the labyrinthlike quality of the book, with all its surprising twists and turns, and its profound openness to otherness and difference that cautions against any totalizing of meaning or understanding. Deconstruction has much to say to us about how many pages there are to live and to die "between the book and leaving the book." Although it is often criticized as nihilistic and frivolous, I align myself with those who see in deconstruction an ethical and a creative possibility.

The Broken Book

The dialogue set up by Jabès between Reb Chemoul and Reb Haggaï bears some similarities to the dialogue between Gadamer and Habermas.[8] Like Reb Chemoul, Gadamer would not want us to "break the book in anger, but in love" — with a deep respect for the book's disclosive ability such that it continually "opens to the divine Word." Habermas, however, might reply in a fashion similar to Reb Haggaï. We have "no need to break the book" because "it is already broken." We need to recognize and uncover the brokenness of the book, the ways the book is deeply implicated in systematic distortions within its own pages. In other words, the book not only opens out toward understanding and disclosure; it is also deeply fissured by false consciousness and ideological distortions.

Hermeneutics of Suspicion

Habermas critiques Gadamer's hermeneutics for failing to pay attention to the way power and domination function within a tradition. He believes Gadamer's hermeneutical project is too concerned with maintaining mutual understanding within a tradition and not concerned enough with uncovering the ways tradition is distorted by hegemonic relations of power and control. According to Habermas, the language of tradition is not only a bearer of meaning and truth; it is "*also a medium of domination and social power; it serves to legitimate relations of organized force.*"[9] Since we cannot leave our language behind, as Gadamer suggests, this means that if our language of tradition and interpretation is itself systematically distorted, hermeneutics has no way of recognizing it. Habermas writes:

> Hermeneutics has taught us that we are always a participant as long as we move within the natural language and that we cannot step outside the role of a reflective partner. There is, therefore, no general criterion available to us which would allow us to determine when we are subject to the false consciousness of a pseudo-normal understanding and consider something as a difficulty that can be resolved by hermeneutical means when, in fact, it requires systematic explanation. . . .This hermeneutic consciousness proves inadequate in the case of systematically distorted communication. . . . The self-conception of hermeneutics can only be shaken when it appears that patterns of systematically distorted communication are also in evidence in "normal". . . speech.[10]

Habermas draws upon both Freud and Marx to suggest that there is not only intelligibility in our language of tradition but also repression and domination. The danger these thinkers alert us to is that the meanings we retrieve from tradition could well be those of a dominant group (Marx's influence) for the sake of keeping the present arrangements of society stable and in conformity with the past (Freud's influence).[11] We could ask, for example, whether the normatively held classics of a tradition endure because of their surplus of meaning, or because of power structures and the repression of rival traditions.[12] Who perpetuates a classic's status as classic? Do the classics represent the tradition of the victors, not the victims?[13] Can we assume that tradition is only a source for truth and disclosure — always meaningful and never distorted? What if we cannot find ourselves in tradition "as in dialogue"?

Alongside Freud and Marx, Nietzsche has also cast a suspicious eye toward the truth claims of tradition. According to Nietzsche (and thinkers after him, such as the French poststructuralist Michel Foucault), knowledge is about the production and control of discourse — it is the "will to power" present under the guise of the "will to truth."[14] The play of tradition is in fact a power play, and the unity of tradition — rather than being something natural or inherent — is in fact one enforced by controlling powers who exclude what is other in order to maintain the place of dominant structures. We need only think of the systematic exclusion of women in the patriarchal ordering of Christian and other Western traditions to feel the scope of this critique.

According to Paul Ricoeur, the great masters of suspicion — Marx, Nietzsche, and Freud — all engaged in programs of suspicion that point to "truth as lying," as the exercise of "false consciousness."[15] For Marx, it was the false consciousness of class bias resulting in domination and submission; for Nietzsche, it was the false consciousness of will resulting in *ressentiment* — the resentment of the weak against the strong; for Freud it was the false consciousness of desire, resulting in repression — where consciousness itself is wounded at its very core.[16] David Tracy notes how these masters of suspicion unleashed a relentlessly negative critique on the "last illusion of the Enlightenment — the illusion that if we are autonomously conscious and rational we need fear no further illusions." Rather, we are now acutely aware that all expressions of consciousness "possess not only their manifest meanings but conceal and distort a series of latent, overdetermined meanings that demand new modes of analysis."[17] In rather dramatic fashion, Terry Eagleton brings to bear the full force of these hermeneutes of suspicion toward Gadamer's dialogical hermeneutics; he points to the hidden dangers of a dialogue that results from a false consensus, a false "we," a false sense of an unbroken stream of community and tradition.

> It might be well to ask Gadamer whose and what "tradition" he actually has in mind. For his theory holds only on the enormous assumption that there is indeed a single "mainstream" tradition; that all "valid" works participate in it; that history forms an unbroken continuum, free of decisive rupture, conflict and contradiction; and that the prejudices which we (who?) have inherited from the "tradition" are to be cherished. It assumes, in other words, that history is a place where "we" can always and everywhere be at home. . . . It is, in short, a grossly complacent theory of history. . . . It has little conception of history and tradition as oppressive as well as liberating forces, areas rent by conflict and domination. History for Gadamer is not a place of struggle, discontinuity and exclusion but a "continuing chain," an ever-flowing river, almost, one might say, a club of the like-minded. . . .
>
> It cannot, in other words, come to terms with the problem of ideology — with the fact that the unending "dialogue" of human history is as often as not a monologue by the powerful to the powerless, or that if it is indeed a "dialogue" then the partners — men and women, for example — hardly occupy equal positions. It refuses to recognize that discourse is always caught up with a power which may be by no means

benign; and the discourse in which it most signally fails to recognize this fact is its own.[18]

Eagleton is deeply suspicious of the way Gadamer's hermeneutics could be appropriated conservatively as a "caretaker" hermeneutics that preserves a tradition in a self-enclosed historical community. Its goal becomes one of aiding the internalization of a tradition's central claims, rather than the critique and reconstruction of the tradition in which we stand.[19] Although my own reading of Gadamer has not led me to a similar conclusion, I do see how he could be read along these lines. Consider, for instance, how an emphasis on tradition and historicity could foster a sense of being confined within a particular religious tradition, coercing all new experience into agreement with the past. In this sense, highlighting the ways in which we are deeply held by the prejudices of tradition could serve as a strong legitimization for the conservative maintenance of tradition. Linell Cady, for example, argues that whereas theology was displaced all through the modern age as a purely subjective discourse, the postmodern situation has provided a new recourse for theology to regain its lost status. However, she worries that many theologians are taking advantage of the postmodern awareness of historicity to legitimate conservative and confessional theologies.[20]

The Enlightenment Legacy: Emancipatory Reason

Whereas both Gadamer and Habermas critique the Enlightenment notion of disinterested and ahistorical reasoning, Habermas believes Gadamer leaves us too bound by the constraints of tradition: "hermeneutics bangs helplessly, so to speak, from within against the walls of tradition."[21] Unlike the empirical-technical sciences or the historical-hermeneutical sciences, Habermas believes the critical-social sciences are governed by an interest in emancipation.[22] In contrast to Gadamer's strong polemic against the Enlightenment, he holds that there is a claim to truth in the Enlightenment tradition that reflects our human quest for freedom.[23] Although Habermas recognizes the need to critique the illusions of Enlightenment rationality, he nevertheless believes the Enlightenment left us a very positive legacy, namely, critical reason's emancipatory interest: its capacity to unmask false consciousness and to free us from oppressive and mystifying traditions, along with the need for civilized discourse that aims at nondistorted communicative speech and action. According to Richard Bernstein, Habermas is writing

> a *new* Dialectic of Enlightenment — one which does full justice to the dark side of
> the Enlightenment legacy, explains its causes but nevertheless redeems and justifies

the hope of freedom, justice, and happiness which still stubbornly speaks to us. The project of modernity, the hope of Enlightenment thinkers, is not a bitter illusion, not a naive ideology that turns into violence and terror, but a practical task which has *not yet* been realized and which can still orient and guide our actions.[24]

Habermas refuses to concede to postmodern descriptions that believe we must give up any hope of knowledge leading to liberation, that any attempt to justify the emancipatory aspirations of the Enlightenment represents just one more "metanarrative" that needs to be eschewed and deconstructed.[25] As Bernstein notes, we live in a time when there is a great rage against reason, humanism, and the Enlightenment legacy.[26] Yet Habermas still holds to the hope, less fashionable yet maybe secretly shared by many of us, "that it is possible to confront honestly the challenges, critiques, the unmasking of illusions; to work through these, and still responsibly reconstruct an informed comprehensive perspective on modernity and its pathologies."[27]

Habermas believes it is possible to uncover repressed or distorted communication within structures of interpretation via a "depth hermeneutic" which he models on Freudian psychoanalysis.[28] According to Habermas, the same problem that occurs on an individual level in terms of repressed and distorted behavior also occurs on a societal level with ideological distortions. Although hermeneutics may uncover the pre-understandings of truth claims, critical self-reflection enables one to reach even deeper into revealing a society's implicit self-understanding — its ideological dimension to which its very pre-understandings are tied. Habermas draws the distinction between hermeneutics that can interpret the meaning of a distorted text and depth-hermeneutics that is needed to interpret the meaning of the distortion itself.[29] In other words, revealing assumptions does not necessarily mean revealing the distortions that may lie behind those assumptions. For this task, a more self-conscious approach is needed than hermeneutics is capable of.[30]

The value of the psychoanalytical model is that it shows how emancipatory interest requires a critical analysis of the self-formative process. In a similar way, society requires a critical reflection on its own formative processes to uncover the interests, assumptions, and ideologies that distort our ways of being-in-the-world. For example, it is necessary that people who are oppressed become aware of their oppression — that blockages imposed by oppressors on the consciousness of the oppressed be removed. Because communication is systematically distorted in favor of the oppressor, these distortions are not recognized as they are part of the interpretations within which people operate. Emancipatory reason offers alternative interpretations to remove these blockages and distortions in communication. Critical reflection frees human communities to recreate their socio-cultural world in emancipatory ways.[31]

The Gadamer-Habermas Debate

Gadamer's reply to Habermas seems inevitable. How is such critical reflection still not inside a tradition rather than outside? Can we ever reach a privileged place of ideological neutrality? How does ideology critique avoid the influence of tradition? How does it escape the confines of the "hermeneutic situation"? How does it rise above hermeneutic limitations to reach a higher position of critique?[32] Habermas, however, believes it is possible to find an objectively given basis or foundation for a critical rationality, while at the same time recognizing that all human knowing is rooted in actual structures of human life. To this end, he proposes a complex theory of "communicative competence" that aims at undistorted, constraint-free communication.[33] He argues that by examining human discourse we can discover the conditions necessary for an "ideal speech situation" that provides a rational basis or a "regulative ideal" for evaluating our communicative actions. An ideal speech situation is one in which there is complete mutuality and intersubjectivity between people. This is conversation that is marked by mutual respect for one another, which is free from domination or manipulation, where there is no compulsion to consensus or decision other than the validity of particular perspectives as they are tested by community discernment. This ideal, while it is always counterfactual, is nevertheless built in to the very anticipation and hopes of every conversation and hence operates as a measure of communication's validity. In other words, every conversation works toward the ideal of mutual and undistorted understanding. The ideal speech situation is always presumed in practical discourse, not as "transcendental criteria" but as that which makes communication possible and as that to which we strive in communication. As such, the ideal speech situation fulfills a regulative function revealing the criteria by which all un-relationship, all non-community, all domination, distortion, and division may be judged. It provides the norms for constraint-free discourse that can guide our praxis as we seek to approximate the ideal of reciprocal and undistorted communication and dialogue with others.[34]

As Richard Bernstein suggests: "If we think of what is required for such a dialogue based on mutual understanding, respect, a willingness to listen and risk one's opinions and prejudices . . . we will have defined a powerful regulative ideal that can orient our practical and political lives."[35] Yet we still need to ask ourselves what it is that prevents or blocks such dialogue and how genuine solidarity and authentic community can be achieved. Georgia Warnke claims that for

Gadamer, the evaluation of tradition cannot be measured against an ideal of constraint-free communication; rather, it should be evaluated

> within a practical context, as that degree of knowledge, enlightenment and openness of which we are capable at a given time. In contrast to the "counterfactual" norm of an ideal speech situation, Gadamer [points to] the way in which prejudices are overcome and ideologies revealed in the continued course of tradition itself.[36]

Gadamer holds that even though we are bound by tradition and its prejudices, the hermeneutical task can be sufficiently critical to be emancipatory. The critical hermeneutics of feminist scholars working within the Christian tradition is perhaps one example of the hermeneutical task being done with a radical and emancipatory interest.[37] According to Gadamer, there seems no reason why hermeneutics should be exclusive of self-critical, emancipatory reflection.

We have come to the crux of the debate between Gadamer and Habermas. Gadamer claims we are always situated within the process of tradition such that a privileged position of critical disconnection is not possible. However, he does not believe this necessarily locks us into distorted practices because we are constantly modifying and reforming tradition according to new applications, new experiences, and risky conversation. Habermas, however, claims that we cannot simply trust ourselves to the conversation of tradition. Rather, he believes that the emancipatory interest of critical reflection does enable us to gain a critical perspective from which to evaluate tradition in order to move beyond its constraints. Shaun Gallagher draws the boundaries of the debate by asking, "Does hermeneutical practice, conceived as a depth hermeneutics, actually move us beyond constrained communication to a reflective emancipation (as claimed by Habermas), or is such critical reflection itself bound by hermeneutical constraints (Gadamer's position)?"[38]

It is tempting to seek ways of reconciling the debate between Gadamer and Habermas. Although I believe this is indeed possible and helpful, it nevertheless seems important to allow the tension between their positions to remain. Bernstein suggests that Gadamer's hermeneutics "can be read as an invitation to join him in the rediscovery and redemption of the richness and concreteness of our dialogical-being-in-the-world."[39] However, Habermas reminds us that the conversation of tradition is never so totally reliable and assured; more often than not it has the character of a battle that is, in Foucault's words, "bloody, lethal, and far removed from the serene ideal of Platonic dialogue."[40] Although I do not share Habermas's concern "to escape from conversation" in order to find a more secure foundation that "lies in the background of all possible conversations,"[41] I do believe he is correct in suggesting that Gadamer's hermeneutics lacks a proper understanding of how hegemonic relations of power and domination function to distort the hermeneutic situation. As Sharon Welch notes, it is vital that we hear this critique, because "it is not easy for Christians to acknowledge the oppression supported and engendered by Christian faith. The ambiguities of discourse that has both oppressive and liberating functions is indeed unsettling."[42] Sometimes we need to write the book "outside the book," from the position of deep suspicion and critique; yet we must nevertheless recognize that it is the book to which we belong that we are rewriting and for which we are ultimately responsible. There is a sense in which the book is, as Jabès says, "written twice: in the book and outside it." This is tradition writing against tradition: "Book rejected and reclaimed by the book."

The positions of Gadamer and Habermas are often distinguished by referring to the former as a "hermeneutic of retrieval" and the latter as a "hermeneutic of suspicion." Yet, as Gerald Bruns suggests, these two positions are sometimes seen "as methodological options that one can pick up as one pleases, but in fact one does not so much choose between them as abide within their oppositional interplay."[43] According to Ricoeur,

> nothing is more deceptive than the alleged antinomy between an ontology of prior understanding and an eschatology of freedom . . . as if it were necessary to choose between reminiscence and hope! . . .
> The moment these two interests become radically separate, then hermeneutics and critique will themselves be no more than . . . ideologies![44]

Ricoeur sees the critical, suspicious, explanatory moment of hermeneutics not in opposition to the hermeneutical quest for understanding, but as a valid and fruitful reflection that enables a fuller projection of possibilities in front of the hermeneutical situation.[45] He reminds us that the practice of suspicion should not be misunderstood as an exercise of skepticism. The great masters of suspicion were indeed "great destroyers," but that should not mislead us because "destruction . . . is a moment of every new foundation," clearing the way for "a more authentic word."[46] As Jàbes suggests, while revolt may represent a torn-out, "crumpled page," often a new writing of tradition "is born from this sacrificed page."

The Absent Book

Jean-François Lyotard describes the postmodern condition as an incredulity toward the "grand narratives" *(grands récits)* of Western history — all those appeals that are made in the name of some metadiscourse or first principle, be it God, the Idea, the Self, and so on.[47] These grand narratives seek to legitimate the contingent social practices that human beings have worked out in the course of history with something that offers itself as a more solid and substantial foundation.[48] In contrast to this Western metaphysical tradition, John Caputo believes that a radical hermeneutics "cultivates an acute sense of the contingency of all social, historical, linguistic structures, an appreciation of their constituted character, their character as effects."[49] And so we are led to wonder: Must we abandon any notion of emancipatory reason premised on the Enlightenment ideals of rational consensus, freedom, and democratic justice? Or any notion of dialogue and conversation in a transformative participation in tradition? "If the flux is all, and linguistic, historical structures are nothing more than writings in the sand which we manage to inscribe between tides, what then?"[50] Are we simply left, in the words of Yeats, spinning in an unknowable and unnameable world?

> Turning and turning in the widening gyre
> The falcon cannot hear the falconer;
> Things fall apart; the center cannot hold;
> Mere anarchy is loosed upon the world. . . .[51]

According to David Tracy, it is this experience of homelessness that is our most fundamental question today, provoking a "not-at-homeness which is one, perhaps the most familiar, kind of experience in our situation."[52] As Richard Bernstein suggests, this is not simply an intellectual question. Rather, it is a question that goes to the heart of "our everyday moral, social and political experiences. . . . At issue are some of the most perplexing questions concerning human beings: what we are, what we can know, what norms ought to bind us, what are the grounds for hope."[53]

The Dizzying Non-Place of the Book

If Habermas stands as the great defender of the unfinished project of modernity and the Enlightenment legacy, then it is probably Jacques Derrida who stands as the great postmodern thinker.[54] Derrida believes we are not in control over language, that we are always in the position of being "inside the text" of our constitutive traditions and that it is futile to look for groundings "outside the text." For Derrida, we must begin by "taking rigorous account of this *being held within* language."[55] In this sense, he shares something in common with Gadamer's view: "Being that can be understood is language."[56] Derrida's now famous phrase, "there is nothing outside the text,"[57] is the recognition that language is the medium of all interpretive tradition. It is not an instrument or tool we use; rather, as Heidegger suggests, it is the house in which we live.[58]

Derrida, however, could be said to stand at the far end of historical and hermeneutical consciousness. For Derrida, "there is nothing outside the text" because there is *only* text, or writing, in which words refer to other words, interpretations to other interpretations, in an endless play of signs without beginning or end. Derrida draws upon the work of Ferdinand de Saussure, who analyzed the workings of language as a system or structure *(langue)*. According to Saussure, signs (or words) derive their meaning only in relationship to other signs. If we ask what it is that our words refer to — that is, what is the relationship between the signifier and the signified — Saussure replies that there is no natural or necessary relationship; rather, in order to understand a sign, we have to see how it is used in relationship to other signs within a language system.[59] Signs get their meaning by functioning differentially, by playing off each other such that a sign has meaning only because of the difference it bears from all other signs. According to Saussure, everything "boils down to this: in language there are only differences."[60]

Derrida, like Saussure, sees language and text as constituted by signs and, again like Saussure, he understands the meaning of these signs to consist in what they are *not,* in their "difference" from other signs within the language system. And since their meaning resides in what they are not, the meaning of a particular sign is absent from itself. Sign is linked to sign, word to word, such that all our signifiers merely bear upon themselves the traces of other signifiers — and thus the very distinction between signifier and signified collapses in upon itself.[61] With the collapse of this distinction, the hope of finding any secure or stable meaning that grounds a text's reference is continually deferred, is never fully present. "There is always an element of 'undecidability' or 'play' in the unstable sign. This leads to an emphasis on the signifier and on textuality rather than the signified and meaning."[62] For Derrida, it is impossible to locate any kind of "presence," any form of being or reality (a "transcendental signified") that lies outside the ongoing play of signification on which our thought and language might be securely grounded. As David Tracy notes, in Derrida's scheme, any hope of a full presence of meaning is lost to us.

> When we use language, we must always defer claims to full meaning, for the differences multiply and the traces of absent meaning are disseminated. We must both differ and defer in order for meaning to happen at all. . . . All is difference, and all difference is always already a deferral of full meaning. Difference has become *différance.*[63]

The result, according to Nathan Scott, is that writing and texts extend into "the abyss of an infinite and ungrounded process of signification initiated by the signs within the text itself, that abyss wherein all signifieds are collapsed within signifiers."[64] Interpretation can only seize on another interpretation that is buried within an ongoing chain of texts. Meaning is always deferred, delayed, or diverted, "caught in a network of contextually bound and generated commentaries."[65] The search for truth is always a search for lost words — words forgotten except for a haunting trace. To bear this pain, we turn to other words in the hope of finding a way again. Words are saved by other words—born of the silence they break, which in turn will break them. We only read words out of their depths, struggling in the pages of the book — a continual flickering of presence and absence.

According to Derrida, therefore, we have no way of getting beyond our being-inside-linguistic-structure. There is nothing we can count on to center language, to ground the free play of endless signification, to establish a stable reference outside of language. His alternative is that we have to learn to live without a center or, at least, to determine *"the noncenter otherwise than as loss of center."*[66] The very idea that language needs a center, a principle or grounding that provides a unified meaning, belongs to the Western metaphysical tradition — and it is this tradition ("logocentrism") that Derrida radically calls into question.[67] "It has always been thought," writes Derrida, "that the center, which is by definition unique, constituted the very thing within a structure which while governing the structure, escapes structurally."[68] Now, however, we must live

> in the absence of a center or origin . . . in a system in which the central signified, the original or transcendental signified, is never absolutely present outside a system of differences. The absence of the transcendental signified extends the domain and the play of signification infinitely.[69]

Openness to Otherness and Difference

Some might read Derrida's decentering project as being nihilistic, frivolous, or anarchical. Yet I believe there is a more positive and fruitful way of interpreting Derrida's deconstructive work.[70] We can ask ourselves, for example, why is Derrida so keen to critique or displace the concept of a "centered structure" that provides a "reassuring certitude" on the basis of which "anxiety can be mastered"?[71] According to John Caputo, the oldest desire (*philia*) of Western philosophy's metaphysical tradition has been to locate a stable, fixed, permanent center (the *arche*, the *principum*, the overarching principle) that "supplies unity which rules over multiplicity, necessity which drives out chance, order which subdues chaos."[72] However, in looking for this center, this unity, this reassuring certitude, Western philosophy has also tended to establish fixed boundaries and hierarchical orderings that do violence to everything which is other or different or unable to fit by excluding and repressing this difference for the sake of an undisturbed sameness and a "metaphysical comfort."[73] Caputo, therefore, defines deconstruction as "an exercise in disruption which displaces whatever tends to settle in place."[74] Its aim is not a cold, despairing, or tragic divestiture of all meaning making, but rather a constant questioning of boundaries that aims at the liberation or emancipation of all that has become fixed, rigid, or closed to otherness and difference.[75] According to Richard Bernstein, Derrida's deconstructive project is not concerned with a celebration of "formlessness and chaos"; rather, Derrida is concerned that we never cease questioning "the status of what we take to be our center, our native home, our *arche*."[76]

David Tracy believes that postmodern writers such as Derrida aim to "deconstruct the *status quo* in favor of the *fluxus quo*."[77] They recognize that indeterminacy, rather than undermining ethical concerns, can actually serve to foster ethical imagination: "otherness, difference, and excess become the alternatives to the deadening sameness, the totalizing system, the false security of the modern self-grounding subject."[78] They want to break down concentrations of power through deconstructive acts of decentering and dissemination.[79] It is probably the Jewish philosopher Emmanuel Levinas who has done the most to bring the issue of "otherness" into the fore of postmodern thinking over against Western philosophy's concern with closed systems and identities. For Levinas, the claim of "the Other" (*L'Autre*) is an ethical-political claim that can release us from our desire for totality and open us toward a more genuine sense of alterity and infinity.[80]

Levinas critiques the dominant tradition of Western philosophy for always seeking to reduce "the other to the same." In this framework, "the other" is construed as something foreign and as an obstacle that needs to be overcome or reduced and absorbed into "the same."[81] This force of exclusion and exile reflects the violence of Western metaphysical thought that aims to dominate, control, and colonize "the Other" into "more of the same" — where all otherness and difference disappear.[82] Gerald Bruns provides us with an example in the relationship between Christianity and Judaism, where Christianity has taken its "own other" — Judaism — and rewritten this "alien discourse" to make it "come out right," that is, according to Christianity's prevailing norms of what is right. "Judaism is no longer the other but is an intelligible component of Christianity and even foundational for the theological narrative of promise and fulfillment by which Christianity understands itself."[83] There are no doubt countless other examples in the history of the West where dominant institutions and discourses have functioned to identify everything "alien" and "other" in terms of itself, as a way of overcoming its suspicion of whatever is not itself and keeping it under control.

"There are winners," said the imprisoned rabbi, the imprisoned saint. "Winners with their arrogance, their eloquence. And there are losers without words and without signs. . . ."[84]

According to Francis Schüssler Fiorenza, the "other" does not merely represent "the other of signification." It also represents the voices of those who are "without words," those who have been robbed of the power to speak — the "losers" who are

> not present within the tradition, are not present within the discourse interpreting the tradition, and have no voice in interpreting their identity and self-determination. In the absence of secure objective or experiential foundations, the community of discourse plays a pivotal role. It becomes imperative that those voices excluded from dominant discourse become introduced to the discourse.[85]

In Bernstein's view, deconstruction represents an ethical-political openness to the claim of the other and the different, the "rebellious" and the "absent." Derrida's deconstructive work has the quality of an "exile bearing witness" to all those who have been excluded and banished from the mainstream discourses of Western tradition.[86] Similarly, for Caputo, deconstruction highlights an ethics that gives priority to the claim of absence rather than presence. It highlights difference rather than sameness.[87] It does not locate itself within the mainstream ordering of Being and presence, but keeps its focus on the rights of the different, the call of the silent and the excluded. "It takes its stand with those for whom the system was *not* designed . . . those who are being excluded by the system."[88]

A questioning that puts principles and grounds into question may at first appear groundless, anarchic, and irresponsible. Yet such questioning is not irresponsible; rather, it is a questioning that takes a measure of responsibility for, or responsiveness to, what has been excluded and marginalized by what calls itself *arche:* the rule of the same, the overarching principle of order. It stands on the side of those elements of a tradition that have been subdued or oppressed by the principal forces of order. It is not so much that deconstruction is simply against principles for the sake of flatly refusing them; rather, deconstruction assumes responsibility for principles by holding them in question, by delimiting the power of the *arche* and seeing what it excludes.[89] In this sense, Caputo sees deconstruction as representing a "responsible anarchy":

> Deconstruction takes aim at the "powers that be," an excellent English expression which shows very nicely the ethical spin which Derrida has put on his critique of the metaphysics of presence. The powers that be: that means the powers that have presence, that claim to "be" rather than to have "become," to have timeless validity rather than historical genealogy. It wants to delimit the *arche* which metaphysics

always sets at the head of every hierarchical system. Yet it does not do this irresponsibly, but with a sense of what might be called "responsible anarchy."[90]

We can hear something of this sense of "responsibility" in an interview with Derrida where he speaks of deconstruction as "a vocation," "a response to a call" — the call of "the other."[91] Bernstein sees this vocation evident in Derrida's ability "to *show* us that at the heart of what we take to be familiar, native, at home — where we think we can find our center — lurks (is concealed and repressed) what is unfamiliar, strange, and uncanny."[92] Bernstein notes some marked vocational similarities between both Derrida and Gadamer in their concern with the call and claim of the "other." Both recognize that

> it is only through an engaged encounter with the Other, with the otherness of the Other, that one comes to a more informed, textured understanding of the traditions to which "we" belong. It is in our genuine encounters with what is other and alien (even in ourselves) that we can further our own self-understanding.[93]

According to Caputo, however, Gadamer's dialogical hermeneutics is not radical enough in allowing the claim of "the other." Gadamer follows the Hegelian model of too quickly subsuming the other into a sameness, "always interested in assimilating the other, making it part of its substance."[94] Otherness becomes only a moment within the Same and is thereby denied its radically strange, different, provoking claim in and of itself.[95] Yet it is difficult to imagine how one could relate to "the other" as totally, absolutely other and foreign. There can never be, as Tracy suggests, a pure encounter with difference and otherness — this encounter will always issue forth as an "identity-in-difference."[96] As Mark C. Taylor notes, difference implies relationality in the sense that "*difference from* the other is at the same time *relation to* the other."[97] We cannot speak of identity without also speaking of difference just as we cannot speak of difference without also speaking of identity. "Difference resists the totalitarianism of identity, just as identity resists the anarchy of difference."[98] Or as Thomas J. J. Altizer suggests, instead of identity diffusing difference, difference actually constitutes identity:

> For we can evoke an actual or real identity only by embodying difference, a real and actual difference, a difference making identity manifest. . . .Only the presence of difference calls identity forth. . . . There is always difference *within* identity and absence *within* presence.[99]

The Wound of Absence in Presence

Charles E. Scott highlights the way Derrida's own exilic experience lies at the heart of much of his work. During his formative years, Derrida experienced a feeling of nonbelonging in which a sense of difference was infused in every moment of his perceived identity. This experience of nonbelonging gave Derrida a profound sense that everything we experience as continuous and abiding and deeply part of who we are stands out for us in the very experience of nonidentity, nonbelonging, and discontinuity: "'something' that identity and belonging do not encompass seems to resonate in the margins and spaces of identity."[100] Derrida "found himself neither properly Jew nor properly non-Jew, neither a proper Algerian nor a proper Frenchman, neither secure in his family nor insecured by his family."[101] He lived in this tension of belonging and nonbelonging, identity, and difference, in which everything was in question and finally undecidable. According to Bernstein,

> Derrida seeks to show us that we never quite are or can be at home in the world. We are always threatened by the uncanniness of what is canny; we are always in exile — even from ourselves. We may long and dream of being at home in our world, to find a "proper" center, but we never achieve this form of presence or self-presence.[102]

Although we can read Derrida's work as an *apologia* for all those who have not found a place in the book — all those who are excluded and thereby cast "outside the book" — Derrida does not provide us with the same hope or assurity (such as Habermas seeks) to find a place outside the constraints of tradition from which the critique of exclusionary practices can take place. For Derrida, everything is always already inscribed in a web of interpretation such that there can be no exit from this labyrinth of interpretive textuality. Faced with this indeterminacy, deconstruction places in doubt both Habermas's belief in the critical power of emancipatory reason and Gadamer's innocent trust in the "good will" of hermeneutical conversation.[103] Nevertheless, Derrida does perform his deconstructive work and in the end he seems close to Gadamer in rejecting the possibility of a critical perspective that gains mastery over the text. For Derrida, the only exit from the book is the one inscribed in the book's pages: "we can pronounce not a single deconstructive proposition which has not already had to slip into the form, the logic, and the implicit postulations of precisely what it seeks to contest."[104] The "movements of deconstruction" do not take place outside the structures they aim to question but rather work inside those structures in a subversive way:

> They are possible and effective, nor can they take accurate aim, except by inhabiting those structures. Inhabiting them *in a certain way,* because one always inhabits, and all the more when one does not suspect it. Operating necessarily from the inside, borrowing all the strategic and necessary resources of subversion from the old struc-

ture . . . the enterprise of deconstruction always in a certain way falls prey to its own work.[105]

On the one hand, Derrida undermines our pretensions for complete mastery and control over language and tradition such that there is no need for further interpretive or deconstructive practice. We can never say "the word" that delivers "full presence." On the other hand, Derrida speaks in the very language he questions and takes apart. We can never say a word against it that is not (at least) motivated by its desire for truth. Here, perhaps, Derrida is like Habermas: we cannot speak a language that would deliver absolute truth and we cannot speak a language that does not claim to strive toward that. Derrida plays "in between" these two poles, between the book of yearned-for presence, and the book of wounded absence.

Derrida works his exilic hermeneutics within and against an overconfident and all-too-often arrogant and violent metaphysics of the West that has sought, both in its philosophical and theological traditions, to secure its home in the world. In the face of the violence and genocide that has befallen even our most recent history, this metaphysics of presence now seems empty and hollow, and we are brought face to face with our own nonbelonging and homelessness. Certainly many readers of Derrida attack him on this very point, suggesting that he is a "clever intellectual fraud, a 'prophet' of nihilism, a whimsical destroyer of any 'canons' of rationality, a self-indulgent scribbler who delights in irresponsible word play, punning, and parody."[106] Derrida's notion of the absence of a "transcendental signified," his critique of "logocentrism" and a "metaphysics of presence," is often read as a bleak parody on modernity's self-dug grave leading to a type of nihilistic sense of absence, loss, and despair; or as a reveling in the *jouissance* of its disintegration and the newfound pleasure of textuality's infinite play.[107] However, in my view, Derrida does not so much celebrate or extol absence as he does make us acutely aware and mindful of it. What he would not have us do is what we have done too often and too confidently, namely, celebrate a presence that becomes so totalizing that we forget (repress/suppress) everything this all-encompassing presence neglects, excludes, and fails to take into account. Derrida's *oeuvre* is not so much a celebration of absence as it is the sharp, dismantling critique of a too confident and undisturbed celebration of presence — a celebration that becomes drunk with its own *veritas,* and that in the end becomes a poisonous party of excluded, unwanted, or unrecognized guests.

Would Derrida have us extinguish any sense of presence? Perhaps we could ask the question this way: Who, in the end, could live their lives in the shadow of an uncompromising absence? Who would choose a fate like that of the Jewish boy whose face we meet in Elie Wiesel's *Night,* struggling between life and death at the end of the gallows rope, with the poignant question haunting the darkness: *"Where is God now?"* [108] It is this very absence we must not — cannot — choose. It is this very absence we have no right to celebrate and every urgency to negate (an absence that is itself the result of a violent "metaphysics of presence"). Our every "yes" must be a "no to this no." [109] In memory of all those who have suffered — and died with a prayer yet still on their lips ("My God, my God, why have you forsaken me?") — in memory of these we cannot let go of our hope in the mystery of a vulnerable yet "commanding presence" [110] — a presence, in other words, not left undisturbed by absence but that commands attention and addresses us from the very wound of absence. In David Tracy's words:

> In that experience, the force of the not-yet unmasks our present bondage and, in that very unmasking, discloses an always-already hope: a hope sheerly there — given, we know not how, or by what or by whom, given as gift, as threat, as promise in an ineradicable, always-already power that we acknowledge as given to us only for the sake of the hopeless. . . . [111]

Neither of these two — absence or presence — can be totalized into frameworks of either nihilistic despair or seamless, uninterruptive wholes. Presence inevitably gives way to that which we have absented, banished, or left unrecognized. Yet when we face the stark realization of how much of our lives are exilically inscribed, we may sense, once again, the uncanny proximity of a presence both rejected and reclaimed. Book written twice. So many pages to live and to die. . . .

> In the relentless waves of negativity . . . we may recognize the presence of an always-already undertow of the sensed presence of some gift, some participation beyond all homelessness and absence in a history that is also a heritage, a fate which has become again a destiny, a culture which can release us, through its very negations to the gift and wonder of a grounding at-home-ness . . . because we finally sense some reality, vague yet important, which we cannot name but which is, we sense, not of our own making. [112]

Notes

The epigraphs introducing part 2 are from the following works of Edmond Jabès: *The Book of Resemblances*, 1. 95; *The Book of Resemblances*, 3. 73; *The Book of Questions*, 1. 191, 367, 43, 333, 160, 215; *The Book of Resemblances*, 1. 74; *The Book of Questions*, 1. 398; The citation from "Reb" Derrida is from Derrida, *Writing and Difference*, p.75; *The Book of Resemblances*, 1. 60, 13.

1. Gustavo Gutiérrez, *A Theology of Liberation*, p. xx.
2. In David Tracy's excellent article "On Naming the Present," Tracy shows how our present age is one that cannot name itself, though he posits three main contenders: moder-

nity, antimodernity and postmodernity. With respect to postmodernity, scholars today recognize that there are a variety of "postmodernisms" and that the opposition "modernity/postmodernity" is a vague and ambiguous yet powerful "mood" that is exerting influence on the ways we think, act, and experience. See, e.g., Richard Bernstein, *The New Constellation: The Ethical-Political Horizons of Modernity/Postmodernity*, pp. 11–12; Andreas Huyssen, "Mapping the Postmodern"; David Tracy, *Plurality and Ambiguity; The Analogical Imagination*, pp. 339–70 and "The Uneasy Alliance Reconceived: Catholic Theological Method, Modernity and Postmodernity"; Sheila Greeve Davaney, ed., *Theology at the End of Modernity;* Walter Brueggemann, *Texts under Negotiation*, pp. 1–25; Gayle Ormiston and Alan Schrift, eds., *Transforming the Hermeneutic Context;* Patricia Waugh, ed., *Postmodernism;* Sharon Welch, *A Feminist Ethic of Risk*, pp. 145–51.

3. Tracy, *Plurality and Ambiguity*, p. 73.

4. Tracy, *The Analogical Imagination*, pp. 358–59.

5. "Deconstruction and the Other: An Interview with Derrida," in Richard Kearney, ed., *Dialogues with Contemporary Continental Thinkers*, p. 118.

6. Edmond Jabès, *The Book of Resemblances*, 1. 19.

7. Habermas's work stands in the tradition of the Frankfurt school of critical theory, which was founded in the 1920s. Max Horkheimer, Theodor Adorno, Walter Benjamin, and Erich Fromm — all Jewish intellectuals — were associated with the school. The Frankfurt school sought to develop philosophy in dialogue with the social sciences, particularly psychology (Freud) and sociology (Marx). They were critical toward Western positivism (as practiced in the Vienna Circle) and Western capitalism. As such, their critical theory emphasized the importance of negativity (iconoclasm, which fit very well with their Jewish roots).

8. By a similar extension, the dialogue could also be read as one between Gadamer and Derrida, though Derrida's understanding of the "broken book" is very different from Habermas's.

9. Jürgen Habermas, "A Review of Gadamer's Truth and Method," p. 239.

10. Habermas, "The Hermeneutic Claim to Universality," p. 254.

11. See Edward Schillebeeckx's essay, "From Hermeneutical Theology to Critical Theory" in *The Schillebeeckx Reader*, pp. 106–19.

12 . The sociological-Habermasian question would be: How is a particular reading of tradition functioning? Freud asks: What is it hiding/masking? Marx asks: Is it functioning to reinforce the status and control of a dominant group? Who is deciding? Who is benefiting? Who is suffering?

13. See, e.g., Walter Brueggemann's chapter "Blessed are the History-makers" in his book *Hope within History*, pp. 49–71.

14. Friedrich Nietzsche, "Beyond Good and Evil," in *Basic Writings of Nietzsche*, esp. sections 36 and 230; Michel Foucault, "Truth and Power," in *The Foucault Reader*, pp. 51–75. Sharon Welch notes that Foucault expands the notion of ideology-critique by revealing how the productive aspects of power are often more dangerous than the distortive aspects. Power relations do more than distort knowledge; they also produce effects that become ingrained in discourses and thereby less evident as distortions. See *Communities of Resistance and Solidarity*, pp. 61–64.

15. Paul Ricoeur, *Freud and Philosophy*, pp. 32–36.

16. Ricoeur, "The Critique of Religion," in Charles Reagan and David Stewart, eds.,

The Philosophy of Paul Ricoeur, p. 214. Nietzsche's notion of *ressentiment* can be found in his work *On the Genealogy of Morals*. By analyzing morals, Nietzsche tries to show that morals which seem very noble are really quite base. They are rooted in the desire for power and control. If we go back to the origin of morality and unmask what it really is, we discover the will to power for domination and control.

17. Tracy, *The Analogical Imagination*, p. 346.

18. Terry Eagleton, *Literary Theory*, pp. 72–73.

19. See Sheila Greeve Davaney's introduction to *Theology at the End of Modernity*, p. 6.

20. Linell E. Cady, "Resisting the Postmodern Turn: Theology and Contextualization," pp. 81–98. A good example of this postmodern confessionalist theology is George Lindbeck's *The Nature of Doctrine*.

21. These are Habermas's words cited by Gadamer in his essay "On the Scope and Function of Hermeneutical Reflection," in *Philosophical Hermeneutics*, p. 31.

22. Habermas, *Knowledge and Human Interests*, esp. pp. 301–17.

23. Richard Bernstein believes that Gadamer's polemic against the Enlightenment fails to take into account its positive value vis-à-vis Gadamer's own notion of "effective history." See *Beyond Objectivism and Relativism*, p. 155.

24. Bernstein, "Introduction," *Habermas and Modernity*, p. 31.

25. See Jean-François Lyotard's critique of grand theories and metanarratives in *The Postmodern Condition: A Report on Knowledge*. See also Richard Rorty's essay on Habermas's debate with the French postmodernists Lyotard and Foucault, "Habermas and Lyotard on Postmodernity," in *Habermas and Modernity*, pp. 161–75. For a review of Habermas's response to postmodernity as developed in his work *The Philosophical Discourse of Modernity*, see Jane Braaten, *Habermas's Critical Theory of Society*, pp. 114–39.

26. Bernstein, "The Rage Against Reason," in *The New Constellation*, pp. 31–56.

27. Bernstein, "Introduction," *Habermas and Modernity*, p. 25.

28. Habermas, *Knowledge and Human Interests*, pp. 214–45, 274–300 (esp. pp. 218–35).

29. Ibid., p. 220.

30. In her work *Gadamer: Hermeneutics, Tradition and Reason*, Georgia Warnke writes: "The crucial point here is that ideology is not the same as prejudice, that there is a difference between calling a perspective ideological and recognizing its historical and social situatedness. What makes a claim ideological is not merely its connection to an unarticulated source, nor its reliance on unexpressed norms and assumptions. Ideological claims do not simply leave the assumptions behind them implicit; they rather articulate them in such a way that it becomes difficult to disentangle the warranted part of the claims from the unwarranted" (p. 115).

31. See also Julia Kristeva's use of psychoanalysis as a form of analytical interpretation in her essay "Psychoanalysis and the Polis," in *The Kristeva Reader*, pp. 302–20 (esp. her summary points on pp. 303–4).

32. See Gadamer's "Reply to My Critics" and also *Truth and Method*, pp. 545–49. In *Hermeneutics and Education*, Shaun Gallagher cites Gadamer's view that a critical hermeneutics can never achieve a privileged ideological neutrality: "My objection is that the critique of ideology overestimates the competence of reflection and reason. Inasmuch

as it seeks to penetrate the masked interests which infect public opinion, it implies its own freedom from any ideology; and that means in turn that it enthrones its own norms and ideals as self-evident and absolute" (p. 18).

33. Habermas, "Towards a Theory of Communicative Competence."

34. See Richard Bernstein's helpful discussion of Habermas's theory in *Beyond Objectivism and Relativism*, pp. 182–97. See also Jane Braaten, *Habermas's Critical Theory of Society*, pp. 51–74; Anthony Giddens, "Jürgen Habermas," in Quentin Skinner, ed., *The Return of Grand Theory in the Human Sciences*, pp. 122–39. A more detailed and elaborate commentary can be found in Thomas McCarthy, *The Critical Theory of Jürgen Habermas*. For discussions of Habermas's theory in the context of theological reflection and religious education, see Dermot Lane, *Foundations for a Social Theology*, pp. 47–55; Nicolas Lash, "Conversation in Gethsemane," in W. G. Jeanrond and J. L. Rilke, eds., *Radical Pluralism and Truth*, pp. 51–61; Thomas Groome, *Sharing Faith*, pp. 102–4, 107–8; and *Christian Religious Education*, pp. 169–75.

35. Bernstein, *Beyond Objectivism and Relativism*, p. 163.

36. Georgia Warnke, *Gadamer: Hermeneutics, Tradition and Reason*, pp. 130–31.

37. See, e.g., Elisabeth Schüssler Fiorenza, *Bread Not Stone* and *But She Said*.

38. Shaun Gallagher, *Hermeneutics and Education*, pp. 239–40. The Gadamer-Habermas debate has provoked much comment and discussion among scholars. See, e.g., Georgia Warnke, *Gadamer: Hermeneutics, Tradition and Reason*, pp.107–38; Richard Bernstein, *Beyond Objectivism and Relativism*, pp. 171–231; Hugh Silverman, ed., *Gadamer and Hermeneutics*, pp. 151–77; Joseph Bleicher, *Contemporary Hermeneutics*, pp. 152–64; Paul Ricoeur, *Hermeneutics and the Human Sciences*, pp. 63–100.

39. Bernstein, *The New Constellation*, p. 49.

40. Foucault, cited in Sharon Welch, *Communities of Resistance and Solidarity*, p. 13. See *The Foucault Reader*, p. 57.

41. Richard Rorty, cited in Bernstein, *Beyond Objectivism and Relativism*, p. 199.

42. Sharon Welch, *Communities of Resistance and Solidarity*, p. 15.

43. Gerald Bruns, *Hermeneutics Ancient and Modern*, p. 196.

44. Ricoeur, *Hermeneutics and the Human Sciences*, p. 100.

45. Various chapters in Ricoeur's *Hermeneutics and the Human Sciences* address this issue: "Hermeneutics and the Critique of Ideology," pp. 63–100; "What is a Text? Explanation and Understanding," pp. 145–64; "Science and Ideology," pp. 222–46.

46. Ricoeur, *Freud and Philosophy*, p. 33.

47. Jean-François Lyotard, *The Postmodern Condition: A Report on Knowledge*, pp. xxiii–xxiv.

48. This is a key theme in Richard Rorty's work *Philosophy and the Mirror of Nature*. See also Richard Bernstein's commentary on Rorty in *Beyond Objectivism and Relativism*, pp. 197–207.

49. John Caputo, *Radical Hermeneutics*, p. 209.

50. Ibid., p. 209.

51. W. B. Yeats, "The Second Coming," from *Yeats Selected Poetry*, p. 99.

52. Tracy, *The Analogical Imagination*, p. 358. More specifically, this is the provoking question of the Western, postmodern, contemporary situation facing a "crisis of history" as it moves through an uneasy critique of modernity. It is a different question than that

faced, e.g., by liberation theologies whose primary concern or question comes from the "underside of history."

53. Bernstein, *Beyond Objectivism and Relativism*, p. 4.

54. For Habermas's views on modernity's unfinished project, see his essay, "Modernity — An Incomplete Project." For a comparison of Habermas and Derrida, see Richard Bernstein's "An Allegory of Modernity/Postmodernity: Habermas and Derrida," in *The New Constellation*, pp. 199–229.

55. Derrida, *Of Grammatology*, p. 159.

56. Gadamer, *Truth and Method*, p. 474.

57. Derrida, *Of Grammatology*, p. 158. The original French, *il n'y a pas de hors-texte*, could be read "there is nothing outside of the text" or "there is no outside-text."

58. Martin Heidegger calls language "the house of Being," see his "Letter on Humanism" in *Basic Writings*, p. 213; see also *On the Way to Language*, p. 63.

59. The traditional understanding of language (e.g., in Aristotle) saw a natural connection between words and ideas or between words and objects. For Saussure, however, words are *arbitrary* signs in which this natural relationship no longer holds.

60. Ferdinand de Saussure, *Course in General Linguistics*, extract reprinted in Philip Rice and Patricia Waugh, eds., *Modern Literary Theory*, p.14. For a general introduction and discussion of Saussure's work, see Manfred Frank, *What Is Neo-Structuralism?* pp. 25–33.

61. See Nathan Scott's discussion of Derrida in "Hermeneutics and the Question of the Self," in Werner Jeanrond and Jennifer Rike, eds., *Radical Pluralism and Truth*, pp.82–83. See also Terry Eagleton, *Literary Theory*, pp. 127–34.

62. Philip Rice and Patricia Waugh, eds., *Modern Literary Theory*, p. 148.

63. David Tracy, *Plurality and Ambiguity: Hermeneutics, Religion, Hope*, p. 58.

64. Nathan Scott, "Hermeneutics and the Question of the Self," p. 83.

65. G. Ormiston and A. Schrift, "Editors' Introduction," *The Hermeneutic Tradition*, p. 3.

66. Derrida, *Writing and Difference*, p. 292.

67. Manfred Frank defines metaphysics as "the belief in the subsistence of a trans-sensual world," "a thinking on the basis of principles," and a "knowledge for mastery" (*What Is Neo-Structuralism?* p. 57). In the foreword to Frank's book, Martin Schwab alerts us to the hold metaphysics has on our thinking: "In each of the following pairs of opposites one of the two terms may be taken to represent a metaphysical 'beyond' to the other: world and god, subject and external reality . . . language or thought and the world they relate to. . . . To reject one of the terms as metaphysical is ipso facto revising the model according to which the other term has been conceived. Antirationalism is thus engaged in a radical revision of hitherto fundamental notions" (xvi).

Similarly, David Hoy notes how metaphysics holds as "natural" such oppositions as mind and body, accident and essence, identity and difference, presence and absence, even male and female. While these oppositions are presumed to be value-neutral, what happens in practice is that one pole is always privileged over the other. See his article on Jacques Derrida in Quentin Skinner, ed., *The Return of Grand Theory in the Human Sciences*, p. 46.

See also Joseph O'Leary, *Questioning Back: The Overcoming of Metaphysics in the Christian Tradition*, pp. 1–55.

68. Jacques Derrida, *Writing and Difference*, p. 279. In the Western philosophical tradition, this "center" has been variously named as God or the Idea or the Self or substance, which has been understood to be prior to all discourse and the foundation of all experiencing and knowing.

69. Ibid., p. 280.

70. In this chapter, I follow very closely those who render an ethical-political reading of Derrida, such as Richard Bernstein and John Caputo. There is, however, a theological reading of Derrida's deconstructive work that highlights its mystical, apophatic, or "originary" dimensions in an attempt to forge a nonmetaphysical theology. See, e.g., Kevin Hart, *The Trespass of the Sign;* Joseph O'Leary, *Questioning Back;* and Thomas J. J. Altizer et al. *Deconstruction and Theology.* Other readings link Derrida's work to the Jewish mystical and rabbinic traditions such as Susan Handelman's *The Slayers of Moses.* Then there are those readings that take up the esoteric, playful, antiauthoritarian verve of deconstruction such as Mark C. Taylor's *Erring: A Postmodern A/theology.* These other perspectives will emerge in subsequent chapters.

71. Derrida, *Writing and Difference*, p. 279.

72. Caputo, "Hyperbolic Justice: Deconstruction, Myth, and Politics," p. 3.

73. See Caputo's article, "Beyond Aestheticism: Derrida's Responsible Anarchy," esp. pp. 62–67. On the need for preserving a "metaphysical comfort," see Bernstein, *The New Constellation*, p. 176.

74. Caputo, *Radical Hermeneutics*, p. 193.

75. See Gerald Bruns's reading of Caputo in *Hermeneutics Ancient and Modern*, p. 219.

76. Bernstein, *The New Constellation*, pp. 183.

77. Tracy, "On Naming the Present," p. 78.

78. Ibid., p. 78.

79. See Caputo, *Radical Hermeneutics*, p. 193.

80. This is a key theme in Emmanuel Levinas's major work, *Totality and Infinity.*

81. See Robert Bernasconi's essay on Levinas, "The Ethics of Suspicion," esp. p. 5.

82. See Bernstein's reflections on Levinas in *The New Constellation*, pp. 68–71.

83. Bruns, *Hermeneutics Ancient and Modern*, p. 203.

84. Jabès, *The Book of Questions*, 1. 50.

85. Francis Schüssler Fiorenza, "The Crisis of Hermeneutics and Christian Theology," pp. 136–37.

86. Bernstein, *The New Constellation*, p. 182.

87. Caputo, "Beyond Aestheticism: Derrida's Responsible Anarchy," p. 66.

88. Caputo, *Radical Hermeneutics*, p. 263.

89. Caputo, "Beyond Aestheticism," see esp. pp. 60–66.

90. Ibid., p. 60. For a similar theme, see also Caputo's work, *Radical Hermeneutics*, pp. 194–95.

91. "Deconstruction and the Other: An Interview with Derrida," in Richard Kearney, ed., *Dialogues with Contemporary Continental Thinkers*, p. 118.

92. Bernstein, *The New Constellation*, p. 174.

93. Ibid., pp. 66–67.

94. Caputo, "Beyond Aestheticism: Derrida's Responsible Anarchy," p. 67.

95. Bernstein makes this similar point in his discussion of Levinas, *The New Constella-*

tion, p. 69. See also his discussion on the function of alterity in the Hegelian dialectic in his concluding chapter, "Reconciliation/Rupture," pp. 293–322.

96. This is a key theme of Tracy's book *The Analogical Imagination.* See esp. pp. 446–56.

97. Mark C. Taylor, *Erring*, p. 108.

98. Ibid., p. 109.

99. Thomas J. J. Altizer, cited in Taylor, *Erring*, p. 49.

100. Charles E. Scott, "Beginning with Belonging and Nonbelonging in Derrida's Thought," p. 402.

101. Ibid., p. 402.

102. Bernstein, *The New Constellation*, p. 179.

103. Derrida challenges this Gadamerian "good will" in his "encounter" with Gadamer at the Goethe Institute in Paris, 1981. For the complete texts of this encounter and commentary, see Diane P. Michelfelder and Richard E. Palmer, eds., *Dialogue and Deconstruction: The Gadamer-Derrida Encounter.*

104. Derrida, *Writing and Difference*, pp. 280–81.

105. Derrida, *Of Grammatology*, p. 24.

106. Bernstein, *The New Constellation*, p. 172 (this is not Bernstein's view of Derrida but rather his depiction of a caricatured reading of Derrida).

107. *Jouissance*, which could be loosely translated as "pleasure," "bliss," or "ecstasy," is a key word in Roland Barthes's work *The Pleasure of the Text.*

108. Elie Wiesel, *Night*, p. 62.

109. See Taylor, *Erring*, pp. 69, 72–73: "The Nay to Nay ends by reconfirming the No within every Yes."

110. The phrase "commanding presence" is Emil Fackenheim's. In his effort to offer a Jewish theological response to the Holocaust, Fackenheim argued that the divine presence is a commanding voice that compels and enables Jews to survive, to endure *as Jews*, and not to lose hope or go mad. Fackenheim draws his insight from the experience of a Jewish woman in the death camps who, faced with the atrocities and inhumanity of the Nazis, found herself clinging to the "command" which addressed her: "I felt under orders to live." See Michael E. Lodahl's reflections on Fackenheim's writings in *Shekhinah /Spirit*, pp. 118–26.

111. Tracy, *The Analogical Imagination*, p. 358.

112. Ibid., pp. 359, 364.

CHAPTER FOUR

RISKING THE BOOK

In the Northern summer of 1993 I had the privileged experience of being a teaching assistant for Gustavo Gutiérrez who was offering a course on liberation theology at Boston College. Naturally, those who came to the course were keen to learn more about Gutiérrez's key themes: the preferential option for the poor, theology from below, basic Christian communities, and so on. However, without once mentioning any of the themes of liberation theology for which he is best known, Gutiérrez spent the entire first week of a two week course outlining the history of Western philosophy/theology, a history with which he is most familiar having been trained himself in this tradition. By the end of the first week, it was obvious that participants were beginning to question the relevance of his presentation.

I remember asking him about this, and he replied that the Western philosophical and theological tradition was *our* tradition, and that the questions facing us are different from the questions facing Latin American theologians. What is our situation, as mostly white, educated, middle-class, Eurocentric Christians (he was, after all, speaking at a prestigious North American, Jesuit university)? Our situation is not that of the "underside of history" which, for Gutiérrez, is the position generating the theologies of liberation in Latin American countries.[1] Rather, it is the situation of a "crisis" or "passage" of history — the passing of a dominant Western Enlightenment culture, the undermining of a confidence in historical progress, the radical questioning of a capitalist economy, individualism, the dominant claims of Christianity, and so on.[2] We live in the postmodern times of a great dismantling of a world constructed through the privilege of a white, patriarchal, Western, colonial hegemony: "it *feels* as though we are reaching the end of a historical era, since we find ourselves in the midst of cognitive, historical, political, socioeconomic and religious changes of vast importance . . . shattering the monolithic character and hegemony of the Western church as a whole."[3] Our situation has become one of a great homelessness, a disturbing absence of meaning, a profound recognition of the pathologies of the modern age, and a sense of our own "lostness" in the world.

This sense of homelessness — this exilic experience — plays a large part, I believe, in the recent phenomenon of the growth of interest in intentional Christian communities within North American, European, and Australian cultures. Their critically suspicious verve is directed not simply toward the institutional church, but toward the whole social-symbolic order of modern, Western Christianity. It is relatively easy to critique the institutional church — besides, there are many institutions that make up church, some of which are healthier than others; it is much more difficult and demanding to engage a hermeneutic of suspicion toward the deeply ingrained systematic distortions present within one's tradition of belonging. Intentional Christian communities engage a variety of theologies (liberationist, feminist, ecological, correlational) to tackle a variety of issues (wealth distribution, racial reconciliation, patriarchal structures, gender issues, homophobia, environment, indigenous peoples, community organizing, respect for diversity, postmodern spirituality, and so on).[4] Such communities recognize that

> Going beyond the modern world will involve transcending its individualism, anthropocentrism, patriarchy, mechanization, economism, consumerism, nationalism, and militarism. Constructive postmodern thought provides support for the ecology, peace, feminist, and other emancipatory movements of our time. . . .[5]

Intentional Christian communities are engaged in what Walter Brueggemann calls the task of funding the postmodern imagination: "to provide the pieces, materials, and resources out of which a new world can be imagined." The struggling efforts of these communities with their diverse, local, fragmentary theologies and actions have little to do with the forging of a new "grand scheme or coherent system, but the voicing of a lot of little pieces out of which people can put life together in fresh configurations."[6]

Theologies of liberation insist on the freedom of Christian communities "to develop theology outside the classic centers of theology, in concrete historical circumstances, in a precise locus or context, in determinate social, political and economic conditions and circumstances."[7] Members of intentional Christian communities are those who find themselves outside the classic centers of dominant institutions, mainstream orderings, established interpretive renderings of tradition, and too-familiar readings of "the book." They are communities that protest "more of the same" for the sake of concrete differences emerging from a dispersed range of places (sometimes far-flung from the center) that generate different readings and renewed writings of the book.

The strategy of deconstruction and the postmodern imagination has much to say that can speak to the experience of these communities. As David Tracy notes, for the postmodern sensibility, "the hope of the present is in the reality of otherness and difference — the otherness alive in the marginalized groups of modernity and tradition alike."[8] Such marginalized communities are those whom the settled centers of power have little interest in hearing and every interest in silencing or subjugating. They are the exiled poets, prophets, mystics, artists, dissenters, visionaries whose daring wanderings outside the book are so dangerous and prophetic to current understandings, mainstream practices, and institutional structures that their critical readings must remain somewhat in a condition of exile from the place of their deepest belonging. Sharon Welch speaks of these prophetic gatherings as "communities of resistance and solidarity," releasing the voices of subjugated knowledge — all those voices exiled and marginalized by the centers of control and power that systematically dominate, regulate, and exclude.[9] As John Caputo notes, deconstruction is interested in recovering the "dangerous memory" of those who have questioned the mainstream hold of tradition.

> When it comes to theology, deconstruction wants to know why everyone is so frightened of the "heretics," and just what it is that tradition wants to exclude. In theology, as elsewhere, deconstruction looks to the marginalized and excommunicated figures, not the classics; the forbidden sayings, not the eternal truths engraved in stone; the suppressed writings, not the ones that sit high on the altar.[10]

The postmodern imagination appeals to intentional Christian communities feeling their marginal status because it can speak to those who have felt the alienation and the pain of being excluded by the prevailing hierarchies embedded in the text of Christianity and the history of the West. So much of the way tradition and history is appropriated is simply the working out of exclusion and the silencing of difference. Edmond Jabès, however, believes that our "master texts" — those texts that are the "houses" of our being — can be read in a way that goes against the order of the house, the master plan of the whole, to find new paths and discoveries through forbidden doors and hidden passages.

> A good reader is, first of all, a sensitive, curious, demanding reader. In reading, they follow their intuition.
> Intuition — or what could pass as such — lies, for example, in the unconscious refusal to enter any house directly through the main door, the one that by its dimensions, characteristics and location, offers itself proudly as the main entrance, the one designated and recognized . . . as the sole threshold.
> To take the wrong door means indeed to go against the order that presided over the plan of the house, over the layout of the rooms, over the beauty and rationality of

the whole. But what discoveries are made possible for the visitor! The new path permits them to see what no other than they themselves could have perceived from that angle. . . .

One needs to have wandered a lot, to have taken many paths, to realize, when all is said and done, that at no moment one has left one's own.

A door towards which we could have bent our steps, moved by I don't know what lost reason, what insatiable desire to unlearn or to founder in the abyss, will never have misled us, will never mislead us. . . .

To forget in order to know; to know in order to fill up the forgotten, in its own time.[11]

A Feminist Ethics of "Reading" and "Writing"

The scholars-practitioners who, I believe, have much to offer the life of marginal/intentional Christian communities are the feminist or feminist-identified people working within and against the presiding order of the Christian tradition.[12] A consistent and recurring theme in feminist theologies is the recognition that our social, cultural, and religious traditions are markedly shaped by a dominant patriarchal ordering. According to Rosemary Radford Ruether,

> women have to suspect that the entire symbolic universe that surrounds them, which has socialized them into their roles, is deeply tainted by hostility to their humanity. . . . An entire social and symbolic universe crumbles within and outside them. . . . They recognize in the familiar the deeply alien.[13]

Feminist theologians have engaged a profound hermeneutic of suspicion, uncovering oppression, alienation, and discrimination against women and other oppressed groups caught in the network of patriarchal hierarchies and dualisms. Their work represents a profound critique on the book's mono-patriarchal inscription that has made women (and others "torn-out" by patriarchal orderings) absent and invisible, and in this sense "outside" the book. As Elisabeth Schüssler Fiorenza notes, feminist suspicion is directed toward patriarchy "as a complex systemic interstructuring of sexism, racism, classism and cultural-religious imperialism that has produced the Western 'politics of Otherness.' "[14] Yet feminist theological work is not only concerned with this critical task; it is also concerned with the task of redefining and reconstructing the social-symbolic order. Feminist theologies have a strong emancipatory interest, creating new discourses and practices from the marginality of women's experience in their struggle for liberation from oppression.[15] As Rebecca Chopp notes, feminist discourse "is not somehow just about women; rather, it casts its voice from the margins over the whole social-symbolic order, questioning its rules, procedures, and practices."[16] Many intentional communities share the concerns of feminist scholarship to work toward liberation from all structures of domination, to engage in an "ethics of reading and writing" that promotes new paths and discoveries against the patriarchal, colonizing, exclusionary orderings of the whole.

Absence and Silence: Filling up the Forgotten

According to the Jewish feminist writer Judith Plaskow, the creation of a feminist Judaism that goes against the order of the house — the master plan of the whole — begins with hearing silence. "It begins with noting the absence of women's history and experiences as shaping forces in the Jewish tradition."[17] As Jabès suggests, "The future carries the burden of all our pasts. That's why it's important to know of how many forgotten words it is made."[18] In order to fill up this forgotten history, feminist theologians also know that "the great silence that has shrouded women's history testifies not to women's lack of historical agency but to androcentric bias that has shaped historical writing."[19] "Over time," writes Plaskow, "we learn to insert ourselves into silences."[20]

Women who stand within a patriarchal tradition face the particular challenge of how they are going to interpret a tradition that has systematically excluded women's voice and experience from its text. It becomes difficult for women to correlate their feminist experience with a tradition that has for so long engaged in a "patriarchal silencing of women."[21] Given this reality, one wonders whether any fusion of horizons is possible between women's experience and a patriarchal tradition. Feminists such as Mary Daly have rejected the possibility of reclaiming a feminist textual or cultural-religious tradition. Daly rages against the patriarchal obliteration of women's history and seeks instead to create a radically new "Otherworld" of feminist time and space that is "absolutely Anti-androcrat, A-mazingly Anti-male, Furiously and Finally Female."[22]

According to Elisabeth Schüssler Fiorenza, however, Daly's radical feminism is "no longer the 'binding of oppressed women struggling for liberation' but the gathering of the feminist elect and holy 'Selves' who have 'escaped' patriarchy."[23] Unlike postbiblical feminists who have rejected patriarchal tradition, Schüssler Fiorenza insists that women must remember the reality of their history which, though not written into the tradition, nevertheless remains powerfully present in its absence and silence. To opt out of Christian tradition is to deny this secret history and succumb to the patriarchal negation of women's experience; it also leaves the patriarchal tradition in power and unchallenged. The fusion that feminist hermeneutics seeks is a fusion between the silent, exiled presence of women in the past with the experience of women today, struggling like their fore-sisters for liberation and wholeness. This means that feminist hermeneutics looks for silences and ruptures within a tradition rather than continuities. They seek out those elements in the past that have been subdued or oppressed by the patriarchal forces of order. According to Schüssler Fiorenza, feminist hermeneutics must

> find ways to "break" the silences of the texts and to derive meaning from androcentric historiography and narrative. Rather than understand the texts as an adequate reflection of the reality about which they speak, [feminists] must search for rhetorical clues and allusions that indicate the reality about which texts are silent.[24]

The Appeal to Concrete Experience

Feminist hermeneutics gives priority to a hermeneutics of suspicion over against a hermeneutics of retrieval.[25] It recognizes that we cannot speak about truth or truth claims without also asking about power and power claims. Schüssler Fiorenza claims that feminist hermeneutics must be one of "critical evaluation" rather than "correlation."[26] Yet the question then emerges as to what *criteria* one can use in order to undertake a critical *evaluation* of tradition. According to Schüssler Fiorenza, the evaluative norm for feminist hermeneutics is not the Scriptures or the tradition but the *experience of women* struggling for liberation. Feminist critical hermeneutics derives its canon "not from the biblical writings but from the contemporary struggle of women against racism, sexism, and poverty as oppressive systems of patriarchy. . . . It places biblical texts *under the authority of feminist experience* insofar as it maintains that revelation is ongoing and takes place 'for the sake of our salvation.'"[27] In other words, the tradition is evaluated according to how it responds or fails to respond to the contemporary experience of women in their search for justice and freedom. Feminist hermeneutics "has to formulate its own criterion, which cannot be derived from biblical texts but must be drawn from Christian communities, to which these texts speak today."[28]

The importance of attending to our current experience in all its concreteness and historical particularity is central to the feminist hermeneutical enterprise. However, this appeal to experience should not be confused with liberal theology's attempt to ground theology's project in an "anthropological universality," that is, an anthropological appeal that tends to universalize as human experience what in reality is always quite specific and interest laden (most typically, the vested interest of a patriarchal understanding of human experience).[29] Moreover, as Francis Schüssler Fiorenza notes, the appeal to experience can all too easily fall prone to the Enlightenment pretense of pseudo-autonomy. As we saw in chap. 1, the Enlightenment sought to replace the authority of tradition with the authority of the subject. However, this shift from external authority to human experience and subjectivity is now also seriously under question. We recognize that human subjectivity fails to provide a foundational certainty, because such subjectivity is itself caught within interpretive webs that we ourselves have spun. There is little that is foundational, solid, or universal about them. The appeal to experience and subjective authority now faces similar challenges that the appeal to the external authority of tradition once faced. If we once sought knowledge in and through the authority and claims of tradition, and if the Enlightenment sought freedom from such constraints through the appeal to experience and the autonomy of a subjective knower, then postmodernism represents a loss of both.[30]

The feminist appeal to experience, therefore, is an appeal to the particularity and concreteness of experience — not a universal human essence — much in the same way that Gutiérrez insists that theological reflection should always take place within the precise locus or context of a community's concrete historical circumstance. This places theological reflection in a "dispersed" context rather than a "centered" context, theologies given to diverse searchings and namings rather than to timeless, perennial essences or unities. Intentional Christian communities, I believe, are communities wanting to search out the particularity of their experience in diverse locations rather than surrender to mainstream renditions or construals of reality that offer only more of the same.

Immanent Critique and Productive Possibility

Although Elisabeth Schüssler Fiorenza grants priority to the authority of present experience over against the authority of tradition, other feminists argue that there is within the biblical tradition (even granting its patriarchal character) a "canon within the canon."[31] Rosemary Radford Ruether, for example, maintains that feminist readings of biblical tradition can discern a critical norm within that tradition by which the tradition itself can be criticized.[32] She locates this critical norm in the prophetic-liberating traditions: "The rediscovery of prophetic content, and its discerning reapplication to new social situations, is precisely what the Bible calls 'The Word of God.'"[33] Schüssler Fiorenza, however, argues that we cannot abstract an essence of revelation from its historical-social context. She claims that "the canon and evaluative norm cannot be 'universal,' but must be specific and derived from a particular experience of oppression and liberation."[34] Similarly, Plaskow says that there simply is no liberating, nonsexist essence to biblical tradition. Even the prophetic tradition disfigures divine female symbolism and perpetuates the patriarchal subordination of women through its sexist imagery. Such a tradition must be dealt with critically before it can serve as a resource for feminist liberation.[35]

I wonder, however, if Ruether is really talking about the prophetic tradition as an abstract critical key. She says it "is important to see that the prophetic-liberating tradition is not and cannot be made into a static set of 'ideas.'"[36] Rather, the central "point of reference for biblical faith is not past texts, with their sociological limitations, but the liberated future. We appropriate the past not to remain in its limits, but to point to new futures."[37] I am reminded of Paul Ricoeur's question: From where does critical consciousness speak, if not from a hermeneutical consciousness? To the critical reader of the Jewish and Christian traditions he might well say,

> It is indeed from the basis of a tradition that you speak. . . . Critique is also tradition . . . the tradition of emancipation rather than of recollection. . . . I would even say that it plunges us into the most impressive tradition, that of liberating acts, of the Exodus and the Resurrection. Perhaps there would be no more interest in emancipation, no more anticipation of freedom, if the Exodus and the Resurrection were effaced from the memory of humankind.[38]

Ricoeur is suggesting that we often engage in a hermeneutic of suspicion because we are interested in a radical retrieval of those traditions that are continually subverting the book in their quest to be free of distortions. Or, as Tracy suggests, "retrieval now demands both critique and suspicion. Indeed, retrieval can now often come best through critique and suspicion."[39] As we noted in the previous chapter, the literature of subversion comes as much from within a tradition as from outside it; tradition spawns its own critique. There is a sense that emancipation operates as a "critique from within," that "every exit from the book is made within the book." In other words, the book is set free and prolonged through its own subversion, transgressing the book in favor of another that will prolong it.

In this sense, we can see the importance of the critical appeal to contextual experience that feminist hermeneutics insists upon. Far from diminishing a text's productive possibility, it enables feminist readers to elicit the referential power of a text to provoke new understanding, new appropriations of meaning, new horizons of possibility for feminist experience. Following Ricoeur's lead, we can see that while a feminist hermeneutical stance leans clearly in the direction of a hermeneutic of suspicion, such suspicion implies that one is at base interested in radical retrieval as much as it implies that one is similarly committed to radical reconstruction.

Sharon Welch echoes this sentiment in her analysis of resistance narratives. She says that these narratives recover the past in order to open up new possibilities for the present and the future. Indeed, the past itself changes depending on what new futures are envisioned or created.[40] Judith Plaskow sees this practice of reconstructing the past according to present concerns and future possibilities as a traditional rabbinic hermeneutic. The rabbis always reconstructed the past to mirror their present experience.[41] Midrash is a traditional strategy whereby "the sages gave the meaning of a text for the present and declared that meaning its meaning for all times. The open-ended process of writing midrash — simultaneously serious and playful, imaginative, metaphoric — has easily lent itself to feminist use."[42] Midrash can float entirely free or it can play with fragmentary clues from the text, combining free-floating midrash with historical reconstruction. "Midrash expands and burrows, invents the forgotten and prods the memory, takes from history and asks for more."[43] In an effort to fill up the forgotten, Jewish feminists listen for the words of women "to rise out of the white spaces between the letters of the Torah" as they remember and recreate the past through the experience of their own lives.[44]

Feminists who are engaged in this constructive theology recognize that it cannot rely solely on classical sources but must draw upon a variety of sources, including pre- and post-Christian traditions.[45] In their search "to produce stories that save our lives," feminists are reading their tradition in the light of older traditions that have been forgotten or buried and newer traditions that are emerging from contemporary experience. In Gadamer's terms, feminist understanding is "understanding differently," because it is understanding that is shaped by different historical concerns and questions in which the tradition is "growing in size," expanding as it opens itself to new experience, coming to be in new form, representing a new happening of tradition: "the book is written as we read."

Discourses That Rend and Renew

Feminist discourse moves against closure toward the openness of possibilities, yet such openness is not one of indeterminate anarchy. Rather, "distinct terms, values and norms emerge to guide feminist discourse."[46] In other words, feminist discourse is not without an ethic, one that emerges from the practice of resisting and transforming dominant orderings of reality. It is an ethic, however, that recognizes the contextuality and situatedness of all discourse and is deeply suspicious of knowledge claims that purport to be objective, universal, or value free. Indeed, it is this very type of ethical reasoning that feminist discourse challenges: reason that purports to be impartial and universally applicable, because of the ways it can function to exclude the unthought, the unseen, and the unheard.[47]

According to Rebecca Chopp, feminist discourse seeks "to rend and renew —

by questioning, interrupting, correcting, and subverting the basic terms of order."[48] It shares an affinity with the revolutionary energy of postmodernity's deconstructionist critique. This critique takes aim at a metaphysics of presence which, according to Iris Marion Young, is "a desire to think things together in a unity, to formulate a representation of a whole, a totality."[49] Such a metaphysics seeks to have everything under control, to eliminate uncertainty and unpredictability, to eliminate concreteness and specificity, otherness and difference, into an overriding, unifying system of order and identity. This metaphysical urge necessarily generates hierarchical oppositions: "Any move to define an identity, a closed totality, always depends on excluding some elements, separating the pure from the impure."[50] The logic of identity creates an inner/outer distinction that seeks to keep these borders firmly drawn. Whole systems of Western thought have been based on hierarchical oppositions such as mind/matter, spirit/body, one/many, perennial/ time-bound, God/world, and so on, in which one side represents the internal unity of the system as good, pure, and normal, whereas the other side represents what is secondary or external to the system as bad, impure, deviant.[51] In other words, a metaphysics of presence tends to create dichotomy instead of oneness. The move to create a single totality, as the logic of hierarchical opposition shows, creates not one, but two: a dualism in which one term is privileged through the divestiture of its opposite.[52] Deconstruction is profoundly suspicious of all ordering and centering principles because such principles, while speaking of unity, are at the same time excluding; while speaking of truth, are at the same time dominating; while speaking of preserving order, are at the same time controlling. The unity they display is not inherent in them; rather, such unity is inscribed by the power of exclusion, by virtue of which they represent precisely this and no other unity. Mark C. Taylor writes:

> The deconstruction of the Western theological network discloses the recurrent effort of human beings to achieve a position of domination. This struggle appears to grow out of the conviction that mastery results from the ability to secure presence and establish identity by overcoming absence and repressing difference.[53]

Feminist discourse aims at "transforming the law of ordered hierarchy" which follows a "monotheistic ordering" of the "one" as opposed to the "other."[54] Women have typically been consigned the role of the "other" within the dominant social-symbolic ordering.[55] A monotheistic ordering presumes that if God is one, truth is one. Upon this reading, "the true is never plural, multiple, and complex but always unified, single, and simple."[56] All that is temporal and in flux is subordinated to a metaphysics of unchanging, timeless truth. Radford Ruether shows that throughout Western history "male monotheism begins to split reality into a dualism of transcendent Spirit (mind, ego) and inferior and dependent physical nature."[57] The bodiless ego is seen as primary and preexistent, and the physical world as secondary and derivative. "Whereas the male is seen essentially as the image of the male transcendent ego or God, woman is seen as the image of the lower, material nature."[58] In such a system, gender becomes the primary symbol for the dualisms of spirit/matter, culture/nature, good/evil, rational/irrational: all patterned on the polarized opposition of male and female, with the former of each pair assuming priority and privilege over the latter.[59]

This framework of a dualistic, ordered hierarchy not only relegates women to absence and invisibility; it also sets up the dangerous equation of otherness with opposition. According to Sharon Welch, "it transforms difference into alienation and conflict." When we imagine the ultimate good as similarity or uniformity, "then difference per se appears to threaten this valued state. . . . Difference comes to be equated not only with 'potential rival' but with potential chaos, something to be eradicated so that the good can be achieved."[60] The twentieth century abounds with examples of how we destroy the "other" in the name of the "good" system of sameness and uniformity. Ours is a world in which difference continually works itself out as domination and subordination: men over women, Christians over Jews, whites over blacks, the First World over the Third World, Eurocentric cultures over indigenous cultures, and so on.

Feminist discourse resists the dominant social-symbolic order, but resists by way of transformation, seeking to provide new discourses: "to transform the ruling principles and order into ones that allow, encourage, and enable transformative relations of multiplicity, difference, solidarity."[61] It is not a matter of balancing or equalizing the hierarchy as it is resisting its codes, concepts, and structures: "allowing differences and connections instead of constantly guaranteeing identities and oppositions."[62] Or, as Taylor notes:

> In place of simple reversal, it is necessary to effect a dialectical inversion that does not leave contrasting opposites unmarked but dissolves their original identities. . . . Unless theological transgression becomes genuinely subversive, nothing fundamental will change.[63]

Elizabeth Kamarck Minnich believes that transforming knowledge is about "thinking ourselves free."[64] It means letting loose, disseminating, or unraveling the texts of our tradition such that "if anything is destroyed in a deconstructive reading, it is not meaning but the claim to unequivocal domination of one mode of signifying over another."[65] Authoritative readings and centers of power and control are radically destabilized through a transformed reading of tradition that asks, "What makes, and keeps, it what, and as, it is?"[66]

Communities of Dialogue and Solidarity

We have seen how feminist discourse is wary of the ways "difference" and "otherness" plays itself out in our world as domination and subordination, and how established identities and unities are typically achieved through the force of exclusion. We have seen the suspicion toward normative traditions and classics that are often read and maintained in ways that privilege the dominant order. It is not surprising, then, that we find feminist discourse valuing the acceptance of difference over against sameness or unified continuities; openness and indeterminacy over against closure and certainty; concrete, specific experience over against universalizing norms. Feminist discourse, however, is not an anarchical free for all. One of the strongest values we find in this discourse is the value of community, in which we can discern specific educational practices of attending to the concrete realities of life, to relational knowing rooted in conversation and dialogue, and to the facilitation of connectedness and solidarity amidst acknowledged differences. As Ruether notes, feminist discourse "reaches for a new mode of relationship, neither a hierarchical model that diminishes the potential of the 'other' nor an 'equality' defined by a ruling norm from the dominant group; rather, a mutuality that allows us to affirm different ways of being."[67]

A central requirement of feminist ethics is that it attends to "the concrete reality of persons, however inevitably partial the insight and provisional the interpretation."[68] Intentional communities of ethical discourse are valued because they represent places where people can intentionally reflect upon, and make room for, otherness and the play of difference. "The condition of overcoming ideology is difference."[69] Such a condition is served in the creation of genuinely pluralistic communal forms, in which there is interaction between "concrete others," dialogue and conversation between diverse experiences and understandings. Welch speaks of "an epistemology of solidarity" that is an attempt, as Groome has also argued, to bring together epistemology and ontology.[70] Our knowledge of ourselves, other people and our world is determined by concrete, specific relations; our way of knowing is shaped by our very way of being-in-the-world. As Heidegger notes, the question of ethics is closely related to the question of *ethos*, which asks about our ways of dwelling or being-in-the-world.[71] Iris Marion Young believes that the disjunction between knowing and being is actually a

> counterfactual construct, a situation of reasoning that removes people from their actual contexts of living moral decisions, to a situation in which they could not exist . . . the deontological self is not connected to any particular ends, has no particular history, is a member of no communities, has no body.[72]

An epistemology of solidarity is more a matter of "responsiveness in relationship" rather than "commitment to obligation." It represents a communitarian "ethics of care" that presumes a social, relational self and espouses the values of responsibility, love, and care amid bonds of sharing and solidarity.[73] Responsiveness in relationship is concrete and specific, and grounds ethical discourse and deliberation in a community of action and reflection. It does not seek out abstract norms then to be applied, nor does it focus on the achievement of predefined goals or ends; rather, it aims at the creation of a matrix in which further reflection and action become possible, the creation of the conditions of possibility for desired changes and, over time, a heritage of resistance and transformation.[74]

Feminist ethics values the openness of conversation in which a plurality of voices and viewpoints can enter into dialogue with one another. As Iris Marion Young notes, this commitment to dialogue implies that reason is contextualized, that answers are the result of a plurality of views that cannot be reduced to a unity. "As long as the dialogue allows all perspectives to speak freely, and be heard and taken into account," such expressions will "not have merely private significance, nor will they bias or distort conclusions because they will interact with other needs, motives and perspectives."[75] To hold to truth as dialogic rather than as objectively given is to live in the openness of ongoing conversation and the continuing transformation of interpretations and practices that genuine dialogue entails.

Feminist discourse offers a deepened appreciation of educational practices that are important to foster in the life of intentional communities. Effective education happens in settings that can direct attention intentionally toward people's experience. The value of the concreteness and specificity of people's experience is vital if we are to avoid the pitfalls of distorting generalizations, totalizing schemes, and hierarchical inscriptions. Moreover, if undertaken in a critical manner, such reflection can enable members of intentional communities to realize that they need not be simple products of dominant social constructions but can imaginatively act to transform their social world. The educational value of dialogue and conversation takes on added meaning as we learn that in conversation between diverse perspectives truth and shared values emerge. Finally, feminist scholars remind us that while our religious traditions are limiting and constraining, they are also the places from which our histories spring and from which we can act in the hope of creating new futures and liberating possibilities.

Critical Thinking and Emancipatory Education

As we saw in chap. 1, we are acutely aware today of how our fundamental perceptions are shaped and conditioned by historical circumstances. Every utterance is historically conditioned and mediated through a perspective. What has come to be known today as the sociology of knowledge received its initial formulation in the work of Karl Mannheim.[76] Mannheim revealed how truth statements are radically de-absolutized by sociological factors such as the culture, social position, and interests of the perceiver's worldview. His principle thesis is that "there are modes of thought which cannot be adequately understood as long as their social origins are obscured."[77]

Mannheim focused on the positive function of ideology.[78] In a similar fashion, Peter Berger argues that every culture and society needs "systems of legitimation" and "plausibility structures" that make social constructions seem both legitimate and reasonable.[79] In organizing our ways of being together, we give everything its proper place: "It goes here!" However, we quickly hide from ourselves the constructed nature of what we ourselves have made, and live as though the order we have chosen exists on its own, independently of us. Religion provides one of the strongest legitimizations of social order, concealing our constructions beneath a sacred canopy that gives cosmological reasons for why "it goes there" ("on earth as it is in heaven").[80]

In this context, we can see why critical theories of education are concerned with the way educational experience serves the cultural reproduction of society, including power relations, economic interests, class, race, and gender prejudices.[81] Similarly, deconstructive approaches to education aim to show how ideas and practices are the effects of larger discourses, or what Lyotard calls "metanarratives." The educational task becomes one of "destroying" the authority of metanarratives by giving them the status of "relativized narratives," and standing in critical opposition to dominant orderings.[82] Caputo, for example, draws attention to Derrida's provoking critique of the university system.[83] Within the university, power relations gather around the concept of reason to defend established positions and exclude new ones, with the result that "the university is put more and more to work by the society to which it belongs," with little or no time for the free play of ideas or the exploration of unestablished and different ways of thinking.[84] "The university becomes an instrument of normalization, of reinforcing and resupplying the existing order, and of the exclusion of those who dissent from it."[85] It becomes a center where everything is centered on the purpose of reproducing established orderings, and where "everything decentering and in free play is held suspect or dangerous," even though such voices of exploration and concern are essential to reason and to honest, open inquiry.[86] "Who is more faithful to reason's call," asks Derrida, "who hears it with a keener ear, who better sees the difference, the one who offers questions in return and tries to think through the possibility of that summons, or the one who does not want to hear any question about the reason of reason?"[87] The strategy is to deconstruct culture and tradition not so much in ways that merely lead to an anarchy of interpretations but in ways that transform educational practices to risk new interpretations, to let loose play and productivity, and to guard against any form of final closure that seals the way things are.[88]

Paul Feyerabend is also deeply suspicious of the monolithic, Western Enlightenment culture with its imposing notions of truth, reason, and reality. He recalls a significant experience in his life as a professor when, in the early sixties, Mexicans, blacks, and native Americans entered the university:

> There they sat, partly curious, partly disdainful, partly simply confused, hoping to get an "education". . . . What an opportunity my rationalist friends told me, to contribute to the spreading of reason and the improvement of mankind! What a marvelous opportunity for a new wave of enlightenment! I felt very differently. For it dawned on me that the intricate arguments and the wonderful stories I had so far told to my more or less sophisticated audience might be . . . just reflections of the conceit of a small group who had succeeded in enslaving everyone else with their ideas. . . . Were [these ideas] the right thing to offer to people who had been robbed of their land, their culture, their dignity and who were now supposed to absorb patiently and then repeat the anaemic ideas of the mouthpieces of the oh so human captors? . . . Their ancestors had developed cultures of their own, colourful languages, harmonious views of the relation between man (*sic*) and man and man and nature whose remnants are the living criticism of the tendencies of separation, analysis, self-centeredness inherent in Western thought.[89]

Feyerabend bemoans the loss of cultural variety and is particularly sensitive to the encroachment of science and its manipulative rationality, which he believes has robbed many cultures and indigenous peoples of their dignity and their means of survival. He advocates instead a "democratic relativism" that affirms difference and otherness and is deeply appreciative of the many ways of being-in-the-world.[90]

As we saw earlier in this chapter, feminist and postmodern discourses share much in common in their attack on the workings of ideologies and power relations within Enlightenment discourses that universalize white, male, Western experience. Both call for new ways of envisioning life in terms of pluralities and diversities rather than unities and universals. Both seek to break the conceptual hold of the Western philosophical and theological traditions that have systematically constructed the world in hierarchical and dualistic frameworks. Both recognize the need for a new ethics that takes account of difference and otherness amid concrete, specific relations.[91]

However, as Patricia Waugh notes, even though feminist discourse draws upon postmodern strategies of disruption to reimagine the world, "it cannot repudiate entirely the framework of Enlightened modernity without perhaps fatally undermining itself as an emancipatory politics."[92] Postmodern narratives, to be sure, tell us that we are recipients of our identity, our world, our tradition, our relationships, before we are agents in, or transformers of, that world. Yet postmodern narratives often fail to foster confidence in effective human agency, leaving us with the "claustrophobic sense" that there can be no real opposition to hermeneutical constraints, because there is no place outside those constraints to effectively stand and act. "Indeed, human subjects generally 'disappear' amidst a theory that leaves no room for moments of self-creation, mediation, and resistance."[93] It is here that the claims of modernity defended by thinkers such as Habermas come to the fore: the ability of critical reason to unmask and demystify oppressive ideologies in ways that lead to a *transformation* of tradition and society. Emancipatory reason highlights the role of public reason and the hope for a genuine, democratic ethos: democratic public spaces that serve a communal, dialogic rationality in search of the Enlightenment ideals of justice, freedom, and equality. Bernstein writes:

> The Enlightenment legacy cannot be smoothed out into *either* a grand narrative of the progressive realization of freedom and justice *or* the cosmic night of ineluctable nihilistic self-destruction. With a stubborn persistence, [Habermas] seeks to keep alive the memory/promise and hope of a world in which justice, equality and dialogical rationality are concretely realized in our everyday practices. . . . He is a "guardian of reason," but the reason he defends is dialogical, intersubjective, communicative.[94]

These Enlightenment ideals of critical reason, dialogue, public debate, and societal transformation are important hallmarks of intentional Christian communities. As *intentional* communities, they have strong purposes that motivate their coming together, particularly their desire to engage the pressing social issues of our time, to effect a critical transformation of societal and ecclesial structures. They share a sensibility with critical thinkers and educators such as Stephen Brookfield, who are extremely suspicious of dominant, established paradigms and therefore passionately committed to the transformative potential of emancipatory education. Brookfield believes that effective education "is present when adults come to appreciate the relative, provisional, and contextual nature of public and private knowledge and when they come to understand that the belief systems, value frameworks, and moral codes informing their conduct are culturally constructed."[95] Emancipatory education involves a continual scrutiny of the conditions that have shaped our private and public worlds, along with a continuing praxis of action and reflection that attempts to reconstruct those worlds.[96]

Brookfield's educational canons are "the twin canons of relativity and provisionality."[97] His educational sensibilities reflect a strong bias toward suspicion and critique. As we noted in chap. 2, many intentional Christian communities also share this predilection. We also noted that a constant emphasis on critique and suspicion (on "continual scrutiny") can be overplayed to the detriment of conversation and constructive transformation of history. We need to learn how to retrieve traditions appreciatively as well as critique them, to recognize that there is transformative wisdom to be found in our cultural and religious traditions. Brookfield makes little or no reference to this aspect of education in his work. However, I do not think he is asking us to critically distance ourselves in a crippling fashion from our cultural and religious traditions. Rather, he sees critical thinking as a profoundly positive and creative activity:

> Critical thinkers are actively engaged with life. . . . They appreciate creativity, they are innovators, and they exude a sense that life is full of possibilities. Critical thinkers see the future as open and malleable, not as closed and fixed. They are self-confident about their potential for changing aspects of their worlds, both as individuals and through collective action.[98]

According to Brookfield, critical thinking revolves around two key activities: "(1) identifying and challenging assumptions and (2) exploring and imagining alternatives."[99] In other words, critical thinking is about recognizing constraints and enabling new possibilities. Brookfield further analyzes critical thinking according to five key characteristics and four key components, as shown in the following table.[100]

Key Features of Critical Thinking	Components of Critical Thinking
1. Critical thinking is a positive, productive, innovative, transformative activity.	1. Identifying and challenging taken-for-granted assumptions (beliefs, ideas, values, ways of doing things) is central to critical thinking.
2. Critical thinking entails a continual process of questioning assumptions. It is not a static activity that leads to final or finished outcomes or certainties.	2. A keen sense of how thoughts and actions are always influenced by context. Critical thinkers need to be "contextually aware" of the hidden forces that shape ways of thinking and behaving.
3. Critical thinking manifests itself in both "internal" personal transformation and "external" structural transformation.	3. Imagining and exploring alternatives to existing ways of thinking and living where these are perceived as inadequate. The fact that knowledge has been construed in one particular way, means it can also be recon-

strued, reconstructed, or imagined in an
alternative way.

4. Critical thinking is triggered by both
positive and negative events: what is
important is the experience of finding
previously held assumptions put in question
through exposure to unexpected
or alternate ideas and possibilities.

4. Critical thinking fosters a sense of
"reflective skepticism" that is suspicious,
distrustful, and scrutinizing of fixed belief
systems, habitual behaviors, hardened certainties
and entrenched social structures.

5. Critical thinking involves both head
and heart, thinking and feeling.

According to Paulo Freire, the task of critical education is to enable people to
deal critically and creatively with their social reality, rather than simply fitting
them into it. People can become either transformers of their world or creatures of
it. The parallel that Habermas draws between the model of psychoanalysis and
the role of critical reason is similar to Freire's notion of "conscientization."
Freire speaks of "decoding" the historical reality which a people's social location
mediates to them as "coded."[101] The process of conscientization (developing a
critical consciousness) is one by which people come to perceive their personal
and social reality along with the contradictions in it, become more aware of their
own perception of that reality, and therefore are able to deal with it in a more critical
and transformative manner.[102] Critical thinking moves beyond "circles of
certainty" enshrined in the "well-behaved present" and the "normalized today,"
to embrace a consciousness that "perceives reality as process and transformation."[103]
Freire writes:

> Radicalization, nourished by a critical spirit, is always creative. . . . The radical,
> committed to human liberation, does not become the prisoner of a "circle of certainty"
> within which they also imprison reality. On the contrary, the more radical they
> are, the more fully they enter into reality so that, knowing it better, they can better
> transform it. They are not afraid to confront, to listen, to see the world unveiled.[104]

Intentional Communities and Public Life

Sociologist Robert Nisbet speaks of our present age as characterized by a
resurgent interest in community: "community lost and community to be gained."
For Nisbet, this renewed quest for community stems largely from Western society's
experience of alienation from the social order, which is found to be
"remote, incomprehensible or fraudulent; beyond real hope or desire; inviting
apathy, boredom, or even hostility."[105] Leonardo Boff echoes Nisbet's findings

Suburbia !

and calls ours an age of "general anonymity," swallowing up persons in the massive structures of macro-organizations and bureaucracies. Yet Boff sees signs of renewed hope in the growing phenomenon of small Christian communities springing up around the world, communities that are characterized by their desire to reclaim a strong commitment to mutual relationships, inclusive participation, and honest dialogue among equals.[106] This relational character of intentional Christian communities represents a significant counter-movement to the sense of isolation and estrangement typical of twentieth-century life.

In *Habits of the Heart,* Robert Bellah and his associates argue that the language of biblical traditions can help us recapture a public philosophy rooted in the "we" of mutuality rather than the "I" of individualism.[107] Bellah's group suggests that people need the nurture of smaller communities that embody alternative symbols, language, and practices to the dominant symbols and practices of society. These "communities of memory" remind us that we are not self-reliant, isolated individuals but that we exist in relation to a larger whole, a community, a tradition. They keep us mindful of the shared, collective histories and traditions from which we emerge as a people.[108] "To acknowledge that one is a member of the public," writes Parker Palmer, "is to recognize that we are members of one another.[109]

According to the authors of *Habits of the Heart,* we generally do not find this well-formed sense of relationality within the public world. They call for "a deeper understanding of the moral ecology that sustains the lives of all of us, even when we think we are making it on our own."[110] Their later work, *The Good Society,* focuses on the institutions that form the fabric of our society and pattern the way we live together in the world. Because our lives are lived in and through institutions, they stress the importance of renewing institutional life, arguing for changes in the way we pattern our lives together that strengthen and allow for active citizen participation and initiative.[111]

The relational charism of intentional Christian communities can make a vital contribution in building a sense of mutual interdependence and connectedness within the public world. That the public world needs such a relational ethic is underscored by the individualism so dominant in Western cultural experience. As Bellah's team suggests, a middle-class language of "individualistic achievement and self-fulfillment . . . makes it difficult for people to sustain their commitments to others, either in intimate relationships or in the public sphere."[112] We suffer such a preoccupation with individuality and self-actualization that we seldom touch our strength in interrelational bonds. We are so concerned with authentic personal existence that we rarely entertain the prospect of authentic *social* existence. In short, public life has given way to private preoccupations.[113]

Seard for
meaning

Mediating Communities

What we are experiencing today is a sharp dislocation between people's experience of private and public life. The public sphere has become a large and alien world extending little welcome to personal and effective participation. The private world has become a haven of retreat in people's quest for meaning and fulfillment and a sense of purpose and belonging.[114] The result is a continuing sense of alienation and isolation from public engagement and social interaction.[115] Nisbet believes we are witnessing a decline in the active presence of smaller groups and associations that have traditionally bridged the gap between private and public worlds, a gap which in our times is growing wider and wider. This prevailing sense of social alienation can only be overcome by finding renewed ways for people to effectively participate in the public sphere. This renewal needs to take place in the realm of the smaller groups, associations, and communities that make up society and which mediate between persons and the larger world of public and political concerns.[116] It is within this area that intentional Christian communities have the potential to act within society as mediating communities providing an effective link between the private and public worlds.

Evelyn and James Whitehead speak convincingly of the potential for intentional Christian communities to function as social settings in and through which people can recognize and participate in the wider, public arena of life. They argue that an intentional community provides a richer context for relationships and a sense of belonging and participation than we find in the anonymity of public life. Discovering a shared commonality in the face of social alienation and isolation is an important function of a mediating community. As places of shared values and common purpose, small communities provide a "larger-than-private confirmation" of the way we would like to be in the world. They provide an important social context to help us clarify and reinforce the values that are meaningful to us in our lives. We do not feel so alienated from the public world because we belong to a community of people who share these same values with us.[117]

An intentional community also provides a greater variety of people, more diversity of interests, and broader purposes than we find in the private world of family and friends. The values and issues that inform a community's life usually find their connection in the public sphere. They stretch us beyond our private worlds toward larger issues and concerns. As communities reflect on and tackle local issues that affect their lives, many of these issues will lead communities into debates of public interest. Especially when intentional communities adopt a praxis of action-reflection that is rooted in the concrete experience of people's lives, intentional communities function as vibrant settings that "educate us (that is, lead us out) into the public realm."[118] In these ways, the social form of inten-

tional Christian communities serves as an educational training ground in the
practice of citizenship, offering a supportive context of smaller size and complexity that can serve as a bridge between the private and public world.[119]

Mediating communities, however, thrive only when they possess significant
social function and authority within the larger social order. Bernard Lee is concerned that intentional Christian communities in Western cultures are having little impact on the larger public/economic/political life in which they are located.
He feels that the power for social change lies with the middle class, which in fact
now has more in common with the lower than the upper class. Lee believes that
intentional Christian communities could play a key role in the social empower-
ment of the middle class to act on justice issues, which would in turn align them
more than they think with the lower class.

> People in the middle are hooked into identifying with the economic classes above
> them, when their actual trajectory is shared more abundantly with the poor. The
> same systematic dynamics which maintain the poor in their poverty are responsible
> for the increasing powerlessness of those in the middle. . . . Alliances between poor
> and middle classes are needed to redress systemic social injustice.[120]

If intentional Christian communities are to exercise a public stance within culture and society, they will need to establish some form of public presence or public visibility to increase their status and credibility within the larger social
systems of society. One way of achieving this would be through organizing a network of intentional communities that could more effectively embody a corporate
presence of the biblical visions of justice and love. Another way would be for
intentional Christian communities to become partners with other forms and
expressions of public life, such as local civic and community groups.[121] The
measure of their success as grassroots mediating communities depends largely
on how well they can visibly connect with other intentional communities and
civic groups to form an appropriate institutional expression of corporate and
social identity.

Intentional communities, therefore, will need to continue to explore the ways
they can effectively organize themselves to find a collective voice from which to
speak, a collective base from which to act. This is especially the case for marginal communities who have adopted a critical distance from mainstream ecclesial structures — such as the parish or diocese — which have traditionally served
the corporate visibility of the church as mediating institutions within society. Particularly for those communities located within the Catholic tradition, there is a
strong call to work toward the democratization of ecclesial structures, which cur-
rently function without democratic accountability and without the active participation of public discourse and deliberation.[122] Many intentional Christian

communities are struggling to find more appropriate ways for expressing the social embodiment of church within society. They are searching for "forms of institutionalizing which are liberating rather than constricting, and not top heavy."[123] According to Eugene Bianchi and Rosemary Radford Ruether, the need for democratic church reform and the quest for a public ecclesial presence that promotes redemptive relations within society is closely tied to the growth and development of intentional Christian communities.

> Perhaps a much simpler structure, in which the church takes primarily the form of intentional communities gathered amid a variety of social relations . . . needs to be imaged. Such communities scattered across all sectors of society could then become ways of deepening relationships and witnessing against unjust and abusive power in many different contexts, economic, political, and environmental, as well as familial. Simple forms of networking, linking such communities together in a sense of common identity as the Christian church, while retaining pluriformity of organization and cultural expression, might be more appropriate than a vast state-like superstructure.[124]

Public Life and the Art of Politics

A common critique of small communities is the concern that they too readily become what Bellah's team calls "lifestyle enclaves," that is, a gathering together of those "who are socially, economically, or culturally similar."[125] According to John Caputo, we need to reassess our understanding of what we mean by community, because we too often use the word in ways that distort its deeper character.

> Communities are defined in terms of unity, the capacity of individuals to swallow their differences and to come to common divergence, to stand as "one." So defined, a community resists otherness . . . and it ends up adopting ex-communicative practices. That is why we need another idea *of* community . . . one which is conceived in terms of its capacity to tolerate difference, its openness to the other. . . .[126]

Iris Marion Young also believes that the word "community" has become too comfortably associated with notions of similarity and unity. She suggests, as an alternative, that we replace the notion of "community" with the metaphor of "the city." In her view, the model of community depends on the desire for social wholeness and a politics of identification and sameness, whereas the model of the city fosters a politics of difference "without domination in which persons live together in relations of mediation among strangers with whom they are not in community."[127] However, as Caputo suggests, perhaps we can still redeem the word "community" by defining it "not by its convergence upon one, as in a metaphysics of presence and unity, but, in a postmetaphysical way, by its high threshold for tolerating dissent and respect for differences [that] can be put to work today in small communities which work together for the common good."[128]

Working for the common good necessarily draws intentional Christian communities into the realm of public life and the art of politics. Given the individualism of our age, Bellah's group believes that people "lack the resources to think about the relationship between groups that are culturally, socially or economically quite different."[129] Yet as Bernard Crick points out, it is the inherently pluralistic and diverse nature of our society that is "the seed and root of politics."[130] Tension, conflict, and uncertainty are inevitable in the political process. Crick reminds us that this need not be a fragmenting, detracting feature of political activity; rather, political conversation involves the free give and take of differing positions, views, and interests that belong to honest, open communication. Crick defends the art of politics as a good and necessary public activity that attempts to find workable solutions to the ever present problem of diversity and the need for conciliation. "The more one is involved in relationships with others," writes Crick, "the more conflicts of interest, of character, of circumstance, will arise."[131] These conflicts "create political activity." Crick defines politics as "the activity by which differing interests are conciliated by giving them a share in power in proportion to their own importance to the welfare and survival of the whole community."[132] Politics involves the ability to live with plurality and diversity without trying to reduce all things to a single unity and without trying to dominate, ignore, or manipulate others.

According to Stephen Brookfield, political learning involves critical analysis, reflection, and action in the world. It takes place in a range of settings and according to differing levels of involvement.

> Politics is a shorthand term for the processes by which decisions are made, wealth distributed, services are regulated, justice is maintained, and minority interests are protected. At its heart, politics is concerned with issues of control and power — how control and power are gained, shared, abdicated, protected, abused, and delegated; how those without power can organize collectively to press for democratic change and a more equitable distribution of power.[133]

Political activity is the search for the common good in the context of a plurality of needs and interests. It reflects the multi-agenda of diverse self-interests that hold public relationships together. Self-interest need not be equated negatively with selfishness. The word "interest" comes from the Latin *inter* ("among," "between") and *esse* ("to be"). In this sense, self-interest is linked with the question, "What is the self connected to, related to, invested in?"[134] Here, the notion of "interest" is closely connected with the notion of the common good as "the pursuit of the good in common."[135] Small, intentional communities, civic groups, and voluntary organizations with broad-based concerns contribute most to the public health. Such groups endeavor to reconnect formerly disempowered people into a web of political concern and political participation, creating a new public space and a new public process for grassroots political action. It is a matter of reclaiming the art of politics and helping people to understand for themselves that they not only can but should actively participate in the political structures that affect their lives. Bellah and his associates write as follows:

> This view of politics depends upon a notion of community . . . importantly different from the utilitarian individualist view. It seeks to persuade us that the individual self finds its fulfillment in relationships with others in a society organized through public dialogue. The necessary dialogue can be sustained only by communities. . . . [Although] this vision remains sporadic and largely local in scope, the larger implications are clear. These local initiatives may be the forerunners of social movements that will once again open up spaces for reflection, participation, and the transformation of society.[136]

In reflecting on our Western, Enlightenment culture, Sharon Welch speaks persuasively of the need to develop an "ethics of risk."[137] She asks why it is that white, middle-class, socially aware people often end up despairing over their lack of ability to effect changes in our sociocultural, economic, and religious institutions. Her answer is that members of the white, educated, middle-class tend to want to see results; they measure their failures against the criteria of effectiveness; they want social programs to work according to the ideals and goals motivating their actions. Over time, however, they begin to realize how ineffective their programs and actions have been, how impossible their ideals and visions, and this leads them to a "cultured despair" and eventually to "giving up."[138] Welch contrasts this with a feminist ethics of risk, one that retains commitment even and especially in the face of uncertainty, the lack of guarantees and the knowledge that things may never change.[139] She sees this ethic operative, for example, in the heritage of resistance that African-American women share. The luxury of despair and giving up is not an option for them. Theirs is an ethic of faithfulness rather than effectiveness — generations of foresisters faithfully struggling, creating a matrix in which further reflection and action becomes possible, a heritage of resistance and hope.

When I think of intentional Christian communities, I believe there is much struggling faithfulness operative in the lives of people who make them up. Although we need to find ways to prompt them toward more effective engagement with the public world, we also need to affirm their small, struggling efforts of faithfulness. These are communities struggling to read their tradition in deep,

searching ways (with all its stain and beauty) and to tackle the issues and concerns of a complex and ambiguous postmodern society (even in the small projects of social concern they may be involved in). There is something about
Welch's book that evokes the staying power of women and the strength of their
attending faithfully to the very basic needs and issues of human life (in contrast
to male notions of what is successful or effective?). There is also much in
Welch's book that would support the long, hard, time-consuming, relational
development of broad-based community initiatives rooted in traditions of justice
and love. Yet, whatever our form of public engagement, the metaphor she
appeals to is faithfulness versus effectiveness, hope versus despair, risking the
book rather than closing it.

Notes

1. Doing theology from "the underside of history" was the central theme of the second
week of Gutiérrez's course: However, Gutiérrez made a point of rejecting the opposition
often set up between liberation theology and European or Western theology. He believes
they can both learn from each other and that each must develop according to its own
specific cultural contexts and questions.

2. See Peter C. Hodgson, *Revisioning the Church*, p. 11.

3. Ibid., pp. 11, 51.

4. These theologies and issues were repeatedly named in a survey I conducted of some
fifty intentional Christian communities (see n. 22 in the introductory chapter). Recently in
Sydney, many members of marginal Christian communities gathered for the "People's
Conference" (sponsored by Catholics in Coalition for Justice and Peace, April 15–17,
1994), and the following issues were raised on their agenda: "What is the role of the
church in political debate? How can we, the church, support Aborigines in the Post-Mabo
era? Is there a meaningful role for the laity in today's church? Is sexism a sin? Is it operative in the church? How? What's to be done? Do ecological questions have anything to do
with us as church? Racism — do we need to address it as a church? as a nation? Patriarchy
— is it the natural law or an historical structural problem?"

5. David Ray Griffin, ed., *Spirituality and Society: Postmodern Visions*, p. xi.

6. Walter Brueggemann, *Texts under Negotiation*, pp. 19–20.

7. Anthony J. Russell, "Theology in Context and 'The Right to Think' in Three Contemporary Theologians: Gutiérrez, Dussel and Boff," p. 283.

8. David Tracy, "On Naming the Present," pp. 66–67.

9. See Sharon Welch, *Communities of Resistance and Solidarity*.

10. John Caputo, "Gadamer's Closet Essentialism: A Derridean Critique," p. 264.

11. Edmond Jabès, *From the Desert to the Book*, pp. 3–4 (adapted for inclusive language).

12. I recognize that while I value the insights of feminist writings, I am not a feminist in
the sense that I know, as only women can, the effects of patriarchal oppression. However,
I do know some of those effects as a man, and I also share the concerns of feminist schol-

arship to work toward liberation from all structures of domination. In this sense, I see myself as a feminist-identified person.

13. Rosemary Radford Ruether, *Sexism and God-Talk*, p. 173.

14. Elisabeth Schüssler Fiorenza, "Justified by All her Children: Struggle, Memory, and Vision," p. 35 n.6. See also *In Memory of Her*, where Schüssler Fiorenza notes that patriarchy is not just about men over women; rather, it "represents a social-cultural system in which a few men have power over other men, women, children, slaves, and colonized people" (p. 29).

15. In speaking of feminist theologies, I am drawing primarily upon the work of Euro-American feminists who continue to locate themselves in biblical religious traditions, albeit from a marginal position. In speaking of feminist experience, it is important to note that this is not meant in any universal sense. Rather, there is great diversity. The womanist critique has made feminists aware that a dominant group (e.g., white, middle-class, educated women) cannot speak on behalf of all women's experience. Womanist theologies raise the concerns of women of color, women who are poor and working class. For an introduction to this tradition, see Delores Williams, "Womanist Theology," in Judith Plaskow and Carol Christ, ed., *Weaving the Visions*, pp. 179–86.

16. Rebecca Chopp, *The Power to Speak*, p. 16. See also Jocelyn Dunphy-Blomfield's fine essay "Suffering," in Morny Joy and Penelope Magee, eds., *Claiming Our Rites*, pp. 99–116.

17. Judith Plaskow, *Standing Again at Sinai*, p. 1.

18. Edmond Jabès, *From the Desert to the Book*, p. 45.

19. Plaskow, *Standing Again at Sinai*, p. 37.

20. Ibid., p. 1.

21. Schüssler Fiorenza, *Bread Not Stone*, p. xx.

22. Mary Daly, *Gyn/Ecology*, pp. 1, 29.

23. Schüssler Fiorenza, *In Memory of Her*, p. 28.

24. Schüssler Fiorenza, *Bread Not Stone*, p. 112.

25. In chap. 1 of her book *But She Said*, Schüssler Fiorenza outlines nine hermeneutical principles that contribute to a feminist hermeneutic:

1. Revisionist: Revise standard accounts of history to recall what is neglected.

2. Text and Translations: Look for correct translations, especially distinguishing between generic versus gender specific language.

3. Imaginative Identification: Retelling stories, imagining the presence of women where they are absent.

4. Women as Authors: Reclaim texts authored by women.

5. Historical Interpretation: Reduces feminist interpretation only to those sources that speak about women.

6. Social-Cultural Reconstruction: Socially and culturally reconstruct the role of women in early Christianity (as Schüssler Fiorenza did in her work *In Memory of Her*).

7. Ideological Inscription: Less focused on historical reconstruction; rather, looks at the biblical texts as literary texts, as "novels."

8. Women as Subjects of Interpretation: Many texts have had an androcentric reception and need to be received in a new way by women.

9. Social Location: Read the Scriptures in view of women's special location (e.g., Latin American, Asian, Womanist positions).

In chap. 2, Schüssler Fiorenza outlines her own position as a critical feminist rhetorical hermeneutic that strives to incorporate many of the above principles as a hermeneutics of (a) suspicion, (b) remembrance, (c) evaluation and proclamation, and (d) creative imagination and ritualization. See also her earlier work *Bread Not Stone*.

26. Schüssler Fiorenza, *Bread Not Stone*, p. xvi.

27. Ibid., p. 14.

28. Ibid., p. 40. See also Schüssler Fiorenza, *In Memory of Her*, pp. 32–34.

29 . See e.g., Francis Schüssler Fiorenza, "The Influence of Feminist Theory on My Theological Work," p. 96.

30. Francis Schüssler Fiorenza, "The Crisis of Hermeneutics and Christian Theology," p. 122. However, as Mark C. Taylor points out, the decentered subject of postmodernity does not mean the disintegration of the self, but recognition of a radically "webbed" self, situated in the midst of multiple and changing relations. See *Erring*, p. 135.

31. Schüssler Fiorenza discusses this approach in *But She Said*, pp. 140–44.

32. Radford Ruether, *Sexism and God-Talk*, p. 23. However, in a later work, Radford Ruether maintains that feminist theology "must create a new textual base, a new canon. . . . Feminist theology cannot be done from the existing base of the Christian Bible [because] in these texts the norm for women is absence and silence." See *Womanguides*, p. ix.

33. Radford Ruether, *Sexism and God-Talk*, p. 31.

34. Schüssler Fiorenza, *Bread Not Stone*, p. 60.

35. Plaskow, *Standing Again at Sinai*, see pp. xiii, 5–6.

36. Radford Ruether, *Sexism and God-Talk*, p. 27.

37. Ibid., pp. 32–33.

38. Paul Ricoeur, *Hermeneutics and the Human Sciences*, pp. 99–100. It is interesting to note that Elisabeth Schüssler Fiorenza herself affirms that it was the liberating/justice traditions of Christianity that first made her aware of feminist oppression by patriarchy. See "Feminist Spirituality, Christian Identity, and Catholic Vision" in Carol Christ and Judith Plaskow, ed., *Womanspirit Rising*, 136–48.

39. Tracy, *Plurality and Ambiguity*, p. 79.

40. Sharon Welch, *A Feminist Ethic of Risk*, p. 142.

41. Plaskow, *Standing Again at Sinai*, pp. 30–36.

42. Ibid., p. 53.

43. Ibid., p. 59.

44. Ibid., p. 54.

45. Ruether speaks of many "useable traditions" and she names five: biblical texts, marginalized or "heretical" Christian countercultural traditions, classical theological traditions, paganism or Goddess religions, and critical or post-Christian traditions. See *Sexism and God-Talk*, pp. 22–45.

46. Chopp, *The Power to Speak*, p. 22.

47. See Iris Marion Young, "Impartiality and the Civic Public: Some Implications of Feminist Critiques of Moral and Political Theory." See also Seyla Benhabib's chapter "The Generalized and the Concrete Other: The Kohlberg-Gilligan Controversy and Feminist Theory," in Seyla Benhabib and Drucilla Cornell, eds., *Feminism as Critique*.

48. Chopp, *The Power to Speak*, p. 23.

49. Iris Marion Young, "The Ideal of Community and the Politics of Difference," p. 2.

50. Ibid., p. 3.

51. Ibid., p. 3. Mark C. Taylor provides an extensive list of these binary oppositions in his work *Erring*, pp. 8–9.

52. Along with Iris Marion Young's article, see also Joan W. Scott, "Deconstructing Equality-Versus-Difference: Or, The Uses of Poststructuralist Theory For Feminism," p. 37: "The Western philosophical tradition rests on binary oppositions: unity/diversity, identity/difference, presence/absence, and universality/specificity. The leading terms are accorded primacy; their partners are represented as weaker or derivative. Yet the first terms depend on and derive their meaning from the second to such an extent that the secondary terms can be seen as generative of the definition of the first terms."

53. Taylor, *Erring*, p. 15.

54. Chopp, *The Power to Speak*, p. 2.

55. Patricia Waugh, however, offers a caution concerning the usual postmodern tendency of using "femininity" to signify "otherness," particularly by male avant-garde writers. See "Stalemates?: Feminists, Postmodernists and Unfinished Issues in Modern Aesthetics," pp. 350–51.

56. Taylor, *Erring*, p. 175.

57. Radford Ruether, *Sexism and God-Talk*, p. 54.

58. Ibid., p. 54.

59. Gender studies abound today which are grappling with the issue of feminist identity. One of the key questions facing feminists is: How can we affirm and celebrate our "femaleness" without falling prone to the subjugated difference of patriarchy's binary oppositions: man/woman, culture/nature, rational/irrational, etc.? In other words, how can feminists reassert an essential and positive gender difference without reinvoking the oppositional structure of patriarchy? For two excellent responses to this dilemma, see Linda Alcoff, "Cultural Feminism versus Poststructuralism: The Identity Crisis in Feminist Theory"; and Beverly Wildung Harrison, *Making the Connections: Essays in Feminist Social Ethics*, pp. 22–43.

60. Welch, *A Feminist Ethic of Risk*, p. 35.

61. Chopp, *The Power to Speak*, p. 68.

62. Ibid., p. 2.

63. Taylor, *Erring*, p. 10.

64. Elizabeth Kamarck Minnich, *Transforming Knowledge*, p. 30.

65. Ibid., p. 148, citing Barbara Johnson, translator of Derrida's *Dissemination*.

66. Ibid., p. 30.

67. Radford Ruether, *Sexism and God-Talk*, p. 20. See also Carol Nicholson's reflections in "Postmodernism, Feminism, and Education: The Need for Solidarity."

68. Margaret Farley, "Feminist Ethics in the Christian Ethics Curriculum," p. 69.

69. Welch, *A Feminist Ethic of Risk*, p. 151.

70. Thomas Groome, *Sharing Faith*, pp. 32–35, 80–84.

71. See Heidegger's "Letter on Humanism," in *Basic Writings*, pp. 233–35.

72. Marion Young, "Impartiality and the Civic Public," p. 60.

73. This is a key theme in Carol Gilligan's work *In A Different Voice*, which contrasts two orientations of moral reasoning, a feminist oriented "ethics of care" and a masculine oriented "ethics of rights." See also Seyla Benhabib, "The Generalized and the Concrete

Other: The Kohlberg-Gilligan Controversy and Feminist Theory," in Seyla Benhabib and Drucilla Cornell, eds., *Feminism as Critique,* pp. 77–95.

74. Welch, *A Feminist Ethic of Risk,* see pp. 20, 137, 182.

75. Marion Young, "Impartiality and the Civic Public," p. 69.

76. See Karl Mannheim's principle work, *Ideology and Utopia.*

77. Ibid., p. 2. Mannheim writes: "We must realize once and for all that the meanings which make up our world are simply an historically determined and continuously developing structure in which humanity develops, and are in no sense absolute. . . . The vain hope of discovering truth in a form which is independent of an historically and socially determined set of meanings will have to be given up. . . . There is no norm which can lay claim to formal validity and which can be abstracted as a constant universal formal element from its historically changing content" (pp. 85, 80, 82; adapted for inclusive language).

78. According to Mannheim, ideology can refer to the way ideas are used "evaluatively" by a dominant group to give a depiction of reality which in fact hides the dominant group's interests. However, ideology can also function as a "non-evaluative" symbolic system of ideas and values rooted in a particular society. In this sense, ideology refers to the necessity of perspective: all knowledge is socially based in particular cultural worldviews. See *Ideology and Utopia,* pp. 80–94, 265–66.

79. See especially the first two chapters (on world construction and world maintenance) in Peter Berger's work *The Sacred Canopy.*

80. Ibid. See also Bernard Lee and Michael Cowan, *Dangerous Memories,* pp. 7–9.

81. Shaun Gallagher, *Hermeneutics and Education,* pp. 246–52.

82. Ibid., pp. 300–304.

83. Derrida, "The Principle of Reason: The University in the Eyes of its Pupils."

84. Caputo, *Radical Hermeneutics,* pp. 230–31.

85. Ibid., p. 231.

86. Ibid., p. 231.

87. Derrida, "The Principle of Reason," p. 9.

88. Gallagher, *Hermeneutics and Education,* p. 296.

89. Paul Feyerabend, *Farewell to Reason,* p. 317.

90. Ibid., pp. 54ff.

91. The convergence between feminist and poststructuralist theory is recognized by many feminist writers. See, for example, Joan W. Scott, "Deconstructing Equality-Versus-Difference: Or, The Uses of Poststructuralist Theory for Feminism"; Patricia Waugh, "Stalemates?: Feminists, Postmodernists and Unfinished Issues in Modern Aesthetics"; Carol Nicholson, "Postmodernism, Feminism, and Education: The Need for Solidarity"; Iris Marion Young, "The Ideal of Community and the Politics of Difference"; Catherine Keller, "Toward a Postpatriarchal Postmodernity," in David Ray Griffin, ed., *Spirituality and Society,* pp. 63–80; Rebecca Chopp, *The Power to Speak;* Sharon Welch, *Communities of Resistance and Solidarity* (Welch draws primarily on Foucault's writings); Morny Joy, "Sainthood or Heresy," in Morny Joy and Penelope Magee, eds., *Claiming Our Rites,* pp. 117–33.

92. Patricia Waugh, "Stalemates?: Feminists, Postmodernists and Unfinished Issues in Modern Aesthetics," p. 349. See also pp. 352ff. See also Linda Alcoff, "Cultural Feminism Versus Poststructuralism," esp. pp. 416–17.

93. Henry Giroux, cited in Gallagher, *Hermeneutics and Education*, p. 249.

94. Bernstein, *The New Constellation*, p. 218.

95. Stephen Brookfield, *Understanding and Facilitating Adult Learning*, p. 293. This point is made repeatedly throughout Brookfield's book; see pp. 58–59, 125, 144–45, 225, 233, 247, 284, 286. Elizabeth Karmack Minnich makes a similar point in her work *Transforming Knowledge*. Challenging assumptions is key to effective learning. If students never feel any anxiety, questioning, disturbance, and so on, then we may wonder whether any effective learning has occurred (see p. 81).

96. Brookfield, *Understanding and Facilitating Adult Learning*, p. 294.

97. Ibid., p. 293.

98. Brookfield, *Developing Critical Thinkers*, p. 5.

99. Ibid., p. 15. Thomas Groome broadens these activities of critical thinking to include analytical and social remembering, critical and social reasoning, and creative and social imagining. See *Sharing Faith*, pp. 104–6, 188–89.

100. Brookfield, *Developing Critical Thinkers*, pp. 5–9.

101. Paulo Freire, *Pedagogy of the Oppressed*, pp. 77ff.

102. Ibid., p. 81. A useful handbook of social analysis is provided by Joe Holland and Peter Henriot, *Social Analysis: Linking Faith and Justice*.

103. Paulo Freire, *Pedagogy of the Oppressed*, p. 65.

104. Ibid., pp. 17–19 (adapted for inclusive language).

105. Robert Nisbet, *The Quest for Community*, p. xxiii.

106. Leonardo Boff, *Ecclesiogenesis*, p. 1.

107. Robert Bellah et al., *Habits of the Heart*, pp. 246–49. The biblical root metaphors of "covenant" and "reign of God" all presuppose a social identity of embeddedness and inter-relatedness. See, e.g., Gerhard Lohfink, *Jesus and Community;* Paul King et al., *Risking Liberation*, p. 175; John C. Haughey, "The Eucharist and Intentional Christian Communities."

108. Bellah et al., *Habits of the Heart*, pp. 152–55, 286.

109. Parker Palmer, *The Company of Strangers*, p. 19.

110. Bellah et al., *The Good Society*, pp. 5–6. For contemporary analyses of Australian culture, see Hugh Mackay, *Reinventing Australia: The Mind and Mood of Australia in the 90s;* and John Thornhill, *Making Australia: Exploring our National Conversation*.

111. Bellah et al., *The Good Society*, pp. 3–18.

112. Ibid., p. 5.

113. For a feminist perspective on the private/public split, see Rosemary Curran Barciauskas and Debra Beery Hull, *Loving and Working: Reweaving Women's Public and Private Lives*, pp. 71–80. On the dichotomy between private and public life in the context of cultural individualism, see Bellah et al., *Habits of the Heart*, p. 163.

114. It is interesting to note that this is a complete reversal of what we find in the political theory of classical Greece. For the Greeks, public discourse and public activity was highly valued as the realm where a person's existence in the world counted most (albeit a male person). Private life was considered too restrictive and limiting in the range of social interaction it allowed. Only within the world of public and civic life could a person's words and actions take on a meaning with larger significance and effect than that which was possible in the private realm. See Hannah Arendt, *The Human Condition*, pp. 22–78. See also Robert Dahl, *Democracy and Its Critics*, pp. 13–23.

115. Evelyn and James Whitehead, *Community of Faith,* pp. 63–71.

116. Nisbet, *The Quest for Community,* pp. 41–65. See also Peter Berger and Richard Neuhaus, *To Empower People: The Role of Mediating Structures in Public Policy.*

117. Evelyn and James Whitehead, *Community of Faith,* pp. 71–76. In a similar vein, Bernard Lee and Michael Cowan write, "The role of mediating structures in social reconstruction is essential. The house churches, the intentional Christian communities, are one such possible agent of reconstruction in our culture. Because of their voluntary nature, they can be one of the most effective means of evangelizing culture. Little systems can better effect big systems than individuals can. Networks of little systems are even more insistent conversation partners with megastructures." *Dangerous Memories,* p. 169.

118. Palmer, *The Company of Strangers,* p. 123.

119. On the relationship between citizenship, religious commitment, and education, see Mary Boys, ed., *Education for Citizenship and Discipleship.*

120. Bernard Lee, "Intentional Christian Communities in the U.S. Church," pp. 183–84.

121. There are many examples of intentional Christian communities exploring these options. To name just a few: The Jeremiah Group of New Orleans (U.S.A.); Salem House Churches (U.S.A.); Communitas (Washington D.C., U.S.A.); Communities Australia, The House of the Gentle Bunyip (Victoria, Aust.); Philip Bay Community (N.S.W., Aust.); The Waiters Union (Qld, Aust.); The Paulian Association (N.S.W., Aust.); Catholics in Coalition for Justice and Peace (Aust.); The Hope Community (U.K.); The Congress of Black Catholics (U.K.); Iona Community (U.K.); and far too many more to name.

122. See the collection of essays in Eugene Bianchi and Rosemary Radford Ruether, eds., *A Democratic Catholic Church.*

123. Ian Fraser, *Living a Countersign,* p. 62.

124. Bianchi and Radford Ruether, eds., *A Democratic Catholic Church,* pp. 12–13.

125. Bellah et al., *Habits of the Heart,* p. 72.

126. Caputo, "Beyond Aestheticism: Derrida's Responsible Anarchy," p. 69.

127. Marion Young, "The Ideal of Community and the Politics of Difference," p. 2.

128. Caputo, *Radical Hermeneutics,* p. 255.

129. Bellah et al., *Habits of the Heart,* p. 206.

130. Bernard Crick, *In Defense of Politics,* p. 66.

131. Ibid., p. 25.

132. Ibid., p. 22.

133. Brookfield, *Developing Critical Thinkers,* p. 164.

134. Ernie Cortez, "Communities and Social Change," notes from a seminar given at Loyola University, New Orleans, 1991.

135. Bellah et al., *The Good Society,* p. 9. The authors note that single-issue groups fail to reflect this principle of the common good. They separate people along absolute lines and thus mar the public realm. Similarly, the language of "rights" — my rights against your rights — tends to polarize groups within society and disables the possibility of a discursive community capable of thinking about the common good. See pp. 138–42.

136. Bellah et al., *Habits of the Heart,* p. 218.

137. Welch, *A Feminist Ethic of Risk.*

138. Ibid., see esp. chap. 6, "The Ideology of Cultured Despair," pp. 103–22.

139. Ibid., pp. 19–20, 67–70.

PART THREE:
IN THE MARGINS
OF THE BOOK

The roads of the book are roads of instinct, listening, attention, reserve, and daring laid out by words and sustained by questions. Road toward the open.

"Writing means going on a journey, at the end of which you will not be the same. . . ." (Reb Denté)

It has the dimensions of the book and the bitter stubbornness of a wandering question.

The question means that, for the time of its formulation, we do not belong. We do not belong with belonging; we are unbound within bonds. Detached, in order to become more fully attached and then again detached. It means we forever turn the *inside out,* set it free, revel in its freedom, and die of it.

"There is no preferential place for the book," he had written, "but there might be a non-place made up of all the thinkable places."

Between one book and the next, there is the empty space of a missing book, linked with we do not know which of the two.

So ever since the book my life has been a wake of writing in the space between limits, under the resplendent sign of the unpronounceable Name.

I have tried to be the word of the book, for the past and future of the book. (Yukel)

"Thus we are led to approach the book. What we read always depends on what remains to be read."

(Thus reading a book in its fullness would mean substituting a different one — identical, but marked by its particular and, often, original approach to the point of being modified; for any reader in the thick of reading is also an unsuspected creator. . . .)

Does reading the book not mean creating it by and by? Taking the book on yourself to such a point, does this not mean being . . . bound to make your own book, that of your spirit, of your soul and your body?

Make allowance for fire where writing spreads. . . . Ah, write, write to keep alive the fire of creation. Raise words from the peaceful night where they lay buried, words still astonished at their resurrection.

You must believe in the book in order to write it.
The time of writing is the time of this faith.

Edmond Jabès

CHAPTER FIVE

MARGINAL HERMENEUTICS

Perhaps it is a false division to speak of "inside the book" and "outside the book," as if the two are opposed to each other. Marginal hermeneutics is at one and the same time both inside and outside the book — the same book only able to be read "twice" (with trust and with suspicion) because the ways of belonging and nonbelonging live off each other's approaches to the book. A marginal hermeneutic is like a "permeable membrane connecting inside and outside. It confuses them with one another, allowing the outside in, making the inside out, dividing them and joining them. It forms an ambiguous transition between one and the other."[1] Perhaps a dialogical hermeneutic seeks to turn the book "inside out" — drawing it out to face new questions and unexpected possibilities. Perhaps an exilic hermeneutic seeks to allow "the outside in" — so that whatever is absent and unwritten can approach and accost the pages of the book. Marginal hermeneutics feels the tension of both these movements, and attempts to allow each its rightful claim. "Inside-out and outside-in — a boundary settlement the interpreter struggles to effect."[2]

Marginal space is a space that confuses oppositions, a space always inscribed in "the between." We need to know the ways of belonging and nonbelonging to recognize that in reality the two reside together in a space of continual to-and-fro: the space of the margins. For Gadamer, the hermeneutical situation is always placed "in the middle of things," between the familiar and the strange, between the written past we dwell in and the unwritten future we project. Derrida also upholds this marginal space that moves between such oppositions as inside/outside, memory/promise, continuity/discontinuity. In Derrida's words, marginal hermeneutics recognizes the depth of our belonging to historical tradition that is continually working itself out as it works through the gaps and interruptions of nonbelonging.

> . . . we must maintain two contradictory affirmations at the same time. On the one hand we affirm the existence of ruptures in history, and on the other we affirm that these ruptures produce gaps . . . in which the most hidden and forgotten archives can emerge and constantly recur and work through history. One must surmount the categorical oppositions of philosophic logic out of fidelity to these conflicting positions of historical discontinuity (rupture) and continuity (repetition), which are neither pure break with the past nor a pure unfolding or explication of it.[3]

To write in favor of a marginal hermeneutic is to face the quandary of not really being able to do so, in the sense of treating it as a separate and distinct type of hermeneutics. In the more usual and ready-to-hand terms, perhaps we could call it a "hermeneutic of creative reconstruction" that is shaped in the interplay between a hermeneutic of retrieval and a hermeneutic of suspicion.[4] We only really capture a sense of it by working through the hermeneutical reflection of being both inside and outside the book. Marginal hermeneutics is this "being both." It is the site of the "between" such that it resists being pinned down (unlike the book's center, where the pages are firmly stapled), just as much as it resists being lost or forced off the page (but rather, claims the margins as the "breathing spaces" of the book). Marginal hermeneutics is what happens when the twin events of belonging and nonbelonging, faith and doubt, trust and suspicion, the written and the unwritten, presence and absence — when these "unresolved two" burst into life in the thin, interpretive edge that both joins and separates them. As Edgerton suggests, the interpretive space of the margins represents the fully claimed, intentional awareness and activity of reading and writing under the sign of Hermes, the god of "boundaries, doors, and roads," and of the doings that transpire there:

> Under the sign of Hermes interpretation we discover a magic theater of desire performed at the place where boundaries meet: the past and present, present and future, inclusion and exclusion, the fixed and the open, poverty and wealth, privileged speech and unprivileged speech, fiction and chaos . . . lie and truth, possible and impossible, living and dead, wild and tame . . . one person and another, what I have done and what I will do. That is, it is a theater of desire — hungry for a different future, which does not transmit, but transforms — performed at the place where the gods and humankind meet.[5]

It is this "theater of desire" I will be exploring in the following two chapters, suggesting that intentional Christian communities are vibrant communities of interpretation — scribbling in the margins of tradition — enacting hermeneutical practices informed by an interpretive wisdom that represents a dramatic, playful, transformative performance of reading and writing in the margins of the book.

Margin Writing

"If we are to approach a text," writes Derrida, "it must have an edge."[6] On the side of the "written" appears what is stable, familiar, privileged, reverberating and enduring. On the side of the "unwritten" appears what is wandering, strange, excluded, secret, and haunting. Between the two, in the margins, there is "writing": interpretation that listens to the written and the unwritten, interpretation that continually shifts and oscillates in and out of the book, moving between what is and what is not to explore possibilities of what could be.

Perhaps one of the best examples of interpretation that takes place at the edge of a text — between the written and the unwritten — is the realm of the metaphor.[7] Metaphorical writing is tensive writing, reminding us that every "is like" contains an "is not like," that everything written is also haunted by the unwritten, that every hint of presence ("is") is also a reminder of absence ("is not"). Metaphorical resemblance implies that one word is like another, yet it also implies that the two are unlike each other. According to Edgerton, metaphor

> produces meaning only where the distance between the two terms is not collapsed, where it is remembered that the terms brought together are *different*. The difference pushes apart, the identity pulls together, and in the space held open between them the meaning of metaphor happens. . . .[8]

We need only think of our language about God to discern the way all interpretive writing lives in this tension between likeness and unlikeness, similarity and difference. However we name God, we know this name both resembles and does not resemble God. Our interpretive namings have some yield, but every naming also hinders and obstructs. As such, dissimilitude and difference intrude upon all our constructions and pronouncements. Indeed, it has long been recognized that religious and theological language has an iconoclastic or apophatic character: we are always "missing the mark" in our language about God.[9] Attention to metaphor reminds us that "all naming is already the withdrawal of the thing named, and it is this withdrawal which keeps language going, forcing us to resume the naming process again and again."[10] Jabès, for example, can say at one and the same time: "God is a word too many," and "a word without words."[11] So many words resemble God that no one word can hold. God: abundant lack.

Perhaps it is this "abundant lack" that deconstruction wants to highlight. It celebrates the superabundance of meaning that issues forth from interpretation that knows full well its lack. According to Sallie McFague, deconstruction underscores "the necessity of developing 'negative capability' — the ability to endure absence, uncertainty, partiality, relativity, and to hold at bay the desire for closure, coherence, identity, totality."[12] Every constructive effort lives in tension — at every moment — with what threatens to bring it down. In this sense, deconstruction calls attention to

> the underside of all our constructions, the "is not," the incompleteness, the partiality, the uncertainty, that must accompany all our creations lest we reify them into absolutes. Deconstruction cautions us against trying to save ourselves through our constructions. The temptation is to seek security, in a vast number of complex ways, against the abyss, the chaos, the different, the other, the unknown — whatever threatens us. By seeking security through our own constructions, we refuse to step outside the houses of language we have erected to protect us from the emptiness and terror we cannot control. Our safe havens, called dogmas and orthodoxy, become absolutes, giving the illusion of being certain, being "on the inside," having the truth.[13]

Interpretive practice cannot live without the unwritten because, as McFague notes, metaphorical naming that loses its shock of negation also loses its shock of recognition.[14] One of the greatest dangers interpretation faces is the tendency to deny or suppress the tension that exists between the written and the unwritten — to resolve the tension by literalizing the "is like" and forgetting the "is not like." According to Edgerton, this is interpretation that refuses to acknowledge its own haunted world — a world "haunted by the unwritten" that undermines the text but also secretly saves and sustains it.[15] For it is the hunger, the thirst, the questions, the untamed, the unacknowledged, the other, the different, that makes all writing, all dialogue, all interpretation possible. Haunted interpretation insists on keeping the tension between the similar and the different, the known and the unknown, the written and the unwritten, the present and the absent, in continual play with each other:

> The written and the unwritten are different; they are Other to one another. Although standing between the two, interpretation stands closer to the place of the written, the place where Otherness is turned into a narrative, into a text, with all the inevitable misperception and miswriting. Nevertheless interpretation insists upon the necessity of the Otherness, the misperception, the misunderstanding. . . . Haunted interpretation refuses literalization of itself or of the Other and reaches toward the scandals of difference and identity which live in the space between.[16]

The unwritten needs a chance to play in the margins of the text, to claim its share of interpretive practice. Listening to the unwritten enables the wisdom of repressed or disallowed voices the freedom to speak and the chance to be heard. As we noted in previous chapters, this is especially necessary in the face of a metaphysics of presence that always attempts to cover up absence and difference in its quest for completeness and totality. Marginal hermeneutics operates at the very edge of the text where meaning is most metaphorical and unresolved, most "in play." It wants "to try out" new metaphors, new writings, new interpretations. As Bruns suggests, marginal commentary is always unsatisfied with respect to whatever is placed before it. "Something is always left unsaid and undone, and it is this unfinished portion that commentary listens for and works for. . . ."[17] In this sense, marginal hermeneutics is destabilizing and experimental because it tries to "find out for itself," to imagine what things might be like if they were different, to see if something else might be the case than is the case.[18] According to McFague, it represents a daring, free, constructive theology that "must be willing to play with possibilities and, as a consequence, not take itself too seriously."[19]

The play of writing in the margins represents an area of freedom where an interpretive community is partially released from the burden of prescribed meanings and weighty, dominant receptions of a text. It is writing relieved of taken-for-granted conventions and established readings of texts that have become ensnared in familiar and set patterns of interpretive construal. Play releases a community into what Roland Barthes calls the "pleasure of the text," the pleasure of interpretive activity that runs freely across the wild and fertile field of the text. Writing in the margins is excessive and indulgent writing that scribbles madly anything and everything that wells up and wants to be written. It is "vitally engaged with the living situations of men and women; it is concrete rather than abstract, displays life in all its rich variousness, and rejects barren conceptual enquiry for the feel and taste of what it is to be alive."[20]

Margin writing revels in and draws attention to its own playfulness. It does not try to pretend to be "serious" or to represent things "as they actually are." Rather, "in the very moment of conveying meaning, it communicates something of its own relative, artificial status as well."[21] It is writing that lives happily in the realm of ambiguity and alternative possibility, purging itself of ideological attempts to write things "as they are," which is really only an attempt to hide the socially relative or culturally constructed nature of conventional language behind the myth of a neutral and colorless language of representation. This latter type of writing, which takes itself too seriously, actually suppresses or denies the productive, playful, creative character of language. It denies that we are continually recreating our world through interpretive language and fosters "the illusion that we are perceiving reality without its intervention."[22]

Margin writing makes no high claims to seriousness, but neither does it succumb to suggestions that it is nothing more than frivolous writing. Rather, it is scribbling at its best — scribbling that dares to write new commentaries because

it knows itself to stand in a long line of descendants who have felt the same interpretive power that issues forth when commentary becomes the very life and
breath of a text. The pages of tradition are crowded with interpretive scribblers
who have run with the wind in the field as their pens have run with the words of
writing. Marginal hermeneutics shifts the role of interpretive communities from
that of *consumers* of a text to that of *producers* of the text.[23] This is a performative hermeneutic directed toward the future of the text; it opens it out, sets it
going, and "gathers it up as play, activity, production, practice."[24] As Jabès suggests, it turns the book "inside out" and sets it free to face a world of pressing,
unexplored, wandering questions.

How much free play can tradition allow? Terry Eagleton, for example,
believes that Gadamer makes interpretive play "too safe." He claims that, for
Gadamer, everything that is scattered, let loose, and surrendered to the winds of
history will finally "return home," because "beneath all history, silently spanning
past, present, and future, runs a unifying essence known as 'tradition.'"[25] However, my reading of Gadamer suggests that margin writing is necessarily bound
to the textual edges of our cultural, linguistic, and religious traditions of belonging. Yet it also seems true to say that margin writing wants to break free from
these constraints — or, at least, it is motivated by a desire to set free the language
of tradition, to release it, to let it loose as much as possible, to extend and enlarge
it.

Gerald Bruns likens margin writing to the writing of poets. Whereas our
received texts come to us with a certain enduring stability, poetry seems to be "on
the loose" in our discourses, "causing things to go out of control."[26] Poetry
listens to that which is unwritten (as disallowed or unable to be written), to that
which lives in the shadows of the texts we have privileged in our tradition. Poetry
"does not try to bring things under control; rather, it lets them go, lets them turn
this way and that, luxuriates in ambiguity."[27] The poet-interpreter is wary of the
way normative tradition can function to keep everything under its control — a
type of discourse that seeks a world "in which things are just so and not otherwise," that "stakes itself on saving us from precisely such things as the 'breakdown of reality by poetry.'"[28] It wants to keep things straight, to pin things down,
to seal itself off from whatever is not itself. As a consequence, it banishes the
poets, the prophets, the margin writers into exile and, like the words they write,
into endless wandering. According to Maurice Blanchot,

> The poem is exile, and the poet who belongs to it belongs to the dissatisfaction of
> exile. [The poet] is outside, far from home. . . . Exile, the poem then, makes the poet
> a wanderer, the one always astray, the one to whom the stability of presence is not
> granted and who is deprived of a true abode. . . . Error is the risk which awaits the

(prophetic)

poet . . . who writes dependent on an essential work. Error means wandering, the inability to abide and stay. . . . The work draws light from the dark. . . . This is the essential risk.[29]

Instead of banishing the poet/prophet/margin writer, can we linger in their company long enough to allow their words a place along the liminal edges of our texts? If we can, we might realize, as Bruns suggests, that "in its heart of hearts hermeneutics is prophetic rather than nostalgic."[30] Indeed, the very name (hermeneutics) is derived from the Greek god Hermes, who is the herald — the announcer or messenger of the gods. Yet this herald speaks in a strange sort of way. The one who communicates God's words does so through lies, theft, and deception.

Cattle-rustling robber, carrier of dreams,
Watcher by night who haunts the gates,
Lucky finder, inventor of instruments, singer of myths;
Eraser of traces, reverser of signs,
Counselor of blindness, deafness, dumbness. . .
Night-time prowler who goes through keyholes as a mist. . .
Liar, maker of false oaths,
Deceiver with words as well as signs,
Who boldly demands justice for what he knows is untrue. . .
Giver of gifts which may be stolen back,
Who desires to know
The mind of Zeus on his own,
Lord of wild and tame beasts,
Messenger to the dead:
This is Hermes, the herald of the gods.[31]

Edgerton notes that Hermes' life "began on the outside, on the margin: the margin of divine society, the margin of day and night, the margin of the fantastic, where 'uncanny deeds came to pass.'"[32] Hermes is the "god of boundaries, doors and roads," the "Wayfinder" who crosses boundaries in order to find a path.[33] The crossing, however, is a kind of transgression, and the finding is a kind of theft. The Hermes-interpreter steals ownership of the text from all those authoritative owners who dominate the text by exercising control over what it means, how it will be used, in what sense, for what purpose, and by whom. "Even the idea of 'meaning' itself," says Edgerton, "can be the owner of a text, as when we say interpretation must be true to the 'meaning of the text.'"[34] Hermes, however, "steals" the text so that it serves instead the voice and intention of the interpreter — and does so in such a way that this theft is craftily hidden under the guise of loyalty to the text. Interpretation gains entry through "taking up and taking over" an established and privileged text. Yet its concern is for its own voice — its own speaking and questions and claims — and for the future. In taking up a text, therefore, "interpretation subverts the direction and purpose of the very text that gives it entry." It vows loyalty to the text; it claims to be speaking about the text and, in some cases, its vow of loyalty even denies that any interpretation is happening! This is the most subversive of vows; it is where the lie, the theft, the invention and the craft of Hermes weaves its most powerful spell.[35] Jabès speaks of the "interpretive theft" and "lying" performed by Hermes this way:

> "If a phrase or line survives the work, it is not the author who gave it this special chance (at the expense of others): it is the reader.
> "There is the lie.
> "The writer steps aside for the work, and the work depends on the reader. . . ." (from the commentary of Reb Ab)[36]

> *(Thus reading a book in its fullness would mean substituting a different one — identical, but marked by its particular and, often, original approach to the point of being modified; for any reader in the thick of reading is also an unsuspecting creator. . .)*[37]

> Does reading the book not mean creating it by and by? Taking the book on yourself to such a point, does this not mean being . . . *bound to make your own book,* that of your spirit, of your soul and your body?[38]

Tradition is dependent on those who read it, and every reader is a potential writer. Tradition is always written differently. This is what wounds it so — it resists what it seeks: a book of pure transparency and clarity, a book that is in no need of further commentary or questioning. Yet this wound insures its life — a book continually making itself, resisting impossible closures for the sake of its openness to the possible. The book's "failure" is actually its "success." Commenting on Jabès's work, Derrida writes: "[the book] encloses in itself the ways out of itself, which includes its own exits, which itself opens its own doors, that is to say . . . *closes itself by thinking its own opening.*"[39] Perhaps Jabès and Derrida are commenting on the ancient torment of Jewish revelation: "No one can see the face of God and live."[40] If the face of God, of life, of tradition were totally self-present, this would be the place where all reading and interpreting would finally end — would be no more — a death.

"The desire of the reader to seek closure must be postponed, the talent for remaking the book endorsed."[41] According to Mark Taylor, the inventive talent and craft of margin writing receives much of its creative, cutting-edge ability because of its wandering, erring, transgressing sensibilities. *"Interpretation is transgression,"* and transgression is "the action of passing over or beyond."[42]

Margin writing transgresses (goes beyond, extends) the text, such that any distinction between the text as written and the text as writing is lost as the book is scattered and sown like the "volatile seeds of flowers." Taylor writes,

> Writing that wanders into this interstitial space will, of necessity, be unsettled and unsettling. Repeatedly slipping through the holes in the system within which it must, nevertheless, be registered, such writing is perpetually transitory and forever nomadic. It is neither simply this nor that, here nor there, inside nor outside. To follow the ways of such vagrant writing is inevitably to err. . . .
>
> *Erring*, then, is "wandering, roaming; deviating from the right or intended course; missing the mark.". . . The liminal thinking of marginal thinkers . . . asks errant questions and suggests responses that often seem erratic or even erroneous. Since their reflection wanders, roams, and strays from the "proper" course, it tends to deviate from well-established ways. . . .
>
> Within the ambiguous space of liminality, hierarchies crumble and boundaries dissolve. . . . Writing is ever errant. Wandering between an Origin that never was and an End that never is, writing has always already begun and never finally ends. The writer, therefore, remains liminal — a trickster, a joker, a clown. . . .[43]

Taylor, however, also ascribes a spirit of generosity to the wandering, risk-taking, erring character of margin writing. It is writing that is willing to lose its way in order to find a way. As Gadamer notes, "all playing is a being-played," in which we lose ourselves and allow the game to play us, rather than we playing it.[44] "Without this self-forgetfulness," writes Taylor, "the generous expenditure of erring is impossible."[45] Margin writing is willing to expend itself in order to "save" the book from premature closure; it replaces sterile stability with creative instability and generous and generative multiplicity.[46] It is writing that is willing to disperse itself so that words can be sown and borne in new contexts and new fields. It is free, gratuitous, grace-filled writing, surrendering itself to the many possible paths of the book into what Taylor calls a "mazing grace."[47] Or, as Jabès suggests (in words reminiscent of Frost), it is writing that follows paths less traveled and that, in the end, makes all the difference.

> Having our paths mapped out for us, why do we usually take the one which leads us away from our goal, leads us elsewhere, where we are not? Perhaps we are there also? Only when guided by inspiration do we choose right, when we are receptive, in a state of grace. But that is rare, even very rare. And those who are (in a state of grace) do not know it. I mean, at the time. The more so, since being in a state of grace often means losing your way, your usual way, to follow another: more secret, more mysterious.[48]

The book, it seems, is "condemned to remain open, both to the past and to the future."[49] Yet one wonders, Is the goal of interpretation simply more interpretation? In a positive sense, interpretive activity could be seen as the "immense hap-

piness" of the book that is continually open to new writings and new interpretations (as the Talmud says: "The words of Torah are fruitful and multiply"). However, it could also be seen as the "immense grief" of the book that knows no end
to the interpretive process (as Ecclesiastes says: "Of the making of many books
there is no end").[50] According to Derrida, maybe the best we can hope for is to
move the past forward in as many different ways as possible:

> Perhaps the desire to write is the desire to launch things that come back to you as
> much as possible in as many different forms as possible. That is, it is the desire to
> perfect a program or a matrix having the greatest potential, variability, undecidabil-
> ity, plurivocality, et cetera, so that each time something returns it will be as different
> as possible.[51]

Interpretation is a kind of reading that is free to produce what it reads — not
the repetition of the same, "but a creative production which pushes ahead, which
produces *as* it repeats."[52] It is as if Derrida is suggesting, in rabbinic fashion, that
unless we are prepared to listen to the book over and over again, it will always
sound the same. "Turn it and turn it," the Mishnah says, "in it all things can be
found."[53] Over and over, yet different, again and again.

Heidegger speaks of the book's happiness and grief as an interplay of joy and
sadness. Knowing vast possibility, openness, and generativity, the book nevertheless also knows no end, seeing only an immense, uncovered distance. The more
joyful the joy of the book, "the more pure the sadness slumbering within it." Yet,
the deeper the book's sadness, "the more summoning the joy resting within it."[54]

According to Gadamer, interpretation never closes; rather it "opens up an open
place."[55] This open place, as we recall from the first chapter, is the place of the
question. "The conversation that we are is one that never ends. No word is the
last word, just as there is no first word. Every word is itself always an answer that
gives rise to a new question."[56] Gadamer translates tradition "into a question for
fear we might someday stop hearing it."[57] We hear according to our questions,
never knowing which comes first (or is more important): the hearing or the questioning. "The question leaves a blank: the page."[58] Rarely do we notice this
blankness in what we read. The blanks, gaps, and loose ends in the text invite
interpretive communities to continually expand and extend the text. "Every reading that seeks understanding," writes Gadamer, "is only a step on a path that
never ends. One must lose oneself in order to find oneself. I believe I am not very
far from Derrida when I stress that one never knows in advance what one will
find oneself to be."[59]

We do not know beforehand whether things will hold together or fall apart.
Margin writing is willing to risk this ambiguous dwelling place for the sake of

keeping the book fluid, open and productive. There are times when we need to let our prior constructions fall apart — yet this breakage can be seen not only as the shattering of past artifacts but also as the breaking open of new, imaginative futures. In other words, we cannot live solely in a deconstructive state. Things could well fall apart — and may need to — yet they also need to be brought together again in new, imaginative construals. Peter Hodgson writes,

> Every construction is preceded and followed by a deconstruction, but the construc-
> tive phase is a necessary part of a larger process, without which we could not dwell
> humanly in the world, for we humans share in the impulse to bring order out of
> chaos that pervades the cosmos. What results, of course, is not a single, lasting struc-
> ture but a network of interrelated, temporary structures, each of which in its own
> way images an unattainable wholeness.[60]

After reading a book like Taylor's *Erring,* one cannot help but wonder, Can we live solely in a state of perpetual liminality, endless wandering, labyrinthlike lostness? While deconstruction is wary of the way we construct grand narratives to secure ourselves from whatever threatens our cherished certainties, this need not lead us to conclude that all grand narratives function in a purely distortive manner. According to Patricia Waugh, such narratives provide us with "ways of formulating fundamental human needs and their 'grandness' is a measure of the urgency and intensity of the need. They are unlikely, therefore, simply to die, though they may need to be profoundly transformed."[61] In a similar fashion, David Hoy notes that while deconstruction may serve as a "useful antidote" to the danger of totalizing narratives, it can also become a "poison" when it obliter-ates the vital "sense-making" activity that hermeneutics performs.[62] In other words, although there are times when we need to lose our way in order to be brought to a place of lostness, where the question can emerge, it is not this lost-ness itself that sustains us; rather, it serves to point us in a new direction, to find another way.

Walter Brueggemann refers to the sense-making activity of margin writing as a "zone of imagination."[63] It does not attempt to write in a literal fashion by means of certitude; rather, it writes by way of a literary, imaginative construal.[64] Imagi-native writing is "the human capacity to picture, portray, receive, and practice the world in ways other than it appears to be."[65] According to Thomas Groome, imagination has a "creative capacity that brings people to perceive what can be and should be, to fashion new possibilities beyond the 'givens' of life."[66] Groome cites Ricoeur to suggest that imagination is prophetic in calling forth new life and new ways of being: "the imagination is, par excellence, the institut-ing and constituting of what is humanly possible; in imagining possibilities, human beings act as prophets of their own existence."[67] For Ricoeur, the world

of the text does not lie "behind it" in the realm of an original meaning or intention, but "in front of it" in the space of interpretation. "What must be interpreted
in a text," writes Ricoeur, "is a *proposed world* which I could inhabit. . . . To
interpret is to explicate the type of being-in-the-world unfolded *in front of* the
text."[68]

The Latin noun *textus* and the verb *texere* refer to the act of weaving.[69] Margin
writing actively weaves, fabricates, and "makes" the text: "the text is experienced only in the activity of production."[70] Interpretation does not unveil established meanings "behind the text"; rather, it produces new meanings "in front of
the text." Alfred North Whitehead reminds us that all our constructions are
metaphorical leaps of imagination.[71] Yet this does not necessarily imply that our
interpretive practices have no reference beyond themselves. As Sallie McFague
suggests, although the relationship of metaphors to reality is never one of direct
correspondence, we can nevertheless still speak of a relationship — one in which
our constructions are "productive of reality." Metaphorical constructions create
new possibilities of human existence in place of others. The reality to which our
constructions refer is reality-as-human-possibility, even though the only way we
have of naming this possibility "is by creating versions of it."[72] The reference of
language is the world of possibility we create and respond to. The way we name
reality makes a difference "in what we understand reality to be and how we conduct our lives in relation to other beings, both human and nonhuman."[73]
McFague writes,

> As with any construction, the most we can do is to "live within" it, testing it for its
> disclosive power, its ability to address and cope with the most pressing issues of
> one's day, its comprehensiveness and coherence, its potential for dealing with anom-
> alies, and so forth. Theological constructions are "houses" to live in for a while. . . .
> They become prisons when they no longer allow us to come and go, to add a room or
> take one away — or if necessary, to move out and build a new house.[74]

Margin-Dwelling Interpreters

The metaphor of "writing in the margins of the book" is drawn primarily from
the rabbinic tradition. Jabès begins the first volume of his *Book of Questions* with
the scene of rabbis going into the house of study:

> "What is going on behind this door?"
> "A book is shedding its leaves. . ."
> "I saw rabbis go in."
> "They are privileged readers. They come in small groups to give us their com-
> ments."

"Have they read the book?"
"They are reading it."[75]

As communities of interpretation, intentional Christian communities have much to learn from this ancient practice of rabbis gathering around an open book. For these sage interpreters, "what matters is that they belong to the Book, and through the Book they belong together. The Book is the world and the world is the Book; to live is to interpret, and to interpret is to live. But they can only do it together, not alone."[76] According to the Talmud, interpretation is very much a social and dialogical activity: "Make yourselves into groups to study Torah, since the knowledge of Torah can be acquired only in association with others."[77] Torah finds its voice in the give-and-take of communal dialogue that takes place in diverse, public situations. Interpretation, therefore, "is bound to be many-sided and open-ended."[78] As Bruns suggests, if Torah is to have any force as a text, it must always be situated in a culture of continuous dialogue and debate, rather than a culture of hierarchical system or dogmatic assertion.

> One understands by getting into the game. . . . Do not think of yourself as an analytical spectator situated outside the text; think of yourself as belonging to the text. Only now you must picture the text not as a formal object (so many fixed letters) but as an open canon whose boundaries are shaped and reshaped by the give-and-take of midrashic argument. This means studying not just an original text but also midrash itself, for the words of the Sages constitute Torah, make it what it is, and above all open it to the present and to the future. The words of the wise are not added to the text; they are the text as well, linking its words not to form an integrated, hierarchical system but an ongoing tradition, a structure of mutual belonging. The Torah emerges as what it is and comes into its own only in the dialogue it generates; and only by entering into dialogue can one enter Torah.[79]

In *The People of the Book,* Samuel Heilman provides a rich account of the time-honored Jewish practice of *lernen,* "the eternal review and ritualized study of sacred Jewish texts."[80] Heilman describes the Talmudic study circle (*shiur*) as a place of communal, interactional drama through which *lerners* play the game of interpretation, taking their cue from the Talmud, which itself is a book of interacting, circling commentaries in the ever-expanding margins of the book.

> Both literally and in effect, the Talmudic page is framed by commentaries: Rashi on the inside margin, his successors the Tosafists on the outside. . . .
> [These commentaries] in turn may be reframed by later commentaries which have been added to the outer margins of the page. . . . With each new edition of Talmud, the publishers may add more commentaries or new appendices — new interpretive keys. . . .
> Passing through layer upon layer of interpretation, [the *lerners*] bring themselves, their ethos and world view to bear upon the subject and animate the whole. . . . As

the folio of Talmud is characterized by commentary, replies, responsa, questioning, debate, information exchange, digression, narrative, and repeated recountings, so the *shiur* is marked by keys of all of these. . . . The conversations during lernen are always something different from the written page, patterned by it but not exactly the same. . . .

So complicated does the process — the *lernen* game — become that . . . one would have trouble determining where the written page leaves off and oral commentary and reframing begins.[81]

As Jabès suggests, the rabbis are not commenting on the book they have read; rather, they are reading the book in their commentary. For Jabès, the book is written as we read. This privileges process over product and values the ongoing event of interpretation. The book points to the one that will follow it, that will prolong it, just as it points to the one that precedes it:

> There is a book that exists inside the book. There is a part that is before the book. . . .
> It is in the book, but it is also the book that has not yet been written. To be before the book is to be in a state of potential, to have the possibility of creating the book.[82]

> *"What book do you mean?"*
> *"I mean the book within the book."*
> *"Is there another book hidden in what I read?"*
> *"The book you are writing."*   — *Reb Haod.*[83]

The rabbis can only read as they write, such that their commentary *is* the text they are reading. This is a difficult notion to grasp, for we typically think of commentary as something we write *after* reading a text, something secondary or subsequent to the text. However, the rabbis confuse this opposition between reading and writing, such that one never knows where the text ends and the commentary begins, for the two are closely interdependent and woven together.

According to David Stern, midrash (from the Hebrew word *darash*, meaning "to search," "seek out," "inquire," "demand," that is, "the act and process of interpretation") operates in the margins of tradition as an interpretive practice that "avoids the dichotomized opposition of literature versus commentary and instead resides in the dense shuttle space between text and interpreter."[84] Midrash finds its life in the relationship between authoritative text and authoritative interpretation. According to the rabbis, there is not one Torah, but two: one is written and one is unwritten (oral), and both are divine. "In the written Torah God has given and intended all, such that everything is filled with intention and meaning, yet always there is more."[85] So much so, that this fully present text is also enigmatically absent — it demands interpretation. "Always there is more" means that what is not yet written has divine status too. Thus "what appears to be fixed, stable, repeatable, referable, is disclosed as fluid, unstable, singular, elusive."[86] The renowned Jewish commentator Gershom Scholem writes of the Jewish interpretive tradition as follows:

> What had originally been believed to be consistent, unified and self-enclosed now becomes diversified, multifold and full of contradictions. It is precisely the wealth of contradictions, of differing views, which is encompassed and unqualifiedly affirmed by tradition. . . In other words, not system but *commentary* is the legitimate form through which truth is approached.[87]

Stern notes that the rabbinic tradition displays an almost total lack of interest in developing a systematic account of its disparate beliefs. However, this absence of a systematic theology is not a failure of rabbinic Judaism but one of its greatest virtues.[88] As Taylor and Barthes suggest, it preserves the book against the *fixing* of meaning and replaces mastery over the book with the free play of writing: "Is it not characteristic of reality to be *unmasterable?* And is it not characteristic of any system to *master* it? What then, confronting reality, can one do who rejects mastery? Get rid of the system as apparatus, accept *systematics* as writing. . . ."[89]

The rabbis can celebrate and play in the Torah's indeterminacy and multiplicity of meanings because they connect "the infinity of God's being with the infinity of meanings to be found in Torah."[90] This is especially true in the Jewish mystical tradition of Kabbalah, where the multiple, conflicting, pluralistic interpretations of tradition are seen as an essential consequence of the unraveling of revelation's infinite meanings. "For the Kabbalists," writes David Biale, "since the source of revelation is a name unbound by any specific meaning, each word in the Torah can be interpreted *equivocally* in an infinite number of ways."[91] Indeed, the Talmud speaks of the great delight God takes in the interpretive play of the rabbis. At the conclusion of a famous debate among the early sages, we are told:

> You have leave to interpret according to your will, and by your will all the worlds will be conducted. Do not think that God feels woe at this sense of being "defeated"; on the contrary, it is a source of pleasure and joy to God. Thus the rabbis said: "What was God doing? Smiling and saying, 'My children have defeated me.'"[92]

Interpretive authority is granted here to the community of interpreters. As Burton Visotzky suggests, "No longer can authority be construed 'as it is written'; a new source of religious authority is now found in the words 'Rabbi X says.'"[93] Scholars recognize that in Matthew's Gospel, Jesus adopted a similar Jewish practice with his "but I say to you" interpretations of Torah.[94]

Another Talmudic passage suggests that, for the rabbis, interpretation is like a hammer that breaks open the book, shattering the meaning of Torah into a multitude of sparks and fragments.

> It was taught in the School of Rabbi Yishmael: "Behold, My word is like fire —
> declares the Lord — and like a hammer that shatters rock (Jer. 23:29). Just as this
> hammer produces many sparks [when it strikes the rock], so a single verse has several meanings.[95]

The splitting open of the book "is the chance of the book," making "production, reproduction, development possible."[96]

Although acknowledging the interpretive genius of the rabbis, Stern nevertheless makes the point that their unique ability to generate and live with a multiplicity of interpretations actually represented a claim to stability rather than (as is often argued by contemporary postmodern writers) its opposite, namely, an indeterminate state of endlessly deferred meanings. Given the particular historical experience of the early rabbis — the vast spectrum of competing religious sects in Palestinian Judaism, the destruction of the Temple, the rabbis' anxiety over how they could survive this fragmented world (and ensure their claim to being the rightful heirs of biblical tradition) — given this tormented situation, midrashic polysemy represented a world in which conflict, difference, and dispute could be held together in a larger context of harmony and textual stability; all these interpretations could actually stand together and exist side by side as guaranteed by the divine authorship of Torah.[97] Stern writes,

> Following the Temple's destruction, the text of the Torah became for the Rabbis the
> primary sign of the continued existence of God's covenantal relationship between
> God and Israel, and the activity of Torah study — midrash — thus came to serve
> them as the foremost medium for preserving and pursuing that relationship. . . . The
> multiplication of interpretations in midrash was one way, as it were, to prolong the
> conversation.[98]

It seems that for the rabbis, as for their ancient ancestors, interpretive activity is closely tied to the experience of absence and loss. As Walter Brueggemann notes, no biblical text existed before the exile of the Israelites; indeed, "the exile itself was an evocative force in generating the text."[99] So much so, "that wherever exilic Jewry opens the Pentateuch it finds itself."[100] Perhaps the Jewish interpretive tradition represents one of the most striking examples of an exilic hermeneutics, one in which "our unresolved negativities exercise a more powerful and finally decisive influence upon our capacity to receive and imagine than any positive counterpart."[101] It is precisely when we experience things falling apart that we are provoked to generate new texts, new interpretations, new meanings, new futures.

Reclaiming Christianity's Jewish Roots

In his work *Rebecca's Children*, Alan Segal reminds us that in their very conceptions Christianity and rabbinic Judaism are more closely aligned than we typically think. We share a common history that has been forgotten and a kinship that could be fruitfully reclaimed. According to Segal, rabbinic Judaism and Christianity emerged together from the ruins of the Temple as two sibling faiths linked by a common parent — ancient Israel. "The time of Jesus," writes Segal, "marks the beginning of not one but two great religions of the West, Judaism and Christianity."[102] Most people associate Judaism's beginnings with a more distant past, with figures such as Abraham and Moses. Yet the biblical Hebrew tradition has undergone many transformations, the greatest of which — contemporary with Christianity — was the emergence of rabbinic Judaism, which became the basis of Judaism's future life. Both Christianity and rabbinic Judaism were formed during a complex period of changing social and historical forces. When Jesus was born, a new transformation was taking place in the early form of rabbinic Judaism, which would eventually enable the Jewish people to survive the next two millennia. Yet during this time, and especially after the upheaval of the war with the Romans and the fall of the Temple (70 C.E.), many avenues were available to Jews for rebuilding their heritage and culture, one of which was the Jesus movement. As Segal notes, at the time of their inception, rabbinic Judaism and Christianity were "twin alternatives for achieving similar goals."[103] They claimed a twin birth and, "like Jacob and Esau, the twin sons of Isaac and Rebecca, the two religions fought in the womb."[104]

J. Andrew Overman offers an interesting study of Matthew's Gospel that reveals the tensions present in formative Judaism during the post-70 period.[105] This was a difficult time of identity formation and social reconstruction for the Jewish people. It was during this same period that the movement started by Jesus also began to take shape in Palestinian Jewish society. Matthew's Gospel gives us evidence of a Matthean Jewish community trying to order and define its beliefs in a similar way as formative Judaism. The two movements shared the same fluid matrix of their times, yet they were often in conflict with one another. There was no sense at this stage of a "Christian" community apart from Judaism. Rather, the people of Matthew's community understood themselves as Jews and, like many of their contemporaries and competitors, as the "true Israel," embodying the hope of Israel's restoration.[106] In the turmoil of the post-70 period, Matthean and formative Judaism represent

> two emerging movements, among several, involved in a process of self-definition and consolidation in a society that was fragmented and divided following the upheavals associated with the Roman period in Palestine. . . . Matthean Judaism and

its struggle with formative Judaism are perhaps the first chapter in the long and difficult separation of these fraternal twins, Judaism and Christianity.[107]

Although the argument between Judaism and Christianity was initially a
"family affair," their kindred relationship very quickly fell apart. As Segal notes,
"After Christianity separated from Judaism, the polemical passages in the New
Testament were read in an unhistorical way, as testimony between two separate
religions, when they should have been read as strife between two sects of the
same religion."[108] Christians came to see their tradition as superseding Judaism,
a distorted interpretation that shaped much of Christianity's anti-Judaic strains.
In later efforts to express more positively the relationship to Judaism, it was said
that Christianity was born out of Judaism. However, both interpretations fail to
do justice to Segal's insight that the two religions are better understood as contemporaries of each other. As brothers or sisters often do, they picked different
ways to preserve their family's heritage. Yet there is much each can learn from
the other.[109] As two scholars of Christianity and Judaism have asked: "Can we
believe that now, after two millennia of doing it badly, Christians are learning
that the two children of Rebecca can live as siblings?"[110] "Is it not time for the
joint heirs of ancient Israel's Scripture and hope to meet once more, in humility,
before the living God?"[111]

According to Susan Handelman, the rabbinic tradition has been repressed
throughout much of Western history under the dominance of Christian and Greek
construals of reality.[112] Yet this is a tradition that can fund the imaginations of
intentional Christian communities who find themselves confronted by inflexible
and reactionary forces within prevailing church structures and by a confused and
insecure postmodern world. The rabbinic tradition provides a strong legitimation
and rich resources for supporting the interpretive activity of intentional communities whose voices sound out from the margins of tradition: voices from feminist
religious experience, voices from indigenous cultures, voices from those concerned with the earth and ecology, voices from those who aren't sure whether
they belong or not — voices from people trying to recover who they are in the
margins of tradition. According to David Tracy, "A greater retrieval of *our*
Jewish roots as Christians and a better understanding of the rich postbiblical Jewish traditions (rabbinic, philosophical, kabbalistic, and post-Holocaust) could
free Christian theologians to think anew."[113]

Johann-Baptist Metz also argues that "the Jewish-formed mode of believing
belongs in the basic situation of the Christian faith."[114] We need to reclaim the
Jewish-influenced synoptic mode of believing that forms the basis of Christian
faith and which was quickly forced into the background by later interpretations.
"Christian theology after Auschwitz must stress anew the Jewish dimension in

Christian beliefs and must overcome the forced blocking out of the Jewish heritage within Christianity."[115] Similarly, Joseph O'Leary claims that overcoming a dominant, Western metaphysics is closely aligned with the exposure of Christianity to its Jewish matrix: "The step back out of metaphysical theology is a step towards the Jewish matrix of all our theology."[116]

David Stern agrees that a renewed attention to Jewish hermeneutical modes can provide a way for seeking an "alternative, nonlogocentric hermeneutics to replace the ruling Western exemplars."[117] However, he cautions us not to overdraw the distinction between Hebrew and Greek or Jewish and Western in a simplistic fashion. He believes the two are marginally related, rather than simply opposed. Rabbinic Judaism "was not so much completely 'other' to, or apart from, Western culture as it was a marginal presence on its borders, a tradition that developed by drawing on Western categories and transforming them without becoming wholly absorbed by them."[118] Nevertheless, although acknowledging that much Judaic wisdom is not totally removed from Greek expression, I think Handelman is correct in drawing our attention to the "rabbinic repressed."[119] I also think she is correct in wanting to reclaim a Judaic wisdom that can provide us with an alternate vocabulary to mainstream Western thought.

Edmond Jabès: Rabbi-Poet of the Book

"Thinking," Heidegger tells us, "goes its way in the neighbourhood of poetry."[120] Certainly, my own thinking throughout these pages has gone its way in the neighborhood of Jabès's writings, the poet-interpreter of the book. Like the rabbinic tradition of reading and writing, Jabès's writings engage a quite different hermeneutical sensibility than the Hellenic modes most familiar to us. We can expect, therefore, that Jabès's words will sound strange to us, yet such words may help us feel and approach the world of the book differently. "After all," writes Brueggemann, "if God has been mediated to us through Jewish consciousness and Jewish rhetoric, and if this word is the word of this irrepressibly Jewish God, we might expect enormous epistemological displacement in our characteristically gentile hearing of the text."[121]

"First I thought I was a writer. Then I realized I was a Jew. Then I no longer distinguished the writer in me from the Jew because one and the other are only torments of an ancient word." (BQ 1. 361)

Edmond Jabès, a Cairo-born Jew, settled in France after being forced to leave Egypt with other Jews during the Suez Crisis of 1956. This event changed Jabès's life. For the first time he experienced the burden of being Jewish, of suffering for no other reason than that he was a Jew. Up until that

"Judaism and writing are but the same waiting, the same hope, the same wearing out." *(BQ 1. 122)*

time, Jabès had never considered his Jewishness more than a cultural given. Now he had a profound and disturbing sense of the Jewish exilic condition. He began studying Jewish texts (the Talmud and the Kabbalah) and this became the impetus for his major works, *The Book of Questions* (in seven volumes) and *The Book of Resemblances* (in three volumes).[122] His themes are God, silence, absence, life, death, love, the question, the void, the book, the word, the desert, and exile. He has been variously described as a "mystic," a "hermetic poet," a "postmodern philosopher," or, as he refers to himself, as a Jew and a writer.

"What do we renounce in being born? — Perhaps what was, for the benefit of what will be. What do we renounce in dying? — Perhaps what will be, for the benefit of what was. So much whiteness in this renunciation, on which we have tried to write. Memory means promise of a future. 'Tell me what you remember, and I shall tell you who you will be,' wrote Reb Horel, one of the imaginary rabbis, sages or madmen whose questions and maxims have helped me break down the walls erected in my way. Rabbis, in front of and behind these walls, whose words link the future to the past, driven by an unquenchable desire to survive." *(BR 3. 79)*

Whilst Jabès writes with a profound feel for an exilic hermeneutic, particularly in the face of the Jewish holocaust, he also writes with a profound sense of our tie and attachment to the book. His is a poetry of interpretation that brings the ethical and the mystical together in the marginal space of rupture and retrieval, negativity and hope. According to Susan Shapiro, such a marginal hermeneutic embraces the sacred through the testimony of radical negation that also pleads for the possibility of affirmation:

How might a hermeneutic be construed or found that situates its own functioning in terms of the radical negativity of the event of the Holocaust, without necessarily succumbing to that negativity? And, conversely, how might a hermeneutic allow for the possibility of recovery without reducing that negativity? For this a hermeneutic of tradition is required that will not at the outset reduce the radical negativity of the event and, yet, will also not foreclose the very possibility of recovery. However, not foreclosing the possibility of recovery must not be construed as a guaranteeing of recovery, for to do so would already reduce the radical negativity of the event. The hermeneutical grounds of the possibility of the recovery of the sacred, therefore, are necessarily tied to a genuine confronting of the radically negative character of the event.[123]

Along with Susan Handelman, I find it helpful to situate Jabès's writings in the context of the rabbinic interpretive tradition.[124] His writings will appear in the

"I left Egypt because I was Jewish. I was thus forced, despite myself, to live in a certain Jewish condition, the condition of exile. . . . I recognized myself in the vocation of that people engendered by an unpronounceable word: to create the book by reading it; to have it read by commenting on it." *(DB, 30)*

margins of our text — a demonstration of the rabbinic practice that the text which gives rise to interpretation is intimately intertwined with the interpretation itself.[125] Jabès helps us reclaim something of the genius of the rabbis: to live in a book that is at once full and yet incomplete, laden with meaning and yet lacking meaning, closed and yet endlessly interpretable, venerated and yet violated. The "Book of Questions" is Jabès's central image, which, like the book of the Jews, generates the spirals of commentary around commentary. It is also an allusion to the hermeneutical condition: the process of interpreting our lives, our tradition, our world is precisely that which brings the book into being.

The Greek and Hebrew Word

"In the back of the book there is the ground of the book. In the back of the ground there is immense space and, hidden in this immense space, the book we are going to write in its enigmatic sequence." *(BQ 2. 121)*

"Then the book is forever nailed to the book and explores without respite its grounding: its own ground?"

"The book dives and drowns in the books still to be written, which are only its repeated effort to escape death, that is, the unreadability to which it is pledged."

"Then we always keep writing the same book?"

"A book that quietly rehashes the despair of knowing that it will never be read in its totality."

"All true reading is marked by this wound." *(BD, 37)*

A particular character of the history of Western thought has been its quest for a foundation upon which to ground its knowledge, a basis for certainty, a secure condition that guarantees thinking's progress. As Bernstein notes, this "Cartesian anxiety" reached its peak in the seventeenth-century figure of Descartes: "*Either* there is some support for our being, a fixed foundation for our knowledge, *or* we cannot escape the forces of darkness that envelop us with madness, with intellectual and moral chaos."[126] A way to pose this question from a hermeneutical point of view is to ask, Do our interpretations refer to anything? Do they extend beyond themselves? Or is the book "forever nailed to the book" such that there is "nothing outside the text," no "referent," no presence or reality that can serve as a foundation or grounding for our valuing and knowing?

Susan Handelman draws a contrast between a Western, Greek response to this question and a more ancient Hebrew

"We know the word which makes us see, hear, dream, and judge does not exist except in terms of the reality it creates and yet eludes."

"Thus opens the book. . . ."

("Day breaks. The night has conceived." — Reb Gani) (BQ 1. 53)

"The Jew and the writer experience the same perpetual beginning . . . the same amazement at what is written, the same faith in what is still to be read and said. God is Word, and this living word must be forever rewritten." *(SB, 28)*

response. For the Greeks, the realm of words is *not* the realm of meaning and truth. Words are merely signs that point to a reality beyond themselves. The Greeks are implored to "see" beyond words. Words represent, mirror, or copy reality but are not themselves the "revealing" of reality. By contrast, the Hebrew word *davar* is active, present, calling into being. The realm of the Hebrew word *is* the realm of being and reality. The Israelites are implored to "listen" to the word, not to look beyond it: "Hear O Israel." The Hebrew word is not a "movement away from itself towards vision or abstraction; the word leads inwards into itself, not outwards towards the 'thing.'"[127]

The movement is not to metaphysics but to interpretation, not to transcendence but to textuality. "For the Greeks, the culmination of theology was a wordless vision of divine being; for the Jews it was commentary on the divine word, a deeper immersion into the text, further interpretation of scripture."[128]

Handelman suggests that one of the reasons we find it difficult to grasp the Rabbinic concept of the text is our immersion in Greek and non-Jewish ways of thinking about language and meaning. The history of interpretation has been determined in part "by the schism between Jews and Christians precisely over the issue of the proper interpretation of the text."[129] Under the influence of Augustine, Christianity established a central hermeneutical distinction between "spirit" and "letter." This distinction played itself out most severely in the early church's overthrow of the authority of rabbinic law. For Augustine, the Jews were slaves to signs; not recognizing their spiritual meaning, they remained in the "dead" letter of the text. The Hebrew scriptures were

mere signs, figures, shadows pointing to the true word, the word of flesh. True reality became again for Christianity substantial being, not verbal pattern; the text was supplanted, the movement of interpretation now directed to the revelation of how all words point to and are fulfilled by the word of flesh.[130]

In the history of the West, this Christian hermeneutic assumed dominance, and Jewish interpretation was suppressed, forcing it underground. The Jews came to be viewed as a blind people in servitude to the dead letter of the text, whereas Christians were liberated by the spirit, which nullifies the written text (the law).

"There is a word inside us stronger than all others — and more personal.

A word of solitude and certainty, so buried in its night that it is barely audible to itself.

A word of refusal, but also of absolute commitment, forging bonds of silence in the unfathomable silence of the bond.

This word cannot be shared. Only sacrificed." *(BS, 1)*

The end of the law (stubbornly adhered to by the Jews) was precisely the end of its commentary "now replaced by its referent, the incarnate divinity."[131] Christianity replaced "the endless discourses of rabbinic interpretation with the decisive act of presence: incarnation."[132] All the gaps and enigmas that generated the rabbinic play of interpretation were now finally closed and illuminated. The incarnation represented the end of the text; the law and the Jewish tradition remained only as "a long deviation, detour and exile."[133] The Jew was seen as the wandering, mourning, condemned outcast, the carrier of the dead letter, condemned to a book without fulfillment.

The Endlessly Interpretable Book

"To remain open. No doubt it is on preserving this openness, so difficult to defend, that our capacity for astonishment depends. A capacity that makes the world seem ever new." *(BM, 140)*

Although Christianity sought to "escape from textuality," the rabbinic tradition immersed itself in the Torah and the possibility of multiple meaning and endless interpretability. The rabbinic word does not press toward fulfillment and transcendence; rather, each word refers to another word, each text to another text. As Handelman notes, nonfulfillment is a characteristically Jewish mode. "Jews are so strangely at home in exile, in the play of signs, in the wanderings of figurative language, and in their own constant physical wanderings . . . without the redeeming ultimate referent of the incarnate word."[134] We are reminded that the practice of interpretation is our only ground — a ground, however, that always shifts under our feet, a ground not unlike the desert sands across which the ancient Israelites wandered. The anxiety of the West — the haunting sense that language involves the absence of its referent — became the very wellspring of Rabbinic interpretation. For the rabbis, "the text is experienced in relation to the sign, *not* the signified."[135] There is, then, no ultimate out-

"This nonexistent center became the favorite place of my pen, the well of dark where the words came to drink before dying on the page. Thus books complete themselves in the book. . . .

(We are not free. We are nailed alive to the signs of the book. Could it be that our freedom lies in the word's vain try to cut loose from the word?")(BQ2, 83, 23)

side point of view.[136] Everything the West thought of "as spirit, or meaning separable from the letter of the text, remains within an 'intertextual' sphere; and it is commentary that reminds us of this curious and forgettable fact."[137]

"And you shall write My Book by falsifying it, and this falsification shall be your torment and leave you no peace.

"My falsified book shall inspire another and so on till the end of time: for your line of descendants shall be long.

"O sons and grandsons of the sin of writing, lies shall be your breath, and truth your silence."

Thus God might have spoken to Moses.

And Moses might have replied: "Why, O Lord, why condemn Your creatures to lying?"

And God might have added:

"So that each of your books should be your truth and that, faced with Mine, this unworthy truth should crumble and fall into dust.

"There is my glory." (BS, 23)

One of the fundamental characteristics of rabbinic Judaism is that the written Torah is incomplete and incomprehensible without the oral Torah. The written Torah is full of gaps and ambiguities, fraught with hidden, indeterminable meanings. According to the rabbis, this divinely authoritative text is meant to be fragmentary and obscure: "What did God give to Moses and Moses bring to Israel? A 'text' for *interpretatio;* not a finished, independent, self-sufficient text, but one which is open and has to remain open to *interpretatio.*"[138] The oral Torah is the "book within the book," probing the obscurities and ambiguities of what is complete-as-written and yet still in process-as-writing. Gershom Scholem goes so far as to suggest that there is no unmediated divine word, no written Torah that comes in an unmediated form. Because the absolute word of God is an incomprehensible and unpronounceable word, it can only be known in a mediated form, only through interpretation. There is only oral Torah because everything is already and always interpretation.[139]

Susan Handelman invites us to consider the radical nature of rabbinic interpretation. "The oral law they created should not be seen as secondary commentary that simply explains, particularizes, and clarifies the written law." Rather, the rabbis freely reshaped and recreated the written Torah "in a new act of weaving undertaken by master weavers of rare power." This is interpretation at its peak, "born of the tension between continuation and rebellion, tradition and innovation, attachment to the text and alienation from it."[140] In rabbinic commentary *interpretation crosses the line,*

"Before me there was the book; after me there will be the book. . . ." (BR 1. 34)

"What book do you mean?"

"I mean the book within the book."

"Is there another book hidden in what I read?"

"The book you are writing."

— Reb Haod. (BQ 1. 291)

"There is no preferential place for the book," he had written, "but there might be a non-place made up of all the thinkable places." (BS, 18)

"Ah, who will ever count the centuries examined in the margins of our books?" wrote Reb Amit.
"I myself have tried, in the margin of tradition and through words, to find again my fountain-head." (BR 1. 11)

edges over to become the text itself.[141] This blurring between the sacred text and commentary is a unique rabbinic move. "The boundaries between text and interpretation are fluid in a way which is difficult for us to imagine for a sacred text . . . this fluidity is also a central tenant of much contemporary literary theory."[142] The idea that the text which gives rise to interpretation is intricately interwoven with the interpretation is an example of postmodern intertextuality (look at a page of Talmud: "texts echo, interact, and interpenetrate") or in Derrida's famous phrase: "There is nothing outside the text" (as the sages say, everything is in Torah: "Turn it and turn it again, for everything is in it"). The talmudic page has a form unlike any other literature. Interpretation is not something separate from the text itself — an external act that intrudes upon it — but rather the continual play of the text: interpretation that opens out into endless interpretation.[143]

The rabbinic tradition runs as a counterhistory to Western culture that has "never been able to accept the finite, situated, dialogical, indeed political character of human understanding and that even now finds midrash to be irrational and wild."[144] It is only recently that we have witnessed the reemergence of this "untamed" rabbinic tradition in such Jewish thinkers and writers as Freud, Scholem, Bloom, Derrida, Jabès — all of whom have been accused as wild and irrational and all of whom have left deep cracks in the foundations of Western philosophy.[145] They take their stand at the dangerous point of *crossing* — "perpetuating the law through its own transgressions."[146] The point where commentary crosses the line to become text itself is the dangerous place where the potential for faithfulness and heresy assume equal power and strength. The book is prolonged through its own subversion and revision.

Questioning is born from a state of rupture. *"This may seem paradoxical, but it is precisely in that break — in that nonbelonging in search of its belonging — that I am without doubt most Jewish." (DB, 64)*
Jabès celebrates the liberty granted him *"to interrogate*

One of the key dynamics of rabbinic interpretation is its *"ability to produce and absorb its own inversions. . . that is, to* absorb interpretive reversal and the sufferings of history back into itself. . . ."[147] Whereas the logocentric tradition of the West represents a gathering of various meanings into a "oneness" — a unifying order, a movement toward the universal — the rab-

Judaism without ceasing to be Jewish." (DB, 58)

This is Judaism's freedom and obsession, that in the end, *"no answer — no matter how persuasive — will ever have enough strength to resist indefinitely the question that sooner or later will summon it." (DB, 1)*

"What's tragic is that the ardor of questioning is always being shattered by an answer that wants to be absolute." (DB, 75) "To be cured of the answer means, maybe, not to expect anything more, except the answer's withdrawal in favour of the question." (DB, 77)

For Jabès, the whole point of granting priority to the question is not to destroy the book, but to prolong it. Answers embody a certain form of power: a power that pushes too hastily toward closure, a power that claims to have already arrived, that seals the way things are, that cannot imagine that something else might be the case. The question, however, is a subversive type of nonpower: one that confounds and disrupts, that questions and interrupts, that renders ambiguous any form of totalizing meaning.

"The book that would have a chance to survive," writes Jabès, "is the book that destroys itself in favour of another book that will prolong it. This is the point, if you will, of my deconstruction of the book." (SB, 22)

binic tendency is toward "differentiation, metaphorical multiplicity, multiple meaning."[148] The "infinity of meaning and plurality of interpretation are as much the cardinal virtues, even divine imperatives, for Rabbinic thought as they are the cardinal sins for Greek thought."[149] According to Gerald Bruns, rabbinic interpretation "is not a method for resolving hermeneutical dispute . . . it is the place where disputes are meant to go on, where there is always room for another interpretation or for more dialogue, where interpretation is more a condition of being than an act of consciousness." The conflict of a variety of interpretations represents a radical hermeneutical openness. In the rabbinic house of study, "words fly back and forth" according to the principle of "now one, now another." Interpretive practice is multiple, heterogeneous, and conflicting, "as within the open indeterminacy of the question rather than the closure of the proposition."[150] This wealth of diverse and often conflicting interpretations is actually preserved and affirmed in the tradition as a sign of its life and vitality. As Gershom Scholem notes, Talmud maintains contradictory views with astounding seriousness. Disputed views are stated no less carefully than established ones.[151] This is a way of "redeeming rebellion through interpretation."[152] It is the heretical return, which puts "heresy at the heart of tradition," thus developing a "heretic hermeneutic" that claims to continue, even as it abrogates, that tradition: the tradition becomes something continuous and discontinuous at the same time.[153]

The Wound and Hope of the Book

For Jabès, the question is, how can a book encompass all reality? Unless it is continually revised and changed, the book would not be able to keep up with the flux of phenomena, the contradictions of experience. The Book of Books would either have to be completely closed or completely open. If it is in constant process, continually recreated, it is also continually destroyed. If it is completely closed, then it is entirely literal, fixed and thus dead. The remarkable achievement of the rabbis — which is also so important for Jabès — is to make the Book at once closed and open, already finished and yet to be begun, an open process and yet a graven law. The Book includes within itself mechanisms to incorporate the changes of time. For both Jabès and the rabbis, the very ambiguities, gaps, disruptions, uncertainties, and contradictions of scripture are the secret of its power. They are, so to speak, the open spaces that generate questions and interpretations in an endless ongoing process, and so make the Book universally valid, a Book of Books.[154]

Though Jabès subverts the book, subjecting it to an onslaught of interrogation, he also surrenders to its inexhaustible dimensions. Reading Jabès is an exercise in honesty and humility; the book of questions is one we must question as much as it is one that questions us. Its power lies in its givenness over us — such that our own writing and interpretation can never capture the unencompassable book that always eludes and outplays us — and equally in our givenness over it, such that the book always remains unfinished and incomplete, "for it belongs to our condition to be always on the way."[155] Between this finished book that haunts our memory as something we never attain, and this book yet to be written and through which our existence strives, lies both our wound and our hope: the desert of the word and the word of longing; the abyss of a wandering existence and the opening of a land yet promised. In one sense, we are defeated by the book, and our only stance can be one of confession and acknowledgment. In another sense, the book is defeated by us; it is subject to endless interrogation that defers any possibility of sufficiency or closure.

"I write by the light of what is not revealed in what I express. Suffering doubly from a silence without words and from words already again silent. . . ." *(BQ 2. 126)*

"I have gotten use to proceeding by words and in the wake of an unknown word. . . . My Bible is the page you cannot choose." *(BQ 2. 14, 141)*

"Between one book and the next, there is the empty space of a missing book, linked with we do not know which of the two." *(BS, 3)*

There is no beginning and no end in Jabès's books; there is just the opening, and for Jabès, the opening of interpretation is extraordinary. It is extraordinary because it grants us the freedom to create new possibilities of human existence, new readings of the book, new interpretations, new modes of understanding, in place of others. The book becomes the site of a vital freedom. However, as Warren Motte notes, this is a paradox central to Jabès's work.

> The problem is that if interpretation is completely open, it is also ungrounded; that is, its very openness testifies that it has no reliable guarantor. Thus, though we are both obliged and privileged to interpret . . . that act of interpretation will take place on terrain that is constantly shifting.[156]

Some of the central metaphors of Jabès's books — desert, exile, absence — attempt to express this paradox: If absence erases any hope of stable meaning, it nevertheless invests the book with the ongoing possibility of new interpretation; if it denies the existence of an origin and guarantor, it proposes the margin as the place of disclosure where the book continuously becomes itself; if it remains suspicious toward the answer, it offers in its place the question.[157] The impossible book, "both enigmatic and revealing," always slips away from us. Yet it is this very withdrawal of certainty that causes interpretation to open.[158] Opening — like a wound — one we should

"The book, where everything seems possible through a language that one thinks one can master and that finally turns out to be but the very place of its bankruptcy. All the metaphors the word can inspire lie between these two extremes. None of them really gets to the heart of it, but, between this all and this nothing, the unfathomable opening takes place. . . ." *(DB, 15)*

not heal too lightly; rather let the wound be felt in the texture of questioning, suffering the book's desire to be. For if we fear that there is nothing outside the text, we also dream of this "all-encompassing Book."[159]

"The experience of the desert is both the place of the Word — where it is supremely word — and the non-place where it loses itself in the infinite. So that we never know whether we catch it at the moment it springs up or at the moment it begins ever so slowly to fade: the dazzling moment of its issue or of its imperceptible vanishing." *(SB, 27)*

Wandering word of God. It has for its echo the word of the wandering people. No oasis for it, no shade, no peace, only the

This opening is both a radical freedom and an infinite abyss; the freedom to interpret is the secret of the text's compelling power, yet its endless interpretability is its infinite well and abyss. Jabès uses the image of the desert: though a vast openness, the desert is also a silent void — a non-place which is the place of the nomad, the writer. Its sands shift, its paths lead nowhere, and whatever track we do find, we follow it only to find it disappearing again under the shifting sands.

Susan Handelman reminds us that the Jewish God was also a nomadic God, moving through the desert with the people of vast and thirsty desert, only the book of this thirst." *(SB, 228)*

Israel — not fixed to any definite place, not even grounded in Being like the God of the Greek philosophers.[160] God, like the Jew, like the writer, is in exile, wandering the desert of the book: unfathomable openness and abyss. If today we question whether there is anything outside the text (any all-present, assuring guarantor of meaning), it was the rabbinic tradition that long ago found its home in the book. Judaism has always understood itself in its relation to language and the sacred book. For Jabès, this means that the book has taken on all the gravity and significance of a homeland. As Eric Gould says: "The contemporary Jewish writer can only be conscious of the ancient relationship of the Jew to the Word, a tradition that had long known the ironies of endlessly open interpretation centuries before Derrida."[161] The postmodern writer has come to share the Jew's historic condition as "exile, alien, wanderer in history, comforted only by their sacred text and their retreat into the world of the word . . . their only refuge and hope. . . . The Jew is a wanderer ["My father was a wandering Aramean"] and a nomad

"Do I know, in my exile, what has driven me back through tears and time, back to the wells of the desert where my ancestors ventured? There is nothing at the threshold of the open page, it seems, but this wound of a race born of the book, whose order and disorder are roads of suffering. Nothing but this pain, whose past and whose permanence is also that of writing." *(BQ 1. 25-26)*

who finds truth in the wilderness and desert . . . who struggles with God through language, dialogue, dispute, and questioning — from Abraham to Job."[162]

For Handelman, the history of the Jewish people begins with the Genesis story of Jacob wrestling with God. The struggle with God is the paradigm of the struggle with writing, the struggle of trying to interpret and understand our world.

"What I mean by God in my work is something we come up against, an abyss, a void, something against which we are powerless. It is a distance . . . the distance that is always between things. . . . We get to where we are going, and then there is still this distance to cover. And a moment comes when you can no longer cover the distance; you get there and you say to yourself, it's finished, there are no more words. God is perhaps a word without words...

"In the Jewish tradition God . . . has an unpronounceable name." *(SB, 19)*

At the origin, at the beginning of a people's collective memory and definition of itself, is an enigmatic struggle with a stranger of night. Henceforth, the people will be called by this name of struggle [Israel: the one who strives with God]; the wounds of wrestling with God will be their history and their fate.[163]

"The readable is perhaps only the unreadable smashed to pieces. . . .

Fragments of fragments." *(BS, 41)*

"The second set of Tablets could not be like the first, being born of breakage. Between them, the bleeding abyss of a wound. . . .

"God was forced by His people to repeat Himself. . . . Thus the law is built on resemblance. . . . And the book, on the hope of resembling the hidden Book." *(BR 1. 64)*

"The book is the place of the power of God and also the place where God loses power; the place of God's omnipotence and God's humiliating capitulation." *(BR 1. 1)*

"This separation is the unbearable absence every word comes up against, as any given name does against the unpronounceable divine Name." (SB, 29)

How is it that the cry of the newborn infant, pushed out of the womb, is a cry of pain? No doubt because in asserting itself, in its own language, as a cry of life, it is already a cry of exile." (SB, 29)

Writing emerges from a lack; it comments unceasingly upon an absence that it tries to make present, for *"every book is a space*

Jabès also struggles with writing and particularly with the impossibility of writing-the-Holocaust.[164] Eric Gould asks, "What does writing do once it has been disabused of the belief that words resemble anything? How does one recount the impossible-to-tell story of the Holocaust?"[165] The impossibility of writing-the-Holocaust coincides with the impossibility of writing and of being a Jew — the pain of being and writing — "the inability to speak, and the inability to remain silent."[166] The Holocaust is an event that cuts human experience with such a deep wound that our attempt to read and understand life, God, and the world can never again be the same, will always be tormented.[167] "The rupture of the Holocaust, its explosion of Jewish history and community, its voiding of all previous meaning is made continuous and discontinuous with the ancient rabbis' own struggle with an ambiguous Sacred Text and an enigmatic God."[168]

Jabès links the Holocaust's shattering of history with the breaking of the tablets of the Law (Exodus 32:15-19). The absence of God in the Holocaust is the absence of God in every word. Words are born of broken words. The writer and the Jew share a similar fate: both are tormented by an "ancient word," whose source lies in a catastrophic event of loss and separation — the breaking of the tablets — a torment that generated the endless ancient practice of rabbinic interpretation in search of the original divine language.[169]

The question of God's absence (versus notions of God's all-presence) is not a theological problem for rabbinic interpreters, nor

*written on by a missing word."
(BR3,22)*

We write *"in the name of a withdrawn word which is not an absence of words but a word of absence, an unfathomable abyss beyond words toward which all words tend. . . ." (SB, 229)*

for Jabès, because the Jewish divine Name (YHWH) has always contained its own absence.[170] The book is not the place where God is simply affirmed but where God withdraws into the word that has been stricken with the inability to name. It leads to "the writer's thirst to fill the space where God has withdrawn."[171] Jabès draws upon the Jewish mystical tradition of Lurianic Kabbalah, which speaks of God's creative act not as an expansive outpouring of Godself but as a withdrawal and contraction of God into Godself (*tsimtsum*). God had to withdraw the divine presence to create a void or empty space — an opening for creation. Gershom Scholem, the great commentator on Kabbalah, notes that Lurianic Kabbalah interpreted *galut* ("exile") not only as a condition of Jewish life, but a condition of the whole universe — a condition even of God.[172] The concentration and concealment of God is an act of self-exile: God "exiled Himself [*sic*] from boundless infinity to a more concentrated infinity. There is a profound inward Galut, not the Galut of one of the creatures but of God Himself, who limited Himself and thereby made place for the universe."[173] Both Jabès and Scholem see in God's self-exile the deepest symbol of exile that could be conceived. Yet this absence constitutes a form of presence. As Handelman notes, the insight of this kabbalistic theory of creation is that "every creative act requires negativity, withdrawal, absence."[174] Jabès's journey into the void does not lead him to forsake the book. Rather, he struggles with God and the book to establish a presence out of the silence.

> In part, this exile is resolved by the making of "exile" the precise metaphor for the act of creation and interpretation. This is a resolution in the Jewish mode, not as fulfillment of signs in the incarnate word, but as the raising of the Jewish historical tradition into a paradigm of existence: to be is to be in exile; to create is to endure catastrophe; to make texts is to already interpret; absence is presence. . . . In exile, a broken people try to heal themselves through ever more complicated figuration, opening, troping of their Sacred Text . . . trying somehow to make the facts of their historical catastrophe agree with the exalted promises of their Sacred Book.[175]

We cannot forget, however, that exile is not the only self-definition of the Jew. Jewish identity is also rooted in covenant and promise. Berel Lang agrees with Jabès that there is a strong convergence between the history of a people and the life of language and discourse, yet this convergence speaks not only of alienation and exile, but also of promise and hope. Language is also a way of dispelling a sense of alienation.[176] "In language, promises — the promises of the covenant — are made; the only truly alien existence is one without language."[177]

We remember that the concluding book of Torah, which begins with the assurance that "these are the words,"[178] ends with the scene of Israel standing on the edge of a promise, on the edge of a book. Israel's primal corpus of literature ends short of fulfillment, with the people of Israel standing beyond the Jordan, overlooking the promised land.[179] The book of words becomes the book of questions. Torah ends inconclusively, and the question of Israel's future is left open ended. Israel stands on the edge of a book, suspended between that which is written and that which remains to be written. Perhaps the life of language and discourse lies here — neither in its exilic structure nor its promise but in the suspension between both which creates continual yearning and hope.

The gaps and absences in Jabès's text are the "breathing" spaces of discourse. Jabès surrounds words with whiteness — with blanks — inviting the reader to help create the meaning of the book.[180] For Jabès, the book is written as we read. He reminds us that we are always projecting the possibility of the book out of our awareness that the book is not closed, that it will never be fully present to us or totally determinate. The book of questions leads to no permanent place, yet this is the very non-place that generates the place of the book in the task of ongoing writing and interpretation. According to Warren Motte, by affirming a text that never completely *is* but is always *becoming*, we are affirming a text that does not present itself as static, finished product, but rather as writing, as dynamic process. It is precisely in this dynamic, this straining toward the book, that the presence of the book may be inferred.[181]

"Make allowance for fire where writing spreads. . . . Ah, write, write to keep alive the fire of creation. Raise words from their peaceful night where they lay buried, words still astonished at their resurrection." *(BS, 99)*

"Book, object of an inexhaustible quest. Is this not how the Jewish tradition sees the Book?" *(BQ 2. 247)*

"Nobody has understood better that writing only means withdrawing what is written in favour of what is in process, their fidelity being faithful to the future." *(BR 1. 85)*

Richard Stamelman notes that Jabès's exilic hermeneutics is a reenactment of *tsimtsum:* as God withdraws the divine presence in order to leave a blank space from which Creation can surge, so too the book leaves blank spaces and gaps from which another meaning, another interpretation, may emerge. Writing, words, interpretations are thus scattered and dispersed across the pages of the book like nomadic fragments yearning to repossess the original wholeness of divine language.[182] Writing, therefore, is also a yearning — a longing for — what the Kabbalah calls *tikkun* — the repair of the world, the restoration of harmony, the reunion of God. In the kabbalistic view, the redemption of the world depends on the mending of a shattered and broken book

"You must believe in the book in order to write it. The time of writing is the time of this faith." *(BR 1. 29)* — strivings toward an impossible though still to be completed task. Out of the book of discord "a living Book emerges, an endless mediation of commitment and concern."[183]

from its exile back to the original divine Word. Jabès's books evoke a longing for *tikkun.* The power of his writing derives from the strivings it arouses within readers

"You are free to call this familiar — wounded — place by the word 'God.'"

"In each word there burns a wick."

"Ever since the book my life has been a wake of writing in the space between limits, under the resplendent sign of the unpronounceable Name."

"Hope: the following page. Do not close the book."[184]

Postscript

"The wind blows where it wills; you hear its voice, but you do not know whence it comes or whither it goes" (John 3:8). Though taken from John's Gospel, we could imagine these words coming from the chafed lips of a wandering, Galilean Jew familiar with the winds and sands of the burning desert. In a similar fashion, Jabès's writing highlights the inescapability of a wandering existence, a nomadic truth, the absence of fulfillment, the endlessly ongoing task of interpreting and questioning. What his writing lacks in terms of stability, boundaries, and constants, it gains in terms of movement, passion, and openness.

"The history of metaphysics," writes John Caputo, "is the story of so many attempts to still the flux, to contain its course, to arrest its play."[185] The history of Christianity also shares this Western tendency to still the life of tradition in favor of explicit truths, timeless essences, and unchanging, dominant orderings. This is why, I suspect, many marginal communities would rather surrender to the shifting flux than to the settled order. This is why many would feel a resonance with the metaphors of Jabès's writing: absence, because marginal people feel their own absence from the dominant orderings of tradition; desert and wandering, because nomadic truth and being on the way feels more hopeful than the settled truth of having already arrived; provoking questioning rather than imposing answers; an open, indeterminate book rather than a closed, completed book.

(Perhaps Christianity can be read in its beginnings as another Jewish story of a "failed messiah." The resurrection is not the moment of completion in the sense that this failure is transformed into a glorious overcoming. Rather, it is the opening of a wound. A crucified messiah is raised — and the wound, the pain, the failure is lifted up before us. This sacrificed word of God brings us face to face with the wounded nature of our existence, with the impossibility of the book, with the failure of our words and actions to attain fullness and freedom. What is it that keeps us going? What kept the first followers of Jesus going or the followers of Martin Luther King after their deaths? Certainly not any unambiguous sense of something having reached completion or fulfillment. Rather, they were carried by a movement of resistance and hope, the commitment to go on, to "go and do likewise." Rather than a sense of attainment, it was the profound sense of human solidarity in suffering, in questioning, in accepting the wound. Deborah, Jeremiah, Jesus of Nazareth, Martin Luther King, and all the prophets open the wound, yet in this very opening we feel their pledge and commitment to the book: to keep speaking, to keep writing, to keep hoping in the light of the book's promise.

"Listen. The wind is back," Sarah had said.)[186]

Notes

The epigraphs introducing part 3 are from the following works of Edmond Jabès: "There is such a thing as Jewish writing . . ." in Eric Gould, ed., *The Sin of the Book*, p. 29; *The Book of Questions*, 1. 169, 26; *The Book of Margins*, p. 165; *The Book of Shares*, pp. 18, 3; *The Book of Questions*, 1. 328, 302; *The Book of Resemblances*, 1. 23; *The Book of Resemblances*, 3. 56; "The Question of Displacement into the Lawfulness of the Book," in Eric Gould, ed., *The Sin of the Book*, p. 238; *The Book of Shares*, p. 99; *The Book of Resemblances*, 1. 29.

1. J. Hillis Miller, "The Critic as Host," in Harold Bloom, et al., *Deconstruction and Criticism*, p. 219.

2. Mark C. Taylor, "Text as Victim," p. 64.

3. "Dialogue with Jacques Derrida," in Richard Kearney, ed., *Dialogues with Contemporary Continental Thinkers*, p. 113.

4. See, e.g., Thomas Groome's threefold hermeneutics of retrieval, suspicion, and creative commitment in *Sharing Faith*, pp. 230–35.

5. W. Dow Edgerton, *The Passion of Interpretation*, p. 40.

6. Jacques Derrida, "Living On: Border Lines," in Peggy Kamuf, ed., *A Derrida Reader: Between the Blinds*, p. 256.

7. I draw primarily from the following works on metaphor: Paul Ricoeur, "Metaphor and the Central Problem of Hermeneutics," in *Hermeneutics and the Human Sciences*, chap. 6; see also Ricoeur's essay "The Metaphorical Process as Cognition, Imagination and Feeling"; Sallie McFague, *Metaphorical Theology*, chap. 1, and *Models of God*, chaps. 1 and 2; Sandra Schneiders, *The Revelatory Text*, pp. 26–33; Bernard Lee, *Jesus and the Metaphors of God*, chap. 1; Mary Gerhart and Allan Russell, *Metaphoric Process*, chap. 6.

8. Edgerton, *The Passion of Interpretation*, p. 111.

9. Sallie Mc Fague, *Models of God*, p. 23. Elizabeth Johnson notes that classical theol-

ogy always taught that no image of God is ever entirely adequate ("divine incomprehensibility"), that all language about God is caught between likeness and unlikeness ("analogical language"), and that this unpronounceability of God's name requires a pluralistic and playful freedom in speaking about God (God has "many names"). See chap. 6 in *She Who Is*. See also Harvey Egan's essay "Christian Apophatic and Kataphatic Mysticisms"; and Michael A. Sells, *Mystical Languages of Unsaying*.

10. Joseph O'Leary, *Questioning Back*, p. 40.

11. Edmond Jabès, *The Book of Resemblances*, 1. 48–49.

12. McFague, *Models of God*, pp. 25–26.

13. Ibid., p. 25.

14. According to McFague, the best metaphorical namings always lead to "both a shock and a shock of recognition. . . . A metaphor that has lost its shock (its 'is not' quality) loses as well its recognition possibilities (its 'is' quality), for the metaphor is no longer 'heard': it is taken to be a definition, not a likely account" (ibid., p. 35).

15. Edgerton, *The Passion of Interpretation*, pp. 108.

16. Ibid., pp. 110–11. According to David Tracy, negations serve "to assure that the similarities remain similarities-in-difference, to assure that the analogous relationships of proportion are related to the uncontrollable event, negations to keep the principles of order and harmony from becoming merely affirmative. The negations function as principles of intensification constituted by the tensive event-character of the focal meaning to negate any slackening of the sense of radical mystery, any grasp at control of the event and the similarities-in-difference of the realities (God, self, world) focused upon and interpreted by that event" (*The Analogical Imagination*, p. 409).

17. Gerald Bruns, *Hermeneutics Ancient and Modern*, p. 14.

18. McFague, *Models of God*, pp. 35–36.

19. Ibid., p. 37.

20. Terry Eagleton, *Literary Theory*, p. 196.

21. Ibid., p. 135.

22. Ibid., p. 136. Richard Rorty, e.g., notes that Derrida wants us to see "writing as writing," so as to highlight its imaginative, metaphorical status over against notions that it is actually representing or depicting reality as real. See "Derrida on Language, Being, and Abnormal Philosophy," p. 678.

23. Eagleton, *Literary Theory*, p. 137.

24. See Roland Barthes, "From Work to Text," in Philip Rice and Patricia Waugh, eds., *Modern Literary Theory*, p. 170. See also James Risser, "Reading the Text," in Hugh Silverman, ed., *Gadamer and Hermeneutics*, p. 97.

25. Eagleton, *Literary Theory*, p. 72. I do not fully agree with Eagleton's assertion that Gadamer views tradition as a "unifying essence." Indeed, a few pages after his critique of Gadamer, Eagleton speaks of "language" much in the same way Gadamer speaks of "tradition" (indeed, the two are the same for Gadamer) to underscore a point that is in many respects similar to Gadamer. Interpretation is not entirely free-floating because, in Eagleton's words, literary texts "belong to language as a whole, have intricate relations to other linguistic practices, however much they might also subvert and violate them; and language is not in fact something we are free to do what we like with. . . . Language is a field of social forces which shape us to our roots, and it is an academicist illusion to see the literary work as an arena of infinite possibility which escapes us" (pp. 87–88).

26. Bruns, *Hermeneutics Ancient and Modern*, p. 229.

27. Ibid., p. 233.

28. Ibid., p. 230.

29. Maurice Blanchot, *The Space of Literature*, pp. 237–39.

30. Bruns, *Hermeneutics Ancient and Modern*, p. 240.

31. Images of Hermes drawn from the "Hymn to Hermes," attributed to Homer, as compiled by W. Dow Edgerton in *The Passion of Interpretation*, p. 18.

32. Ibid., p. 23.

33. Ibid., pp. 28–29.

34. Ibid., p. 34.

35. Ibid., pp. 33–36.

36. Jabès, *The Book of Questions*, 1. 39.

37. Jabès, *The Book of Resemblances*, 3. 56.

38. Jabès, "The Question of Displacement into the Lawfulness of the Book," in Eric Gould, ed., *The Sin of the Book*, p. 238.

39. Derrida, *Writing and Difference*, pp. 298–99 (italics mine).

40. See Exodus 33:20.

41. Eric Gould, "Introduction" to *The Sin of the Book*, p. xviii.

42. Taylor, "Text as Victim," p. 64.

43. Taylor, *Erring*, pp. 11–13, 18.

44. Gadamer, *Truth and Method*, p. 106.

45. Taylor, *Erring*, p. 160.

46. Ibid., p. 144.

47. Ibid., pp. 168–169.

48. Jabès, *The Book of Questions*, 1. 54. The allusion to Frost to which I refer is from his poem "The Road Not Taken," in Robert Frost, *Selected Poems*, p. 77.

49. Paul Rabinow and William Sullivan, "The Interpretive Turn: Emergence of an Approach," introduction to *Interpretive Social Science*, p. 18.

50. See Warren Motte's commentary on Jabès's evocation of the circle and the point in *Questioning Edmond Jabès*, p. 131. The talmudic verse is *Hagigah* 3b (cited in Gerald Bruns, *Hermeneutics Ancient and Modern*, p. 104). The biblical verse is Ecclesiastes 12:12.

51. Derrida (*The Ear of the Other*, p. 158), cited in Richard Bernstein, *The New Constellation*, p. 173.

52. John Caputo, *Radical Hermeneutics*, p. 3 (see also pp. 120ff.). See Gerald Brun's commentary on Caputo in *Hermeneutics Ancient and Modern*, pp. 213–16.

53. From a famous passage about Torah found in the Mishnah. See Burton Visotzky, *Reading the Book*, p. 225; and Barry Holtz, ed., *Back to the Sources*, p. 185 for particular citations.

54. Heidegger, *On the Way to Language*, p. 153.

55. Gadamer, *Philosophical Hermeneutics*, p. 228.

56. Gadamer, "Letter to Dallmayr," p. 95.

57. Jabès, *The Book of Resemblances*, 1. 39.

58. Jabès, *The Book of Margins*, p. 165.

59. Gadamer, "Reply to Jacques Derrida," p. 57.

60. Peter Hodgson, a respondent in the *Journal of Feminist Studies in Religion* round-

table discussion led by Francis Schüssler Fiorenza, "The Influence of Feminist Theory on My Theological Work," p. 111.

61. Patricia Waugh, introduction to *Postmodernism*, p. 9. In a similar fashion, Bernard Lee believes we need to leave room for "mega-stories," which postmodern theories tend to disallow. "The challenge to a mega-story is how to let the 'is not likes' of foundational metaphors keep a ghostly presence in the plot." See *Jesus and the Metaphors of God*, p. 23.

62. David Hoy, "Jacques Derrida," in Quentin Skinner, ed., *The Return of Grand Theory in the Human Sciences*, p. 58. Hoy notes the way Derrida takes up Plato's reference to writing as a drug—a *pharmakon*—suggesting that writing is both a "poison" and a "cure" (see p. 58).

63. Walter Brueggemann, *Texts under Negotiation*, pp. 62ff. See also Brueggemann's essay "Monopoly and Marginality in Imagination," in *Interpretation and Obedience*, chap. 9.

64. This point is also made by Mark Taylor in *Erring*, pp. 66–67.

65. Brueggemann, *Texts under Negotiation*, p. 13. See also Sandra Schneider's discussion on the role of constructive imagination in *The Revelatory Text*, pp. 102–5.

66. Thomas Groome, *Sharing Faith*, p. 196.

67. Ibid., p. 196.

68. Paul Ricoeur, *Hermeneutics and the Human Sciences*, pp. 141–42.

69. Werner Jeanrond, *Theological Hermeneutics*, p. 85. See also Mark C. Taylor, *Erring*, pp. 177–82; and Elisabeth Schüssler Fiorenza, *But She Said*, p. 52.

70. Roland Barthes, "From Work to Text," in Philip Rice and Patricia Waugh, eds., *Modern Literary Theory*, p. 167.

71. Alfred North Whitehead, *Process and Reality*, p. 4.

72. McFague, *Models of God*, p. 26.

73. Ibid., p. 28.

74. Ibid., p. 27.

75. Jabès, *The Book of Questions*, 1. 16.

76. Edgerton, *The Passion of Interpretation*, p. 45.

77. *Berekoth* 63b. Cited by Gerald Bruns, "The Hermeneutics of Midrash," in *Hermeneutics Ancient and Modern*, p. 107.

78. Bruns, "The Hermeneutics of Midrash," p. 107.

79. Ibid., p. 116.

80. Samuel C. Heilman, *The People of the Book*, p. 1. For an introduction to the classic Jewish texts (including the Bible, the Talmud, the midrashic literature, the mystical texts of the Kabbalah and of Hasidism, the medieval philosophical works and commentaries, the prayerbook), see Barry Holtz, ed., *Back to the Sources: Reading the Classic Jewish Texts*.

81. Ibid., pp. 124–25. Though traditionally a male activity, Jewish feminism is reclaiming women's space and women's experience in shaping new communities of Jewish interpretive practice. See Judith Plaskow, *Standing Again at Sinai: Judaism from a Feminist Perspective*.

82. Paul Auster, "Book of the Dead: An Interview with Edmond Jabès," in Eric Gould, ed., *The Sin of the Book*, p. 14.

83. Jabès, *The Book of Questions*, 1. 291.

84. David Stern, "Midrash and Indeterminacy," p. 132. For descriptions and definitions of midrash, see Jacob Neusner, *What Is Midrash?;* Gerald Bruns, "The Hermeneutics of Midrash," pp. 104–23; Barry Holtz, "Midrash," in *Back to the Sources*, pp. 177–211.

85. Edgerton, *The Passion of Interpretation*, p. 47. Torah is a rich word: it can refer to the first five books of Scripture (the Pentateuch); in wider use, it includes the books of the Prophets (*nebi'im*) and the Writings (*ketubim*); in a still wider sense, it includes the written and oral Torah, the whole body of sacred texts and instruction and its evolving tradition. It can also refer to the scroll from which Scripture is read in public worship. See Jacob Neusner, "Introduction: From Scroll to Symbol" in *Torah: From Scroll to Symbolism in Formative Judaism*, p. 16.

86. Edgerton, *The Passion of Interpretation*, p. 105.

87. Gershom Scholem, "Tradition and Commentary as Religious Categories in Judaism," p. 27.

88. Stern, "Midrash and Indeterminacy," p. 146.

89. Taylor (citing Barthes), *Erring*, p. 91.

90. Stern, "Midrash and Indeterminacy," p. 151; see also p. 141.

91. David Biale, *Gershom Scholem: Kabbalah and Counter-History*, p. 93. For the Kabbalists, it is not only each word, but letters, numbers, omissions, repetitions, anagrams, and so on, that are open to interpretation. Nothing in the text is there by accident. Biale maintains that Jewish mysticism "was a movement at the very heart of rabbinic Judaism and not at its periphery" (p. 115; see also p. 123). Burton Visotzky shows how the rabbis freely employed a great variety of interpretive strategies: allegory, pun, gematria, anachronism, parable, eisegesis, narrative expansion, and so on. See *Reading the Book*, pp. 225–40.

92. This is a Hasidic text cited by Arthur Green, "Teachings of the Hasidic Masters," in Barry Holtz, ed., *Back to the Sources: Reading the Classic Jewish Texts*, p. 384. It is a commentary on the famous passage of the Babylonian Talmud tractate *Bava Metziah* 59b, which concludes, after a debate among the sages, with the words "My children have defeated (outwitted) me." See Burton Visotzky's rendition of this story in *Reading the Book*, pp. 51–56.

93. Visotzky, *Reading the Book*, p. 44.

94. See, e.g., E. P. Sanders, "The Life of Jesus," in Hershel Shanks, ed., *Christianity and Rabbinic Judaism*, pp. 70–73. There has been considerable discussion regarding the influence of the Pharisees on the teachings of Jesus. This is a difficult area because no writings of the Pharisees have survived, and it would be anachronistic to assume that later rabbinic materials reflect the times of first-century Pharisaism. They are more likely to reflect later editorial assumptions than earlier ones. Yet Geza Vermes believes that rabbinic writings "include a large quantity of traditions traceable to the first century" which can be critically recovered as useful sources ("Jewish Studies and New Testament Interpretation," p. 12). Michael Cook, in his article "Jesus and the Pharisees," does not see Jesus as part of the Pharisaic movement, yet he does cautiously recognize parallels between Jesus' teachings and parables of rabbinic literature which include the following: a king who hires laborers who later complain about the way in which wages are distributed; a king who gives a banquet and finds his invited guests fail to come; a father who lovingly accepts his wayward son; lost coins and hidden treasure; and so on (see p. 457). Bernard Lee also sees "deep resonances between the proclamation of Jesus and the teach-

ings of the Pharisees. . . . The tragedy for Christians is that we have steadfastly missed the genetic connection between Jesus and the Pharisees. There is more insight into Jesus in his continuity with them than in his discontinuity" (*The Galilean Jewishness of Jesus*, pp. 105, 13). Edward Schillebeeckx believes that "the Pharisaic movement made 'the phenomenon of Jesus' historically possible" (*The Church with a Human Face*, p. 17).

In a bolder move, Rabbi Harvey Falk, though he does not deal critically with the dating problems, sees Jesus as standing within a particular "school of Pharisees," *Bet Hillel*, rather than their opponents, *Bet Shammai*. In interpreting Torah, Jesus was following good rabbinic practice. See Falk's work, *Jesus the Pharisee*. See also Leonard Swidler, *Yeshua: Model for Moderns*, pp. 55–64, and John Pawlikowski, *What Are They Saying about Christian-Jewish Relations*, pp. 93–107.

95. Babylonian Talmud, *Sanhedrin* 34a (see also *Shabbat* 88b). Translated and cited by David Stern in "Midrash and Indeterminacy," p. 135.

96. Jabès, *The Book of Questions*, 1. 367; and Taylor, citing Derrida, in *Erring*, p. 92.

97. Stern, "Midrash and Indeterminacy," see pp. 153–56.

98. Ibid., p. 153.

99. Walter Brueggemann, *Texts under Negotiation*, p. 63.

100. Thomas Mann, *The Book of Torah*, p. 158.

101. Brueggemann, *Texts under Negotiation*, p. 63.

102. Alan Segal, *Rebecca's Children*, p. 1

103. Ibid., p. 2.

104. Ibid., p. 1.

105. J. A. Overman, *Matthew's Gospel and Formative Judaism*. "Formative Judaism" is a term used to emphasize the fluid nature of Judaism during this period that "was in a process of *becoming*, that is, of consolidating, organizing and obtaining a structure to ensure its existence" (p. 35).

106. Ibid., pp. 1–5. Similarly, Anthony Saldarini describes Matthew's community of believers in Jesus as a reformist sect of "deviant Jews." Like other sectarian groups of the time, Matthew's community was too enmeshed in Judaism to be cut off; rather, "the Matthean community is a fragile minority still identified with the Jewish community by others and still thinking of itself as Jews." See "Social History of the Matthean Community," p. 36.

107. Overman, *Matthew's Gospel and Formative Judaism*, pp. 3, 4.

108. Alan Segal, *Rebecca's Children*, p. 142.

109. Ibid., p. 179.

110. Harvey Cox, "Rabbi Yeshua Ben Yoseph: Reflections on Jesus' Jewishness and the Interfaith Dialogue," in James Charlesworth, ed., *Jesus' Jewishness*, p. 47.

111. Jacob Neusner, *Judaism in the Matrix of Christianity*, p. 143.

112. Susan Handelman, *The Slayers of Moses*, pp. xiii–xv.

113. David Tracy, *The Analogical Imagination*, p. 440 (n. 7).

114. Johann-Baptist Metz, "Facing the Jews: Christian Theology after Auschwitz," p. 31.

115. Ibid., p. 31.

116. Joseph O'Leary, *Questioning Back: The Overcoming of Metaphysics in Christian Tradition*, p. 128. See also p. 209.

117. Stern, "Midrash and Indeterminacy," p. 133.

118. Ibid., p. 134.
119. See Susan Handelman's fine educational essay "Emunah: The Craft of Faith," p. 300.
120. Heidegger, *On the Way to Language*, p. 69.
121. Brueggemann, *Texts under Negotiation*, p. 59.
122. This section on Edmond Jabès's writings follows closely my essay "Edmond Jabès: Rabbi-Poet of the Book," in *Pacifica* 7/1 (February 1994), pp. 13–30. Jabès's writings will be referred to by the following abbreviations. See the bibliography for further details.

BQ 1: *The Book of Questions: The Book of Questions, The Book of Yukel, Return to the Book*

BQ 2: *The Book of Questions: Yaël, Elya, Aely*

BR 1: *The Book of Resemblances*

BR 2: *The Book of Resemblances: Intimations, The Desert*

BR 3: *The Book of Resemblances: The Ineffaceable, The Unperceived*

BD: *The Book of Dialogue*

BS: *The Book of Shares*

DB: *From the Desert to the Book*

BM: *The Book of Margins*

SB: *The Sin of the Book* (edited by Eric Gould. Four essays by Jabès appear in this book. I have referred to them simply by page numbers).

123. Susan Shapiro, "Hearing the Testimony of Radical Negation," in Elisabeth Schüssler Fiorenza and David Tracy, eds., *The Holocaust as Interruption*, p. 9.
124. See Susan Handelman, " 'Torments of an Ancient Word': Jabès and the Rabbinic Tradition," in Eric Gould, ed., *The Sin of the Book*, pp. 55–91.
125. Handelman, *The Slayers of Moses*, p. 49.
126. Richard Bernstein, *Beyond Objectivism and Relativism*, p. 18.
127. Handelman, *The Slayers of Moses*, p. 31.
128. Ibid., p. 84.
129. Ibid., p. xiv.
130. Ibid., p. 32.
131. Ibid., p. 119.
132. Ibid., p. 193.
133. Ibid., p. 88.
134. Ibid., p. 120.
135. Ibid., p. 80 (citing Roland Barthes).
136. Susan Handelman writes: "With the recognition that the metaphysical realm is at bottom metaphorical, and that there is no independent essence 'beyond' (*meta*), the realm of language retains its *physis*, its concreteness, and is preserved. The claims of the letter are vindicated again" (*Slayers of Moses*, p. 20).
137. Ibid., p. 204 (citing Geoffrey Hartman).
138. Ibid., p. 42 (citing Simon Rawidowicz).
139. Gershom Scholem, "Tradition and Commentary as Religious Categories in Judaism," pp. 28–31.
140. Handelman, *The Slayers of Moses*, pp. 41–42.
141. Ibid., p. 204.

142. Ibid., p. 41.

143. Ibid., pp. 47–49. Handelman notes that the Talmud has no beginning (no page one) and no end; it continues today.

144. Gerald Bruns, "The Hermeneutics of Midrash," in *Hermeneutics Ancient and Modern*, p. 112.

145. Handelman believes these contemporary postmodern writers stand in a much older rabbinic tradition and the ancient relationship of the Jew to the Word.

146. Handelman, *The Slayers of Moses*, p. 166.

147. Ibid., p. 195.

148. Ibid., p. 33.

149. Ibid., p. 21.

150. Gerald Bruns, "The Hermeneutics of Midrash," pp. 114–15.

151. Gershom Scholem, "Tradition and Commentary," pp. 27–28.

152. Handelman, *The Slayers of Moses*, p. 195.

153. Ibid., pp. 204–7.

154. Handelman, " 'Torments of an Ancient Word': Jabès and the Rabbinic Tradition," p. 62.

155. John Caputo, *Radical Hermeneutics*, p. 214.

156. Warren Motte, *Questioning Edmond Jabès*, p. 11.

157. Ibid., p. 148.

158. See Jabès, *From the Desert to the Book*, p. 82.

159. Handelman, "Torments of an Ancient Word," p. 63.

160. Ibid., p. 70.

161. Eric Gould, "Introduction," *The Sin of the Book: Edmond Jabès*, p. xiii.

162. Handelman, "Torments of an Ancient Word," p. 57.

163. Ibid., p. 55.

164. Running throughout *The Book of Questions* is the story of Sarah and Yukel, a story never fully told because it cannot be told, the story of two young lovers during the time of the Nazi deportations. Sarah returns insane, and Yukel commits suicide. "This is the 'central text' of the first volume of the series" which is "submitted to extensive and elusive commentaries in Talmudic fashion." See Paul Auster, "Book of the Dead: An Interview with Edmond Jabès," in Eric Gould, ed., *The Sin of the Book*, pp. 4–5.

165. Gould, "Introduction," *The Sin of the Book*, p. xiii.

166. Paul Auster, "Book of the Dead," p. 6.

167. At the center of Jabès's *Book of Questions* lies the "shrillest of all aphorisms . . . the most direct of all responses: the scream which emerges from the gap in every word, which insists on the impossibility of writing-the-Holocaust even while the attempt must be made" (Eric Gould, "Introduction," *The Sin of the Book*, pp. xvi–xvii). The scream pierces the silence and in this silence the wounded word is heard again.

168. Handelman, "Torments of an Ancient Word," pp. 67–68.

169. Richard Stamelman writes: "Jabès' language of separation transports the absences and losses of Jewish history into the Diaspora of the book. The white spaces between words, the margins that surround the writing, the open-ended quality of the discourse, the infinite play of questions [which find no resolution, provoking only more questions], the fragmentary quotations of imaginary rabbis, the absence of narrative continuity . . . these are the hallmarks of Jabès' *oeuvre* which . . . not only recreate the experience of exile;

they *are* the experience." See "Nomadic Writing: The Poetics of Exile" in Eric Gould, ed., *The Sin of the Book,* p. 95.

170. Susan Handelman notes that as a result of Greek ontology, Christianity became so invested with the notion of God as Being and presence that little attention has been given to the notion of God's absence. It is almost as if God's absence is unthinkable in the Western tradition — God is too well grounded in the Being of the Greek philosophers. Perhaps this is why Nietzsche's reflections became so overwhelming to us, that in the end we could not speak of God's absence except by declaring God's death. Yet "the crucial point is that absence does not equal nonexistence. Absence, silence, withdrawal are decisive realities." See "Torments of an Ancient Word," pp. 70–71.

171. Eric Gould, "Introduction," p. xx.

172. See Gershom Scholem's commentary on the doctrine of creation in Lurianic Kabbalah in *Kabbalah,* pp. 128–44. See also Lawrence Fine, "Kabbalistic Texts," in Barry Holtz, ed., *Back to the Sources,* pp. 305–59. Kabbalah also speaks of a second stage of creation. The process of *tsimtsum* is followed by the manifestation of God's divine presence in ten circles of light contained in "vessels." The vessels, however, cannot contain the strength of the divine light and they shatter and break in the world, leaving a scattering of shards or "sparks of holiness." Susan Handelman writes: "Thus in the Kabbalah, it is not only the Tablets of the law that are broken. The universe itself has undergone a primordial shattering; God has withdrawn; the Vessels are broken; the divine sparks lost. . . . Kabbalah is the great myth of exile, a passionate opening of the sacred text to the sorrows of a people in exile from whom the face of God is all too hidden, and to whom the world appears as a shattered vessel. And the great themes of Kabbalah as an extreme opening of the rabbinic text — exile, God's negation of God, absence, shattered light, separated lovers — are the great themes of Jabès" ("Torments of an Ancient Word, p. 76).

173. Richard Stamelman (citing Scholem), "Nomadic Writing: The Poetics of Exile," in Eric Gould, ed., *The Sin of the Book,* p. 102.

174. Handelman, "Torments of an Ancient Word," p. 74.

175. Handelman, *The Slayers of Moses,* pp. 222–23.

176. Berel Lang, "Writing-the-Holocaust: Jabès and the Measure of History," in Eric Gould, ed., *The Sin of the Book,* pp. 191–206.

177. Gould, "Introduction," p. xxiii (commenting on Lang's essay).

178. The traditional title for the book of Deuteronomy, *Debarim* ("words"), comes from its opening verse, "These are the words" (1:1).

179. Thomas Mann, *The Book of Torah,* pp. 157–61.

180. See Maurice Blanchot's essay "Interruptions" for this idea behind Jabès's work (in Gould, ed., *The Sin of the Book,* pp. 43–54). See also Paul Auster's interview with Jabès, "The Book of the Dead," p. 15.

181. Motte, *Questioning Edmond Jabès,* pp. 7, 99.

182. Stamelman, "Nomadic Writing," pp. 108–10.

183. Edward A. Kaplan, "The Problematic Humanism of Edmond Jabès," in Gould, ed., *The Sin of the Book,* p. 120.

184. *BD,* p. 45; *BQ* 1. 18, 328, 344.

185. John Caputo, *Radical Hermeneutics,* p. 257.

186. *BQ* 1. 157.

CHAPTER SIX

REWRITING THE BOOK

There is an old midrashic saying: "All beginnings are difficult" — to which one could add: "so, too, all endings." In this final chapter, I feel as though I should be coming to an end, a culmination, the long-awaited concluding word. The same feeling of trying to begin now returns with a vengeance as I try to end. Every beginning is laced with the anticipation of what is to come, and every writer is paralyzed by this large, hoped-for expectation. Every ending, similarly, carries the burden of a nervous, anticipated, final word. To begin and to end are difficult things in life. Most of our time is spent in the rambling, wandering middle part — trying to work it out.

It is this middle part — this between — that I call a marginal hermeneutics (a hermeneutics trying to work it out). It is a hermeneutics caught between a beginning we do not seem to know, yet nevertheless strikes us as important, and an ending we continually project and hope for but which, in the end, we can never finally name. The middle, therefore, finds its power between a certain uncertainty (our thrownness in tradition going we know not where), and an uncertain certainty (an unforeseeable future projected from a given past). The very act of writing (or any interpretive act that ends with "-ing") is inscribed between these two moments of inexplicable givenness and untellable futureness.

Marginal hermeneutics, therefore, is a hermeneutics of the "-ing": reading, writing, questioning, hoping, acting. It is perennially active, present-making, calling into being.

"The way which leads me to you is safe even when it runs into oceans."
(from the commentary of Reb Daber)

"I went to God, because God was my fate.
"I went to the word of God, because the word of God was my fate."
"I went to the word
"to make it my gesture.

"I went
"And I am going."[1]

The word of God — we never really get it, do we? We never really hear it, or say it, or write it, or do it. Yet we move toward it — we feel its pull and its power — and we find ourselves, suddenly, on the way: going, listening, writing, doing, hoping. Marginal hermeneutics is a hermeneutics of "being on the way." This, it seems, is where hermeneutics leads us: not to a conclusion that offers comfort but to a clearing that opens up, not to a closure but to a disclosure, not to a final word that ends the journey but to an adventure that sets us going, "for it belongs to our condition to remain always on the way."[2] This condition, as J.-B. Metz suggests, is the condition of faith, which "means above all a being-on-the-road, a being-underway, even a being homeless, in brief: discipleship."[3]

Margin Wisdom

Being on the way does not mean we are left in a vague state of directionless wandering. Rather, it represents "a state in which something is always called for in the way of decision and action."[4] The marginal space of interpretation is not so much a dwelling place as it is a threshold — the place of comings and goings. Intentional Christian communities live in this space only in the sense that they are continually "playing the game in the middle" — mediating the claims of their tradition of belonging and the claims of their contemporary situation. To be on the way is to be in a continual state of discerning, deciding, choosing. According to Gadamer, it is to embrace a way of knowing that is well suited to the educational life of intentional Christian communities. This way of knowing is *phronesis* — the way of practical wisdom.

Phronesis is an interpretational virtue that functions "in between" the written and the unwritten, a practical wisdom "that knows the rules of the past, but also sees visions of the future."[5] It is a term that Gadamer borrows from Aristotle.[6] In contrast to theoretical knowledge (*episteme:* "knowing that") and technical knowledge (*techne:* "knowing how"), *phronesis* is a practical wisdom that mediates between the universal/general and the concrete/particular or between the familiar known tradition and the unfamiliar novel situation. *Phronesis* is not a matter of applying the universal (the tradition) to the particular (the situation). Tradition is never given over-and-above history as though we could know it as a pregiven universal. Rather, in *phronesis* we approach an understanding of tradition in light of the concrete particular, just as we approach an understanding of our situation in the light of historical tradition.[7] According to John Caputo, this means that "reason is emancipated from the rule of method and becomes a more plastic, flexible, and spontaneous faculty of application."[8] Reason is not understood as an objective, methodological, autonomous knowing; rather, it is understood in terms of a *sensus communis,* a practical wisdom of interpretive communities who know their way around, "whose judgment has been sharpened by making decisions in the concrete."[9]

Caputo, however, wonders how dependent *phronesis* is upon a stable paradigm, a trusted and established tradition: "Aristotle conceived of the functioning of *phronesis* within a fundamentally stable *polis,* not within a period of revolutionary conflict."[10] How suited is *phronesis* in a world marked by radical plurality and ambiguity? How suited is it for members of intentional Christian communities who do not find themselves standing securely in a religious tradition but rather are questioning the very established modes of a tradition's normative discourse and patterns? I think Shaun Gallagher is correct in his twofold response to this question. He argues that while our world today is very different from the stable *polis* of Aristotle's time, we are never totally in a situation outside of the effective history of our tradition. No matter how uncertain our situation may be, no matter how foundering, it is still a hermeneutical situation.

> We never find ourselves thrown into an *absolutely unfamiliar* situation. There is always some basis on which to interpret that which falls outside of established paradigms, simply because we are always situated, located at some already familiar locale. Our educational experience, our past, our traditions, our practical interests, always condition our situation. . . .[11]

In other words, "if we do not operate out of a position of certainty, still, we do not operate outside of a hermeneutical situation within which we find some degree of familiarity."[12]

Although Gallagher believes that our situation is never totally tragic, he also argues that whenever we do find ourselves caught in the grip of tragic consequence, it is this situation itself that gives *phronesis* its interpretive force.[13] The particular value of Gadamer's retrieval of *phronesis* is that it is *not* a method of knowing that applies an established, preexisting schema that would therefore founder when that schema is in jeopardy. Rather,

> it is precisely the interpretational virtue that one can fall back on when the hermeneutical situation is uncertain. . . . *Phronesis* depends upon educational experience, is to be relied upon precisely on those occasions when no formula is known in advance, in those situations where . . . we must act . . . according to reason formed in educational experience.[14]

Stephen Brookfield sees small "educative" communities as primary settings for developing a practical wisdom among adult learners. According to Brookfield, much significant adult learning is of a nontechnical kind and more akin to *phronesis:* "It is concerned with the resolution of moral difficulties, with the development of self-insight, with acquiring the capacity to explore the world view of others, with reflection on experience."[15] *Phronesis* has a quality of play to it and, like all playing that is done well, it is a constructive and recreative activity. Particularly when we play a game with which we have a deep familiarity and affinity, we do not need to keep calling to mind the rules and contours of the game; rather, they have become part of us. The process has the quality of a virtue that one lives out of, rather than a technical know-how that one applies. It is "essentially artistic, that is, the practitioner makes judgments and exercises skills for which no explicit rationale has been articulated but in which she nevertheless feels an intuitive sense of confidence."[16]

Phronesis is well suited to the interpretive life of intentional communities who find themselves jarred by imposing institutions that establish norms and givens external to the questions and concerns of contemporary experience. It is an interpretational virtue that enables intentional communities to "work out the rules in and for local interpretations."[17] *Phronesis* involves a fundamental shift from a model of interpretation that seeks explicit, determinate norms as a preexisting condition of knowing, to a model of interpretation that emphasizes practical wisdom in discerning the way ahead through deliberation, conversation, and decision making in specific, local, concrete situations among communities of interpreters. It is "a form of reasoning that is concerned with choice and involves deliberation. It deals with that which is variable and about which there can be differing opinions."[18] In terms of a community's educational life, Elizabeth Karmarck Minnich suggests that what it does is to open up space (marginal space, breathing space) "for the renewal, discovery, creation of ways of thinking that are compatible with diversity, plurality, particularity, change — and relationality."[19]

According to John Caputo, "the problem with reason today is that it has become an instrument of discipline, not a mark of freedom, and that, when it is put to work, it is taken out of play."[20] It is precisely here that I think the marginal life of intentional Christian communities has much to offer. So many of our institutions (be they political, educational, ecclesial, or otherwise) place "little confidence in the play of things and a great deal of reliance on constraints, authority and institutional structures." The result is that we are "overrun with creeds and criteria" and that no matter how much we are encouraged to think freely and creatively, "there are always those who are threatened by such emancipation and who insist on knowing what the 'criteria' are. . . ."[21] All of a sudden, play becomes deadly serious, rather than playfully serious.

The choice, however, is not so much between rational, serious thinking and a type of playful, relativistic form of irrationalism. This is a misleading dichotomy that forces all dissenters (or explorers of new ideas and modes of being) to appear absurd and frivolous because they do not subscribe to the dominant paradigm of what is considered rational and acceptable. Caputo reminds us that "subversive-ness is structurally necessary to normalcy."[22] It allows for creative break-throughs, which may at first appear to us as breakdowns. In play, "something breaks through because the constraints we impose upon things breaks down."[23] Caputo is suggesting that if we remove the ruling principles (the *arche*) and admit the possibility of many different ways of being, we will reach a freer and better understanding of reason that stresses its playful, practical character.[24]

Far from undermining reason, *phronesis* brings out the best in our reasoning capacities. Interpretive scribbling is not just a fringe activity: it is what the best hermeneutes do. Reason at its best is reason that is playing, discovering, trans-forming. *Phronesis* opens up a creative space for intentional communities to play in the margins of tradition. This is an interpretational activity that operates at its best when the way ahead is not established but in the making: "then reason is fully at work, which means fully at play."[25] It is a practical wisdom that "knows its way about, even and precisely when the way cannot be laid out beforehand."[26] Richard Bernstein suggests that this practical wisdom cannot be found in a theory of truth but only in dialogic communities of spirited discourse and praxis.[27] We are confronted with a very real need: the imperative to create forms of intentional communal life in which the practice of communal reflection, con-versation, and deliberation can be nurtured once more. The wisdom that emerges in ongoing discourse and dialogue — in speaking back and forth, around and about, risking and imagining, acting and reflecting — forms and informs a com-munity's character and virtue. *Phronesis* releases interpretive activity among communities of interpreters into the realm of play and to-and-fro conversation as a transforming, engaging, practical knowing.

According to Thomas Groome, our educational approaches need to be shaped anew by a reuniting of knowing and being — of epistemology and ontology.[28] Knowledge of the world can never be detached from being-in-the-world, and if we want to know (if we want to understand), we need to engage our whole way of being-in-the-world: our memory, our imagination, our feelings, our thinking, our actions, and our critical, appreciative, and creative capacities. The result is a knowing that leads to wisdom, which brings a far richer significance to education than the typically narrow learning outcome of knowledge.

One of Groome's overriding concerns has been a recovery of the primacy of praxis. A praxis way of knowing operates out of a practical reason, in contrast to the speculative reason of *theoria*.[29] Praxis holds theory and action together as "dual and mutually enriching moments of the same intentional activity."[30] The two cannot really be separated, just as knowing and being cannot be separated. When we speak of hermeneutics or education as having to do with understanding, the temptation is to place the emphasis on reflective or theoretical knowing at the expense of practical or active knowing. "Practical" may not be the best word, if we take "practical" to mean the application of prior systematic understandings. In hermeneutical theory, "practical" carries a different sense, referring to the way in which all understanding is always engaged, interested, historically situated, and applied — such that any true understanding always begins to show itself in action.

Various political, liberationist, and feminist theologies all stress the primacy of praxis, emphasizing the historical and societal character of reason itself and insisting on the transformative nature of practical reason with its emancipatory interest. Many of these theologies have emerged from the praxis of intentional Christian communities located in the midst of life, at the grassroots level, by people reflecting deeply on reality as they experience it. As Lewis Mudge and James Poling suggest, theological reflection and education takes on a different character when it is relocated at the heart of communal life. Interpretive communities "must be the living, reflecting, social reality inside which the theological task is carried on. If theology is to recover its reality reference, it must be meaningfully resituated in the *ekklesia* . . . in the midst of the community's thought and action."[31] Intentional communities need to be supported and encouraged as one of the most viable options open to us for praxis-education. According to Richard Bernstein, we are being constantly drawn in the direction

> of a politics of everyday life in which individuals act together to form new specific and local forms of community. . . . It becomes all the more imperative to try again and again to foster and nurture those forms of communal life in which dialogue, conversation, *phronesis*, practical discourse, and judgment are concretely embodied in our everyday practices.[32]

Margin Justice

John Caputo has written an interesting essay on the interplay between law and justice, which draws some parallels between Gadamer's notion of *phronesis* and Derrida's project of deconstruction.[33] Caputo argues that law (which has to do with governing the *polis*) can never attain justice, even though it yearns for justice and is motivated by justice's claims. Laws, however, have a tendency to equate themselves with justice, and this is where they become dangerous. Undeconstructible laws, laws without resistance, no longer serve justice, but act to hinder justice. "That is why the revisability and repealability of law, even the resistance of law, is structurally part of the law."[34] Laws are deconstructible precisely because they have been constructed in the first place. They have not fallen from the sky, rather they have been drawn up, made, written — and thus the possibility of their deconstruction (remaking, rewriting) needs to be built into them.

We never attain justice, even though it is what we desire; justice must come, yet it forever eludes us. When we think our love of law and order has brought us to the place of justice, we are suddenly interrupted by the very call of justice — a call that comes from the chaos and singularity of each complex situation that demands action. The reason laws need to be deconstructed (or, if you like, continually reinterpreted, remade, interpreted differently) is to keep them open to the particular, to changing historical demands, to the turn of events that lie out of the law's control, to the call of justice that calls out from concrete, particular situations — and in whose very name the law has been written.

Deconstruction has a "civic duty" toward the *polis*. Its task is "to keep the singular one in view, to keep traversing the space between the universal and the singular, between the law and justice, between the calculable and the incalculable, to keep the lines of communication open between them."[35] This is akin to Gadamer's understanding of the functioning of *phronesis*. Caputo cites Derrida to suggest that simply conforming to the law does not necessarily insure justice. "Rather the law requires a 'fresh judgment,' a judgment which 'conserves the law and also destroys it or suspends it long enough to have it reinvented in each case.'"[36] The universal never completely fits. It can never entirely anticipate the "disruptiveness of the singular" or fully prepare itself for the complexities of each and every specific situation. According to Derrida, the law must always pass through the ordeal of having to decide, of having to make an uneasy choice amidst singular complexity: "there can be no moral or political responsibility without this trial and this passage by way of the undecidable."[37]

The call of justice haunts our every move; it "demands immediate justice, justice for this singular one here."[38] It is the cry of "the singular one who calls from beyond the law, whom the law misses."[39] It is like the call of the Hebrew prophets — "Justice come!" It is a cry against injustice. It has a mytho-prophetic tone that "calls from beyond the universal, from the abyss of singularity. It calls upon us, calling for a response, calling upon our most secret responsiveness and responsibility."[40] According to Richard Bernstein, we are always moving in the marginal space of a dual allegiance to both the ethical mores of our tradition and the call and claim of justice.

> We cannot assume a permanent frozen stance of *an-arche*. For this is another fixed metaphysical position. We cannot escape responsibility, decision, and choice. They are thrust upon us by the Other. Furthermore, we cannot simply dismiss or ignore those ethical and political principles that are constitutive of our traditions. The prob-lem — and it is a problem for which there cannot be any final or permanent "solu-tion" — is to live this perpetual uneasiness in a way in which we "gesture in opposite directions at the same time," where we keep alive the distance of question-ing and are prepared to act decisively "here and now" — where we do not hide in bad faith from the double binds that we always confront.[41]

While we need to acknowledge the call of the Other — the call of justice that irrupts in our lives — we also need discourses of memory to remind us of that call. According to Thomas Groome, the Jewish tradition of *shalom* and the Chris-tian tradition of God's reign both have to do with a deep, mythic desire for "peace, justice, love, freedom, equality, gentleness, wholeness, well-being for us and for all creation. . . ."[42] They also have to do with the most dangerous and subversive memories of the Hebrew and Christian Scriptures, the memory of the exodus and the memory of the cross and resurrection. Such memories speak to us of injustice and liberation, of "the suffering of humankind and its resistance to every form of oppression with the hope of new life and freedom for all."[43] These traditions are constitutive of who we are and continually evoke and stir up the call of justice that arises from the depths of our being.

Walter Brueggemann, for example, offers a rich account of the exodus narra-tive, which represents Israel's deep yearning for liberation.[44] This narrative func-tions as a classic text that holds an enduring power to provoke and sustain each new generation's commitment to transformative, liberating action. The narrative begins with an ideology critique of the imperial power structures of the pharaoh and the Egyptian empire. The purpose of the narrative is to deconstruct the impe-rial system, to assault it in a conflictual, disjunctive way. Feeling themselves enmeshed in this system, the narrative's second movement tells how Israel cried out "with a profound yearning and desperate hopeful pain with no assurance of being heard."[45] At first the cry goes out to no one; yet, in a surprising and deci-sive moment, it evokes a response from the desert-crossing God. "God heard their groaning. . . . And God saw the people of Israel, and God knew their condi-tion" (Exod. 2:24-25).

Brueggemann notes that before any social transformation can occur, there must be this "public processing of pain."[46] If pain is only experienced privately and in isolation, no social energy can be released. But when there is a public outcry, "there is a social anger which generates risky, passionate social power."[47] The public cry of pain and the ideology critique that uncovers the sources of that pain lead to the third movement of the narrative, "the release of new social imagination."[48] Things *can* be different. There *is* hope for liberation. "The cry of pain begins the formation of a counter-community around an alternative perception of reality."[49] It generates renewed social energy to undertake transformative, liberating action. That is why this narrative is such a dangerous one to any system of established power (religious, social, or political). Each new generation that participates in this narrative "knows that the dominant ideology will be destroyed by the proper telling of the story."[50] That is why so many communities of women and men, struggling to imagine and build a better world, have "loved to tell the story" — hungering and thirsting to hear it and tell it and enact it again and again.

According to John Caputo, "religion does not begin with God but with suffering, and it invokes God to make its protest heard."[51] In a similar fashion, Sharon Welch notes that when we refer to God as a "liberating God," the referent "is not primarily *God* but *liberation*." It refers to the actual creation within history of communities of peace, justice, and liberation.[52] In the face of suffering, religious faith is faith in a God of life, a God who is in solidarity with those who suffer. This is what it means for there to be a God. A religious stance is one of both hope and defiance. It is an affirmation of life and a protest against suffering. "It speaks in the name of life and against the powers that demean and degrade life." God signifies a presence that stands "always and necessarily on the side of those who suffer . . . who intervenes on behalf of the sufferer."[53]

Caputo takes up Metz's theme that religion speaks from the dangerous memory of suffering.[54] According to Metz, "every rebellion against suffering is fed by the subversive power of remembered suffering." And according to Caputo, "it is a deconstructive memory which will not let us forget, will not let us settle down into the complacency of well-fed presence."[55] This is what lends such memory its dangerous and liberating character. It remembers the subversive histories of the defeated and forgotten, against the metaphysical histories of presence, of the triumphant and dominant.[56]

Perhaps the deconstructionist project, such as Derrida's, aims to keep alive the deep, mythic longings for justice not so much by destroying traditions but by keeping them open. Perhaps Derrida shares the deconstructionist sensibility of that other margin dwelling Jew who once spoke of going to the open roads and alleys to invite the uninvited to be guests at the banquet.[57] Indeed, Caputo notes how Jesus was often misunderstood as a transgressor of the Law — a "deconstructionist":

> What seems to have been preeminently "ethical" to him was openness to the differ-
> ent . . . the Samaritans, the lepers, the oppressed, the lost sheep and prodigal sons,
> even tax collectors and outright enemies. . . . . The mark of divinity for Jesus was
> otherness, difference. . . . He found the face of God in the different.[58]

Margin justice knows that every tightly organized structure is prone to systematically dominate, regulate, and exclude what is other and different. It aims,
therefore, to release "all the loose ends in the system," yet it does this "not by any
show of strength of its own but by letting the system unravel, letting the play in
the system loose."[59] Margin justice recognizes the need for normative judgments, for ethical mores, for developing the law as a guide and way of life, yet at
the same time it recognizes the need to remain open to challenge and interruption, to the ongoing need for redoings and rewritings:

> It distrusts all schemes and programs . . . on the assumption that every such program
> harbors within it an exclusionary gesture, a repressive act, a movement of normal-
> ization and leveling. It suspects that after a certain point every good idea becomes
> inflexible and repressive, that schemes cling tenaciously to life and presence long
> after they have spent their capital and done their work. But it is not opposed to insti-
> tutional organization or the notion of community. It requires rather the hardiness
> (*virtus*) . . . to keep all such institutions free, to keep them mobile, in motion, flex-
> ible, in flux, reformable, repeating forward.[60]

The hope, according to Walter Brueggemann, is "to keep the conversation
going without excluding any voice," a conversation that is "attentive to the role,
function, gift, and claim of different voices."[61] In a similar fashion, Richard
Rorty believes there is a place alongside our mainstream discourses for an
"abnormal discourse" that challenges the authority of every "privileged set of
descriptions" and protests all "attempts to close off conversation."[62] Abnormal
discourse, however, is an "edifying" discourse in the sense that it is productive of
"finding new, better, more interesting, more fruitful ways of speaking." Such discourse wants to keep the conversation going by taking "us out of our old selves
by the power of strangeness, to aid us in becoming new beings."[63] According to
Georgia Warnke, the point of edifying discourse is not to discover "foundations
for our beliefs" or "a final, irrevocable understanding of 'truth.'" Rather, its point
is "to foster an awareness of different possibilities of coping with the world, of
different life-options and, indeed, of new modes of self-description."[64] Such discourse requires a practical wisdom that is able to deal with ambiguity, with a plurality of options, and that can discern the way ahead not so much by knowing
truths as by knowing how to live through questioning in the openness of conversation and dialogue with others.[65]

Marginal hermeneutics affirms the imaginative, productive, creative process of interpretive writing. It is a free, playful, generous, and generative writing. It does not seek sterile stability but rather yearns for movement — to get going, to be underway, to break free, to move in wider and wider circles, to weave and create, to enlarge and extend. Yet it is also a serious, deliberative, hard-working writing of enactment. Whereas nonmovers resist change, margin writers recognize that life is continually moving, and they cannot stand disconnection from the momentum and energy of life itself. Nonmovement is a type of powerlessness. Movement keeps us alive to the possibility of choice and decision — "to refuse to allow parts of ourselves to shrivel and die that have the potential for growth and fulfillment."[66] There is a defiance and a refusal in margin writing that listens to what has been left out, left behind, left unsaid, left powerless. Yet margin writing is eminently hopeful even as it is eminently risk taking. It is willing to err, to deviate, to experiment in the service of life and the possibility of a renewed and transformed world.

Margin Truth

What does the marginal space of hermeneutics teach us? What can intentional Christian communities learn from marginal hermeneutics, from all those messengers of the margin whose voices have been speaking throughout this book? One of the things we learn from marginal hermeneutics is that religious traditions constantly live within the tension generated by two interplaying needs: the need for identity, continuity, guiding norms, and the need for new understanding, relevance, and responsiveness to changing situations. This hermeneutical tension raises a key educational question: how can a religious tradition creatively norm itself to take account both of its need for continuity in identity, and its need for relevance in a discontinuous moment of new interpretation? According to Walter Brueggemann, "education must attend both to processes of continuity and discontinuity in order to avoid fossilizing into irrelevance on the one hand, and relativizing into disappearance on the other."[67] Brueggemann links this educational task with the task of hermeneutics by undertaking an exploration of the Hebrew scriptural canon (the *Tanakh*). "Canon" suggests a privileging — yet it is a privileging of that which we want to endure, not as a fixed and frozen moment; rather, so that it can continue to reverberate. "Canon both binds and frees, freeing us from its binding, and binding us to its freedom."[68]

Brueggemann's analysis of canon suggests that normative parameters are crucial because they act as horizons of meaning through which understanding first becomes possible. We always interpret as members of historical, cultural, linguistic communities. Yet canonical literature is also minimal because it still leaves "all our interpretive work in front of us. . . . It permits and requires endless ongoing interpretation which claims always to discern new meanings." The task of interpretation is not to "find the faithful interpretation, because it has 'not yet' been found — always 'not yet'. . . . Serious concern for canon moves us not toward canonical text but toward canonical interpretation."[69] In other words, the interpretive *act* is the revelatory event as the place where the text comes to mean for us something new, something different, something we have reconstructed in the serious play of interpretation.

Brueggemann finds in the Hebrew canon an invigorating structure that invites and enables interpretive communities to continue the canonizing process. What is normative in the Hebrew canon is not so much the canon itself but the *process* of canonizing: "*the process of canon is a main clue to education,* a process which partakes of stability and flexibility, continuity and discontinuity."[70] In the Tanakh we discover a "book of words" that is disclosive and binding (the Torah), a "book of questions" that is disruptive and transforming (the prophets), and a "book of writings" that is discerning and explorative (the writings). This threefold structure suggests that the canon itself urges tradition to pay attention to three dynamic and interrelated norms: the normativity of *answer* (exemplified in the Torah), the normativity of *question* (exemplified in the prophets), and the normativity of *experience* (exemplified in the writings, particularly the wisdom traditions).[71]

The Book of Words

As a hermeneutical exemplar, the Torah reminds us that we ourselves live in the pages of the book. We are constituted by a past in the sense that we are always already part of tradition and shaped by it. This is Gadamer's great insistence: we must necessarily engage in a hermeneutic of retrieval; we cannot reshape our tradition in the present or for the future without reshaping our past, because our present grows out of our history. "It is a challenge," writes Edgerton, "to name one's person, place, and commitments at what some might call the simplest level (or others might call the most fundamental), and to recognize that the work of interpretation originates there."[72]

The challenge is particularly acute in our own times where we find ourselves surrounded by a whirl of competing narratives. Amid this plurality, our culture makes it difficult for people to remember or reclaim their roots, to listen or open themselves to words and stories that speak of communal places of belonging.[73] Instead, many people become ensnared in a debilitating ideology of radical individualism, one that has produced a "a society of empty, disengaged, drifting

selves incapable of memorable experience or coherent expression."[74] Relativism
of this sort thrives in the individualism of Western culture, and its danger is not
so much that we end up with no truth, no objective reality; rather, that we end up
with individualized truth — my truth for me. This is the "I" who claims independence and the self's own certainty, an "I" in control, neither dependent nor receptive. A self such as this "is not connected to any particular ends, has no particular
history, is a member of no communities, has no body."[75] These autonomous
selves no longer know how to engage in fruitful and meaningful dialogue with
others. They claim an individualized notion of truth as "my truth" and "your
truth" (and "if our paths should happen to meet, that would be fine, and maybe
beautiful — if not, then nothing is lost"). This is the pluralism of the shopping
mall; it is a normless world, a "Torah-less" world, a world that, ultimately, leaves
us impoverished and unfree. It is also a world which, for many members of intentional communities, they do not wish their children to be lost to. As Brueggemann notes: "The Torah is Israel's yearning that its children should not grow up
in chaos, in alienation, in narcissistic subjectivity."[76]

"Life must be a gift before it can become a task."[77] In the midst of the marked
plurality, ambiguity, and confusion of our world, our religious heritage comes to
us first as a gift. "Knowing is fundamentally collective knowing. . . . It presup-
poses a community of knowing which grows out of a community of experiencing."[78] Our religious tradition of belonging is a gift of words, a gift of a language,
a gift of a way of seeing and being in the world. It offers us deep memories, communal stories, ethical wisdom, symbolic imaginings — not to turn us inward, to
become insular, but as a way to enter into conversation with others. Far from
being a constraint upon us, these "words" enable us to enter the wider conversations of our time, to engage the leading ethical, social, and political questions of
our day. They offer a place in which to stand and from which to move; they help
us to speak and they help us to listen; they help us to encounter and engage in
dialogue with others. This is why Gadamer's dialogical hermeneutics is so
important for members of intentional Christian communities today. He is "constantly directing us to a critical appropriation of the traditions that have shaped
us, but he is motivated by the practical-moral intention of searching for ways in
which we can live 'here and now.'"[79] Gadamer is asking us to be mindful of the
historical traditions shaping us so that we can live within these traditions positively and creatively, drawing on their wisdom and, through them, finding fruitful ways to encounter and dialogue with others. Gerald Bruns writes as follows:

> Sometimes hermeneutics gets taken as, and in a certain sense is, a theory of confine-
> ment, because it is preoccupied with our belongingness, or, roughly, with the idea
> that none of us ever comes floating freely into the world; rather, we are from the start

initiated into ongoing forms of life or contexts of practice and action that make themselves felt internally not only as claims upon our ownmost existence but as indispensable features of our self-recognition. We are social before we are individual, and so we are always to some extent "individual" in quotation marks, and perhaps one ought to come out and confess the point that hermeneutics . . . is frankly anti-individualist, a beneficiary (at least) of the many-sided critique of the subject that characterizes so much of twentieth-century intellectual culture; and it is also true, as a further twist, that hermeneutics is drawn historically toward a Levinasian ethics of vulnerability that turns the self or the ego inside out, defines it as responsibility for another.[80]

A certain view of the human subject, deeply flattering and attractive to modern persons, is one of disengagement — of "liberation through objectification."[81] This disengaged identity has created vast distortions in the modern age with its mindset of mastery and control over the world through a technological and disengaged thinking. Modern thought is still swayed by an enlightened scientific rationality that pictures the human subject as "a brave naked will surrounded by an easily comprehended empirical world."[82] Liberated thinkers (so-called) are those who can distance and detach themselves from the situations in which we find ourselves (or the traditions in which we live, the forms of life in which we participate, the texts we read, the people with whom we exist, or the natural world in which we live). We associate freedom with being in control, keeping things at a distance, manipulating the world according to our desire (our fear?) to claim an autonomous, instrumental control over things.[83]

Against this scenario we can hear Gadamer's question, in the words of Jocelyn Dunphy-Blomfield: "Is it possible to speak to 'disengaged' modern philosophers of experience conceived as 'engaged,' caught up, affected by passion or suffering?"[84] As Bernstein suggests, we have been taught well enough in this enlightened age how to be sharp, critical, autonomous thinkers. We have "perfected our adversarial skills but we have carried them to excess. In this respect, our practices reflect what is occurring throughout society. 'We' need to counter-balance these practices by cultivating dialogical encounters."[85] For Gadamer, such dialogue is based on receptivity rather than mastery, responsiveness rather than control, openness rather than distancing. "There is no such thing as interpretation at a safe distance."[86] Understanding means allowing the subject matter (whether this be another partner in a conversation, a text, or a tradition) to "play us" rather than us to control it, to let the subject matter "lead us" into understanding. It is a participation in the subject matter that is an "encounter with" rather than a "control over." It means being receptive to the "other," risking our pre-understandings and allowing the play of to-and-fro questioning, dialogue, and conversation. Gadamer offers us renewed hope in the "good will" of hermeneutical conversation. Some may see this as a naive hope; yet we find ourselves in the world today wondering: what happened to those words of mist, spoken, it seems, so deeply in the past — strange vowlike words, like promise, covenant, dialogue, fidelity, trust, mutuality, commitment? Do we not feel an absence of these words in our society today? Does not our world sometimes appear to us as so fractured and divided — "a jungle of competing, savage interests"?[87] Can intentional Christian communities become deep retrievers — messengers from the margins — of these Torah-like words, words that help us to choose life, words that guide us on our way? "Beyond the desert of criticism," writes Paul Ricoeur, "we wish to be called again."[88]

The Book of Questions

"Be careful how you interpret the world, it *is* like that."[89] Our second hermeneutical exemplar — the prophets — reminds us that our reading of the book can become distorted and can serve to oppress rather than liberate. This is Habermas's insistence: although he does not entirely disagree with what Gadamer means by dialogue, conversation, and questioning, he is nevertheless "constantly drawing our attention to those systematic features of contemporary society that inhibit, distort, or prevent such dialogue from being concretely embodied in our everyday practices."[90] Habermas wants us to be more careful, more self-conscious, more critically aware of the way we are interpreting, lest our interpretations simply reflect the dominant interests of those *who have the say* over against those *who have no say*. We cannot always presume a communal "we" and speak of "our" tradition, "our" consensus, as though the "we" were already given and established. Habermas is concerned that interpreters too often take the "we" for granted, a "we" that is often distorted by hegemonic practice. This is why he calls for a more emancipatory "depth-hermeneutics," one that is continually looking for ways of making the "we" possible rather than uncritically presumed.[91] For Habermas, critical reason is necessary to unmask oppressive ideologies, yet the "reason he defends is dialogical, intersubjective, communicative."[92] Reason that is working well is reason that is working toward emancipation, toward the Enlightenment ideals of justice, freedom, and equality.

In the prophetic exemplar we find the Jewish genius of creating canonically normative space for prophecy and self-critique. If we ask the prophets whether they have read the book, we can only reply that they *are* reading it — even though it appears they have taken leave of it. Within the book itself there is a way that can be found to exit the book; the book inscribes within its own pages the resources needed for a new exodus to freedom. A hermeneutic of suspicion is as important to a community's norming process as is a hermeneutic of retrieval. According to Brueggemann, the prophets of Israel tend to be the voices of peripheral communities, such that "the texts that we regard as authoritative and canonical are in fact marginal in their origin and claims."[93] The prophetic word is a free, irreverent, nonconsensual word that speaks against the book for the very sake of the book.

> The word of the prophet is something immediate, intrusive, and surprising. . . . It is not known in advance. It is a way of knowledge that is not known until it is uttered. When it is uttered, its function may be to break the Torah, to challenge the consensus, to practice criticism on that which, until now, has been beyond criticism. . . . The prophets use Torah to argue against Torah.[94]

The wandering question, the unsettling critique, the cry of pain and protest, the refusal to be tamed by custom and convention, to take what is given for granted — this is the function of the prophets. Here, tradition is disrupted, its distortions unmasked, its settled ways turned upside down. Like Derrida's deconstructionist project, the prophetic exemplar is intent on disrupting all repressive and centrist discourses — "every discourse which tends to create undisturbable limits and order, hegemonic rule, privileged, hierarchized oppositions, etc."[95] Unlike Gadamer, who wants to show continuities and affinities between the past and the present, to enable a "fusion of horizons," deconstruction seeks to highlight the breaks and ruptures within the discourses of tradition.[96] In this sense, the prophets are those who disrupt smooth continuities; they "say no with thunder, for all who say yes, lie."[97] This is a "no" of protest and disruption against the tendencies of tradition to settle down into complacency and indifference. However, as Habermas reminds us, it is a "no" that must always be spoken in the name of liberation and emancipation. It is a "no" that believes in the possibility of historical transformation, that refuses to accept that we are "totally imprinted by history" and unable to break free from the structures that bind us.[98] Prophetic protest enables intentional Christian communities to claim a sense of agency in challenging and transforming the negative determinations of tradition.

To suggest that prophetic communities use the book to argue against the book is to suggest that they uncover the dangerous and subversive memories of tradition, those memories that threaten the status quo of present power arrangements. The prophetic exemplar, therefore, also draws its impetus from an exilic hermeneutic, a hermeneutic which recognizes that there is, as Edgerton suggests, "wrong done by words," that words not only offer truth and guidance and wisdom; they can also hurt and distort and exclude. The prophets cry out, and these cries of pain and protest are not simply the interruption of interpretation, "they are its reason for being and its judge."[99] According to Derrida, the necessity of commentary and questioning is given in the shape of "exiled speech." When people feel exiled from the promise, we learn from their cries that the book can still speak, that words want to grow, and that writing and commentary takes root in a wound.[100] When theologies of liberation speak about the "preferential option for the poor," or the "hermeneutical privilege of the oppressed," they are suggesting that "every interpretation must be weighed against tears, and tears will show its true value."[101] Edgerton writes as follows:

> There is indeed a sign which is sovereign among the signs humankind makes: the sign of tears. There is also a speech which is privileged and takes precedence over other speech, even speech in the words of scripture: the cries of the wronged. The cries of the wronged both prove and declare. . . .
>
> There is only one constant, one reading that is not undone, and remains as judge of each interpretation: there is wrong done by words, and the cries of those wounded by words will be heard in Heaven, and God will take their side. . . for tears are the human speech God privileges above all others. . . .
>
> Interpretation exists because of tears and for the sake of tears. Only with the wiping away of tears, only with the last of tears, would interpretation come to an end.[102]

The Book of Writings

Hope comes from tears. Who hopes? Not those who enjoy a "well-fed" presence, those who imagine that the promises are already fulfilled, that everything is already complete and the order of things already worked out. Those who hope are those who know that this is not true because they know that there is much that has been "written out," forgotten, excluded, left without voice or text. Through their cry of protest they begin to see that things can be otherwise, that new imaginings, new choices, new "writing" is possible. Hope keeps the book open and provisional, continually under scrutiny, and continually open to new possibility.[103] According to Brueggemann, there is no power in critiquing and dismantling the dominant consciousness unless it also leads to a creative imagining of an alternative consciousness. The task of critique is to show that the dominant consciousness "will indeed end and that it has no final claim upon us." The task of imaginative writing is "to present an alternative consciousness that can energize the community to fresh forms of faithfulness and vitality."[104]

The hermeneutical exemplar of "the Writings" reminds us that we must resist the "systematic attempt to repress the play, to hold it in check: to create the illusion of abiding truth over and against the flux; to posit metaphysical grounds that cannot be shaken; to establish stable and transparent signs which lead us straight to pure presence."[105] The Writings remind us that we must remain radically open to new experience, to the unexpected, to letting go. "Truth is no longer what fits but what goes free."[106] Here, our reading of the book is no longer a mastery over, but a reading as rewriting. The paradox is that if the rewriting of the book is disallowed, we become unable to read it. In this sense, the value of rewriting is warranted by the contemporary readability it brings to the book.[107] New experience necessarily invites intentional Christian communities to new writing — to a hermeneutic of creative reconstruction. This time of writing is the time of faith. We must believe in the book in order to write it, and we must believe in ourselves and our own experience. This too carries normative weight. The Writings open up the whole vista of people's experience in the world — in the flux of life — and say that this too has a normative, canonical character for tradition.[108] As we noted in the previous chapter, the rabbinic tradition has continued this sensibility for ongoing interpretation — their tradition is filled with *writings*, with ongoing commentary and question and dialogue. The "book of writings" represents the Jewish genius of creating canonically normative space for openness to new experience and for anticipating the future life of tradition in the multiple possibilities of its continuing interpretations.

How, in the end, are we to evaluate the truth of our interpretations? David Tracy recognizes the complexity of this question and in one place suggests that perhaps the best guide will always be the ethical; in other words, whatever leads to justice, equality, and freedom from oppression is a good interpretation.[109] In other places he argues for the criteria of adequacy to our situation (whereby an interpretation makes sense or rings true with our experience) and appropriateness to the tradition (whereby an interpretation is coherent with the central beliefs and practices of a tradition).[110] However, beneath our questions concerning interpretive criteria there lurks a persisting "Cartesian anxiety."[111] We want to know if anything is constant, stable, or the same amid the changing, shifting, historical flux. Even if we could name such criteria (such as consistency, adequacy, intelligibility, appropriateness, and so on), it seems they still do not help us much. They are values on which everyone can probably agree without agreeing on what they mean or how they should be put into practice. Maybe criteria can emerge only after the fact. Maybe it is only after we have engaged in interpretive conversation, application, and new possibility that we can retrace our steps to see what in the final analysis won the day.[112] This would give a priority to praxis so that every arrival, every decision, every action is followed by an evaluative reflection, which in turn prompts further action and further deliberation. The result is an ongoing practical wisdom that builds an interpretive community's character and virtue.

Francis Schüssler Fiorenza suggests "integrity" as the interpretive criteria rather than "coherence" or "appropriateness." To inquire about the integrity of an interpretation is not so much to ask how well an interpretation coheres with a tradition's beliefs or practices; rather, integrity asks about what change or expansion is required of tradition in the face of inconsistencies and conflicts.[113] Integrity emerges as a result of a conversational hermeneutics "that has to deal with conflicts of interpretation and divergent priorities concerning the meaning of Christian identity."[114] Meaning and evaluation take place not in the realm of abstract principles but in communities of discourse, located within specific historical and linguistic traditions. As such, a tradition "develops and changes in a way that constantly reconstructs what it considers to be paradigmatic to its vision."[115] The best safeguard seems to be a community of interpreters. The search for criteria always ends up being a search for inclusive, dialogical, intentional community — for places of discourse in which we can engage in communal reflection, deliberation, and interpretive conversation; places in which we can risk and imagine, reflect and act, bringing our tradition and contemporary horizon into a vigorous and mutually critical conversation with each other.

Margin Faith

To write is to take the book to places it has not yet been, and at the same time, to follow its leading. According to Brueggemann, to venture into this unknown territory is to venture into the realm of mystery.

> We are in touch with a mystery that cannot be too closely shepherded, as in the Torah, or protested against, as in the prophets. There is here a not-knowing, a waiting to know, a patience about what is yet to be discerned, and a respect for not knowing that must be honored and not crowded. This way does not seek conclusions for immediate resolutions. It works at a different pace because it understands that the secrets cannot be forced.[116]

In discernment and judgment, prior to making the essential cut, we wisely allow for a margin of error. We take into account factors that may be (and usually are) out of our control. Every attempt at accuracy is, oddly enough, made with this measure of flexibility — the margin of error — which means we try to anticipate the surprise, the play of things, the unexpected. The only way we can do this is to leave some room that provides us with the clearance or allowance we need to venture forth. We must necessarily allow a margin of error if we are ever to approximate a measure of truth.

According to Sharon Welch, "the courage to act and to think within an uncertain framework is not easily achieved. It may be that this is what is meant by faith . . . not the denial of risk, but living within the fragile balance of absolute commitment and infinite suspicion."[117] Similarly, Caputo suggests that those with eyes of faith are those who are good at making their way through the dark, "at keeping on the tracks of the divine."[118] This is a faith that does not so much see God everywhere; rather, it is a faith that leans in the direction of the God who withdraws, the God whose very self-giving is self-deferring. Divine presence is "always caught up in the play of presence and absence.The faith of the believer consists in staying in play with that play, which involves maximum risk and uncertainty."[119]

Margin writing is a time of faith, faith measured by trust and commitment as much as it is measured by doubt and suspicion. It is a time when we must make a wager and, as it were, finally put pen to paper.[120] What we write, the actions we take, the future we imagine — these "words" are written in the difficult margin moment of choosing, of deciding, of attending each time to the present. Although clothed in ambiguity, margin writing is nevertheless immersed "most openly and most deeply in the present at hand, attended by the living past in each moment and accompanied by the meanings portended for the future."[121]

The difficulty lies with choosing — with trusting risk, and risking trust. At times it means releasing ourselves — letting go — and choosing that which escapes and runs freely, that which goes exuberantly into passionate, untamed futures. At other times, no less, it means exposing ourselves to a responsibility — holding fast — and choosing that which we are bound to, that which resists and attests to our dependence on an essential work. According to the poet Rainer Maria Rilke, that which is most alive and open to movement and growth is also that which is most difficult.

> If only we could arrange our life according to the principle which counsels us that we must always hold to the difficult . . . everything alive holds to it — then that which now seems to us the most alien will become what we most trust and find most faithful. . . . For this reason it will not cease to be difficult, but for this reason it will not cease to grow.[122]

Notes

1. Edmond Jabès, *The Book of Questions*, 1. 44–45.

2. John Caputo, *Radical Hermeneutics*, p. 214.

3. Johann-Baptist Metz, "Facing the Jews: Christian Theology After Auschwitz," p. 31. Bernard Lee notes how the early followers of Jesus understood themselves as disciples of "the way." See *The Galilean Jewishness of Jesus*, pp. 104–5.

4. Bruns, *Hermeneutics Ancient and Modern*, p. 11.

5. Rebecca Chopp, *The Power to Speak*, p. 97.

6. See Aristotle, *Nicomachean Ethics*, esp. book 6.

7. Gadamer, *Truth and Method*, pp. 312ff. According to Gadamer, practical reason is "concerned with reason and knowledge, not detached from a being that is becoming, but

determined by it and determinative of it" (*Truth and Method,* p. 312). It is closely linked with Gadamer's collapse of the distinction between understanding and application: "Application is neither a subsequent nor merely an occasional part of the phenomenon of understanding, but codetermines it as a whole from the beginning" (*Truth and Method,* p. 324). See also Gadamer's reflections on "practical philosophy" in *Reason in the Age of Science.*

8. Caputo, *Radical Hermeneutics,* p. 210.

9. Ibid., p. 210.

10. Ibid., p. 217. This is also Richard Bernstein's question; see *Beyond Objectivism and Relativism,* p. 157.

11. Shaun Gallagher, *Hermeneutics and Education,* p. 341.

12. Ibid., pp. 341–42.

13. This argument is also made by Gerald Bruns, *Hermeneutics Ancient and Modern,* p. 226.

14. Gallagher, *Hermeneutics and Education,* p. 342.

15. Stephen Brookfield, *Understanding and Facilitating Adult Learning,* p. 142.

16. Ibid., p. 247.

17. Gallagher, *Hermeneutics and Education,* p. 342.

18. Richard Bernstein, *Beyond Objectivism and Relativism,* p. 54.

19. Elizabeth Kamarck Minnich, *Transforming Knowledge,* p. 166.

20. Caputo, *Radical Hermeneutics,* p. 211.

21. Ibid., p. 211.

22. Ibid., p. 220.

23. Ibid., p. 270.

24. This point is also made by Paul Feyerabend, *Against Method,* pp. 218–19. It is also a key theme in Thomas Kuhn's work *The Structure of Scientific Revolutions.* For commentary on both these authors and their relevant themes, see Richard Bernstein, *Beyond Objectivism and Relativism,* esp. parts 1 and 2.

25. Caputo, *Radical Hermeneutics,* p. 226. See also p. 219.

26. Ibid., p. 213.

27. Bernstein, *Beyond Objectivism and Relativism,* pp. 157–59, 223.

28. This is a key theme in Groome's work *Sharing Faith.* He introduces it in the prologue and in chap. 1.

29. Among others, Groome traces the notion of praxis to Aristotle, who spoke of three kinds of knowing: *theòria* (the speculative life), *praxis* (the practical life), and *poiesis* (the productive life) — all structured with *theoria* in the privileged place, as the first and highest form of knowing. See *Christian Religious Education,* pp. 153–57.

30. Ibid., p. xvii.

31. Lewis Mudge and James Poling, eds., *Formation and Reflection: The Promise of Practical Theology,* p. xxiii.

32. Bernstein, *Beyond Objectivism and Relativism,* p. 229.

33. Caputo, "Hyberbolic Justice: Deconstruction, Myth, and Politics." The following represents my own reading of some of the main ideas presented in Caputo's article.

34. Ibid., p. 5.

35. Ibid., p. 9. The sentiments expressed here are similar to those contained in Gadamer's discussion concerning legal hermeneutics; see *Truth and Method,* pp. 324–30.

36. Ibid., p. 10.
37. This quote from Derrida is cited by Richard Bernstein in *The New Constellation*, p. 222; see also p. 214. See also Mark Taylor's reflections on this theme in *Nots*, pp. 86–94.
38. Caputo, "Hyperbolic Justice," p. 17.
39. Ibid., p. 9.
40. Ibid., pp. 17–18.
41. Bernstein, *The New Constellation*, p. 215.
42. Thomas Groome, *Sharing Faith*, p. 17.
43. Ibid., p. 233.
44. Walter Brueggemann, *Hope within History*, pp. 7–26. The following represents a brief account of Brueggemann's chapter.
45. Ibid., p. 19.
46. Ibid., p. 16.
47. Ibid., p. 17.
48. Ibid., p. 20.
49. Ibid., p. 17.
50. Ibid., p. 15.
51. Caputo, *Radical Hermeneutics*, p. 283.
52. Sharon Welch, *Communities of Resistance and Solidarity*, p. 7.
53. Caputo, *Radical Hermeneutics*, p. 280.
54. See J.-B. Metz, *Faith in History and Society*, esp. pp. 109–15.
55. Caputo, *Radical Hermeneutics*, p. 281. The citation from Metz is quoted by Caputo.
56. Ibid., p. 281.
57. See Luke, 14:21–24.
58. Caputo, "Beyond Aestheticism: Derrida's Responsible Anarchy," pp. 71–72.
59. Caputo, *Radical Hermeneutics*, p. 260.
60. Ibid., p. 263.
61. Brueggemann, *Interpretation and Obedience*, p. 132.
62. Richard Rorty, *Philosophy and the Mirror of Nature*, p. 377.
63. Ibid., p. 360.
64. Georgia Warnke, *Gadamer: Hermeneutics, Tradition and Reason*, pp. 156–57.
65. Ibid., see pp. 160–65.
66. Morny Joy (citing Luce Iragaray), "Sainthood or Heresy," in Morny Joy and Penelope Magee, eds., *Claiming Our Rites*, p. 127.
67. Brueggemann, *The Creative Word: Canon as a Model for Biblical Education*, p. 1. In his article "Identity and Change in Religious Education," Thomas Groome notes, "Christian faith recommends education that informs and forms people in both identity and openness to change" (p. 38). This is also a key theme in Mary Elizabeth Mullino Moore's work *Education for Continuity and Change*.
68. David Jasper, "Art and the Biblical Canon," *Religion, Literature and the Arts* Conference Proceedings, edited by Michael Griffith and Ross Keating (North Sydney: Australian Catholic University, January 1994), p. 51.
69. Brueggemann, *Interpretation and Obedience*, pp. 120–22.
70. Brueggemann, *The Creative Word*, pp. 6–7. This is also a key theme in Michael Rosenak's book *Commandments and Concerns: Jewish Religious Education in Secular Society*. Rosenak argues that the Jewish religious tradition is continually mediating

between the community's normative wisdom (what he calls "explicit religion") and the community's contemporary struggles and questions (what he calls "implicit religion"). He suggests that no religious tradition can be sustainable over time without this ongoing interplay between stability and flexibility, norms and context, trusted answers and provoking questions (see especially part 2 of Rosenak's text). For two other texts that take up the theme of canonical hermeneutics, see James Sanders, *From Sacred Story to Sacred Text;* and Francis Schüssler Fiorenza, "The Crisis of Scriptural Authority."

71. Brueggemann, *The Creative Word*, pp. 8–13. This is my reading of Brueggemann's text, adapting his analysis of the Hebrew canon's threefold structure to my phrases "book of words," "book of questions," and "book of writings." I have also adapted his words *ethos, pathos*, and *logos* with my words *answer, question*, and *experience.*

72. W. Dow Edgerton, *The Passion of Interpretation*, pp. 41–42.

73. This is a key theme in the work of Robert Bellah and team, *Habits of the Heart.* See, for example, pp. 80–81 and 152–155.

74. Bruns, *Hermeneutics Ancient and Modern*, p. 250.

75. Sharon Welch, *A Feminist Ethic of Risk*, p. 137 (citing Iris Young).

76. Brueggemann, *The Creative Word*, p. 20.

77. Ibid., p. 20.

78. Karl Mannheim, *Ideology and Utopia*, p. 31.

79. Bernstein, *Beyond Objectivism and Relativism*, p. 228.

80. Bruns, *Hermeneutics Ancient and Modern*, p. 249.

81. Jocelyn Dunphy-Blomfield, "Suffering," in Morny Joy and Penelope Magee, eds., *Claiming Our Rites*, p. 110.

82. Bruns, *Hermeneutics Ancient and Modern*, p. 250 (citing Cora Diamond).

83. Ibid., pp. 258–59. See also: Hans-Georg Gadamer, *Reason in the Age of Science*, esp. pp. 69–87; Martin Heidegger, "The Question Concerning Technology," in *Basic Writings*, pp. 283–317; Neil Postman, *Technopoly: The Surrender of Culture to Technology.*

84. Dunphy-Blomfield, "Suffering," p. 110.

85. Bernstein, *The New Constellation*, p. 338.

86. Bruns, *Hermeneutics Ancient and Modern*, p. 162.

87. Brueggemann, *The Creative Word*, p. 20.

88. Paul Ricoeur, *The Symbolism of Evil*, p. 349.

89. Sallie McFague, *Models of God*, p. 28 (citing Erich Heller).

90. Bernstein, *Beyond Objectivism and Relativism*, p. 228.

91. See Bernstein's reflections in *The New Constellation*, pp. 51–52, 244–47.

92. Ibid., p. 218.

93. Brueggemann, *The Creative Word*, p. 50.

94. Ibid., p. 41.

95. Caputo, "Three Transgressions: Nietzsche, Heidegger, Derrida," p. 75. See also Derrida's discussion of the prophetic resonances of deconstruction in "Deconstruction and the Other: An Interview with Derrida," in Richard Kearney, ed., *Dialogues with Contemporary Continental Thinkers*, p. 119.

96. Bernstein, *The New Constellation*, see p. 26.

97. David Tracy, *The Analogical Imagination*, p. 416.

98. The phrase "totally imprinted by history" is Michel Foucault's, in *The Foucault Reader*, p. 83.

99. Edgerton, *The Passion of Interpretation*, p. 62.

100. See Derrida's commentary "Edmond Jabès and the Question of the Book," in *Writing and Difference*, esp. pp. 64–67.

101. Edgerton, *The Passion of Interpretation*, p. 62.

102. Ibid., pp. 61–62

103. Brueggemann, *Hope within History*, for this theme see pp. 80–91.

104. Brueggemann, *The Prophetic Imagination*, p. 62.

105. Caputo, "Three Transgressions," p. 74.

106. Bruns, *Hermeneutics Ancient and Modern*, p. 261.

107. Joseph O'Leary, *Questioning Back*, pp. 4–5, 41.

108. Brueggemann, *The Creative Word*, p. 73.

109. See David Tracy's contribution to the *Journal of Feminist Studies in Religion* roundtable discussion led by Francis Schüssler Fiorenza, "The Influence of Feminist Theory in My Theological Work," pp. 122–25. For a similar view, see also Marjorie Hewitt Suchocki, "In Search of Justice: Religious Pluralism from a Feminist Perspective," in John Hick and Paul F. Knitter, eds., *The Myth of Christian Uniqueness*, pp. 154–60.

110. Tracy, *Blessed Rage for Order*, pp. 64–81.

111 Bernstein, *Beyond Objectivism and Relativism*, pp. 16–20.

112. See John Caputo's reflections in *Radical Hermeneutics*, pp. 218, 261, 310 (n. 10).

113. Francis Schüssler Fiorenza, "The Crisis of Hermeneutics and Christian Theology," pp. 137–40.

114. Ibid., p. 140.

115. Francis Schüssler Fiorenza, "Systematic Theology: Tasks and Methods," p. 74.

116. Brueggemann, *The Creative Word*, p. 71.

117. Sharon Welch, *Communities of Resistance and Solidarity*, pp. 78, 91.

118. Caputo, *Radical Hermeneutics*, p. 279.

119. Ibid., p. 280.

120. The metaphor of a "wager" is taken from Paul Ricoeur, *The Symbolism of Evil*, p. 355.

121. Larry E. Axel, "Reshaping The Task of Theology," in William Dean and Larry E. Axel, eds., *The Size of God*, p. 61.

122. Rainer Maria Rilke, *Letters to a Young Poet*, pp. 53, 69, 72.

A COMMENTARY

Margin writing is willing to expend itself in order to save the book from premature closure; replacing sterile stability with creative instability and generous and generative multiplicity. It is writing that is willing to disperse itself so that words can be sown and borne in new contexts and new fields. It is free, gratuitous, grace-filled writing: surrendering itself to the many possible paths of the book into what Taylor calls a "mazing grace."[1]

I am somewhat wary of endings and conclusions, because of both their seeming impossibility and their tendency to finalize and close off. Indeed, this has been a strong theme throughout this book, arguing as it does for a hermeneutical and educational preference toward openness, generativity, questioning, being on the way, and so on. When I came to bring this book to a close, I found myself wrestling for many weeks with the question, What type of ending seems fitting? As I puzzled over this, I found in my desk drawer a folder full of cluttered paper with notes to myself, reflections, reminders, and a host of bits and pieces. I read through them, and it seemed I was reading a commentary on my own text. "Maybe this is the place to end?" I thought. "But all these notes seem too messy, too unfinished." Yet I found this notion appealing and decided, "Well, maybe I can take up my own commentary, and then let it go. Perhaps this is the best way to end — for now."

I have lived with this text for quite a few years, and I am not sure whether I have written it or it has written me. I suspect more the latter — for if this were not the case, I doubt I could have written anything. The same seems true for the many texts I have read and that form the fabric of this text. They have been reading me all along the way, more so than I reading them. I have felt myself part of an intertextual web that is also an experience of participation in something larger than myself. There is no one author or writer of a text, just as there is no one reader or reading of a text. There is just the sense of being caught up in something larger and compelled to bring it up and behold it, then let it go and release it. In the following commentary, my aim is not to present a systematic application of all that has been written up until now. Rather, I want to note some questions and comments that seem relevant to the life of intentional Christian communities from my own reading of the previous chapters.

Hermeneutics, as I mentioned in the introduction, is a word that has become familiar in many disciplines — philosophy, theology, literary theory — to name a few. When I began reading hermeneutical literature, I was both amazed and bewildered at the vast labyrinth of new and exciting worlds opening before me. Yet in all this complexity, I began to feel that I had found a place, almost like a wild and fertile field, in which my own troubling and searching questions could take root and find life again. I was also reminded of a book I had read some years back in my youth, about Joseph Knecht, an academic master who played the game of scholars in a detached, elite school — forgetting the world outside for a life dedicated to aesthetic vision and pristine intellectual pursuits.[2] The world of hermeneutics can easily become a world like this. This is where my interest in small, intentional Christian communities has been important to me. I have been a member of such communities for most of my adult life. Whatever renewed energy and vitality I have found in hermeneutical literature, I believe this literature can also inform the educational life and praxis of intentional Christian communities.

Marginal space is the gap in which hermeneutics begins, and ends. . . . It begins in the recognition that there is a gap between our tradition and our lives. What is a gap, except perhaps a space — a blank space, a space like that of the margin? A blank space represents a lack or an absence, yet it also represents a hunger or a search. It is as much about what is missing and excluded as it is about the hope or vision for what could be, for new possibility. My sense is that intentional communities are living in this gap, this marginal space, along the edges of Christian tradition: a tradition in which they feel themselves both radi-

The metaphor I find helpful for creatively establishing the interpretive position of intentional Christian communities is one that locates them "in the margins of the book." If we think of any book that truly engages us — a book that we read well — we read it in the margins. Here we scribble the response of our lives in the form of commentary and question. The margins represent the place of disclosure, the place where the book becomes itself. It is in the margins that we rewrite the book — interpret it — in such ways that the book continuously becomes itself in ways both similar and different to itself. The margins depict the fine, edged space between the written and the unwritten, the familiar and the strange, the named and yet to be named. Hermeneutical theory enables marginal communities to find and *cally immersed and disturbingly alienated. They live both inside and outside of a religious tradition that both provokes their existence as possibility and haunts their existence as non-possibility. . . .*

The issue before us is how this state of suspension between trust (belonging) and suspicion (nonbelonging) can be redeemed as a creative juncture for hermeneutical engagement. . . . exploring ways in which this marginal space can be reclaimed as a creative, productive, vital site of critical and receptive engagement with a tradition's enriching and distorting effects, and with our own contemporary issues and concerns.

reclaim their place in the margins of tradition. Unless we allow this thin, uneasy space to thrive, many marginal communities will take their questioning edge to other places and leave us all the poorer for the loss of their keen and honest voices in the margins of our text. Part of my interest lies in rescuing the term "marginal" from its negative connotations as "on the outside," "separatist," or "insignificant." The position of marginality is often seen as a negative place of withdrawal or isolation, a place that need not be taken seriously because it lacks significance. However, I believe marginality means "between" rather than "outside of." Too often it is read as a separatist word rather than a joining word, yet it is a word that both joins and separates: inside and outside, belonging and nonbelonging, presence and absence.

The marginal life of intentional Christian communities typically begins among groups of people who experience a profound sense of alienation from current ecclesial practices. Initially, this experience of alienation reaches a critical point where people find that they can no longer participate in the established forms of ecclesial expression, namely, the parish or congregation. In the Catholic tradition, this feeling of frustration and anger is often felt intensely by people who can no longer tolerate the exclusionary practices they see operative in the liturgies, theologies, and decision-making structures of mainstream church life, and in the conservative and reactionary forces emanating from Rome. Intentional communities, as Margaret Hebblethwaite notes, receive their initial impetus among people "wandering an ecclesial desert" in search of an alternative place to gather and to be: "that is why we all come here, all of us are refugees from parishes, because we want something different from the parish. Being not-a-parish gives us more freedom to do new things, not less. . . ."[3] The issues facing intentional communities here are: What pattern of communal life do they want to create? What is required to create and sustain the resources needed to function as a Christian community? How do they maintain their distrust of institution while recognizing that healthy institutional expression is a necessary way for embodying the public concerns of Christian discourse?

The move out of parish and into intentional Christian community is not always a simple and smooth transition. People often bring with them unresolved feelings of negativity toward their religious tradition, directed not simply toward dominant institutional structures but also toward conservative and confessional theologies that provide little room for movement or exploration, that fail to fully resonate with contemporary issues or questions, or to provoke imaginative and challenging futures. The feeling here is one of confinement within a tradition that wants to coerce all new experience into a bland agreement with the past. The central claims of tradition are felt as a dominating and regulating force that disallow any expansive reading or rewriting of tradition. Moreover, some of the distortions present within tradition seem so deep that many people begin to wonder whether there is any hope for a renewed dialogue and reconstruction of the tradition in which they stand. The issues facing intentional Christian communities here are: What does it mean to belong to a religious tradition? How does "the past" function in our lives? In what sense are our lives dependent on an essential work? How do we reengage a vital, vigorous, and productive conversation with tradition? Can we move out of a paralyzing mode of alienation into an open mode of commentary, questioning, and new writing?

In their search to find renewed and meaningful places of religious belonging, many members of intentional Christian communities turn their attention to alternative religious traditions and practices. Some find themselves attracted to the wisdom of the classical Eastern traditions such as Buddhism and Hinduism; others search for deeper connections with earth and ecology through the wisdom of indigenous cultures; others turn to reclamations of pagan and goddess traditions. The issues facing intentional Christian communities here are: How can these encounters with other religious traditions be brought into fruitful conversation with one's own tradition of belonging? How much "size" and expansion is our own tradition capable of? How do we live within our own tradition in deep openness to other traditions without succumbing to a shopping-mall pluralism, or to a faddish, designer religion?

It is not uncommon to encounter members of intentional Christian communities who express little interest in reforming the church and who direct their attention primarily to the need for the transformation of society. Typically, they claim a core truth to the Christian tradition that stands over and above both the church and society as a transformative, prophetic force. Root metaphors such as the "kingdom" or "reign" of God serve as their rallying point to motivate and inspire their communal gatherings and their actions in society. The issues facing intentional Christian communities here are: Can we simply bypass the effective history of a tradition to highlight its liberating effects to the neglect of its deep,

systemic distortions? Conversely, can we focus so much on a tradition's exclusionary practices that we neglect to hear its provoking, transformative, dangerous
claims? Moreover, given the complex social, political, economic and cultural
questions of our day, do we not need spirited, intentional faith communities that
can participate in the larger public conversation by drawing on the generative
wisdom and insights of a vibrant religious tradition?

There are also many members of intentional Christian communities who experience a profound attachment to their tradition of belonging, yet their attachment
is one of loyal opposition. They sense that there is more to the past than meets the
eye — that there are alternate readings, deeper and more radical retrievals, that a
tradition's heretics have as much to say to us as its saints. Not only is there more
to the past, there is also more to the future. Their sense is that tradition is capable
of this "more," that it can exceed present arrangements in very startling and
transformative ways. Their interest lies in exploring alternate theologies that are
not tied to established understandings and mainstream practices. The issues facing intentional Christian communities here are: How much free play is tradition
capable of? What role does nonconformity and deviance play in the life of tradition? In what ways can a transgressing and erring community facilitate a heretical hermeneutic in the service of imaginative exploration and creative
experimentation?

In all of the above scenarios, there is a sense of loss, of absence, of nonbelonging, yet there is also a profound sense of promise, of affirming the possibility of
renewed relations between a people and their tradition, between tradition and the
cries of a broken world, between the past and the present, the present and the future.
Exilic experience claims a priority in the educational life of intentional Christian
communities. It is a profound teacher. Yet it represents a strange type of *educare* — a
strange type of "leading out." Grasped by a disturbing sense of brokenness, alienation,
loss, and a voidlike wandering — led out into this desert — intentional communities
yearn ever more deeply for the book's promise, for a world in which healing, inclusiveness, passion, discovery, and newness can take root again. Marginal experience is
closely bound to exilic experience. It evokes

It seems that for the rabbis, as for their ancient ancestors, inter-pretive activity is closely tied to the experience of absence and loss. As Walter Brueggemann notes, no biblical text existed before the exile of the Israelites; indeed, "the exile itself was an evocative force in generating the text." Perhaps the Jewish inter-pretive tradition represents one of the most striking examples of an exilic hermeneutics, one in which "our unresolved negativi-ties exercise a more powerful and finally decisive influence upon our capacity to receive and imagine than any positive coun-

Relevant today? (margin annotation)

terpart." *It is precisely when we experience things falling apart that we are provoked to generate new texts, new interpretations, new meanings. . . .*

the desire for a new, transformed sense of belonging that comes out of the very experience of exilic nonbelonging. In the margins of the book, intentional communities learn once more the power of trust, of a renewed dialogue and engagement with tradition, yet always with a measure of suspicion. They learn the power of naming themselves and their reality, yet always with a sense of silence and absence; they learn the possibility of freedom and liberation, yet always in the context of limitation and constraint; they learn ways of renewed commitment, yet not without feelings of loss and renunciation; they find fresh inspiration, yet always tied to an unfulfilled yearning; they experience new motivation, yet colored with a tinge of reluctance.

A key educative task for marginal communities is to find ways that can lead them back into a vital and vigorous conversation with tradition. . . . Gadamer's hermeneutics is helpful in suggesting that tradition is not a static entity we consent to; rather, it is a living, dynamic activity we participate in — and through that participation, tradition is constantly "happening," "occurring," "coming to be."

According to Gadamer, "this occurrence means the coming into play, the playing out, of tradition in its constantly widening possibilities of significance and resonance . . . something comes into being that had not existed before and that exists from now on . . . something emerges that is contained in neither of the partners by themselves."

The educative task is to help communities realize that the "way out" — the "exodus" — from alienation to freedom is to enter into a vigorous, honest, and searching conversation with their tradition in both its enriching and distorting effects.

To recognize and claim this tensional space of "the between" as a *generative space* of the margins is a vital educational task for intentional Christian communities. How does a marginal hermeneutic facilitate this task? It provides a "bridge" for linking a community's experience of alienation and nonbelonging with a renewed sense of possibility for creative participation and hermeneutical engagement. By "bridge" I am thinking of all that Gadamer's dialogical hermeneutics teaches intentional communities about the "to-and-fro-ness" of interpretation, about listening and questioning, about trust and risk, about conversation and dialogue. Gadamer brings marginal Christian communities face to face with the tradition of their belonging — the tradition that in many ways has spawned their exilic wandering — and suggests that this is the place to take up the questions, to engage the conversation, to find seeds of freedom, to reclaim the possibility of new, transformative futures. When I have presented the metaphor of

Conversation suggests that what is at stake for the educational life of intentional communities is not a critical distancing from tradition but a critical engagement with tradition. It also suggests a two-way process, a to-and-fro, a dialogue in which neither partner in the conversation assumes dominance and neither can come away from the conversation unchanged.

Gadamer tells us that "only the person who knows how to ask questions is able to persist in their questioning, which involves being able to preserve their orientation toward openness." The same holds true in our conversation with tradition. The wandering question always has priority over the settled answer. Knowing that we do not know is to live within the openness of a question, of the still undetermined possibilities of both the situation and the tradition in which we find ourselves. . . . "To be in the book," Jabès says, is to belong to the "book of questions" — to "evoke the book and provoke the questions."

As Gallagher suggests, "education is not the mere reproduction of tradition any more than it is an escape from tradition. The truth lies somewhere between these two extremes in the notion of a 'transformation' of tradition."

Sharon Welch notes, "it is not easy for Christians to acknowledge the oppression supported and engendered by Christian faith. The ambiguities of discourse that has both oppressive and liberating functions is indeed unsettling." Sometimes we need to write the book

the margins to intentional Christian communities in this fashion — as a vital, productive space of interpretive questioning and conversation — I have perceived a noticeable shift in their understandings of themselves and their understanding of what it means to be "intentional communities of interpretation." They discover a renewed sense of their own productive agency as participants in shaping the life of tradition according to their own particular questions, experiences, and situations. They discover that their voice matters. Their readings of texts and their experimentation with new ritual forms and symbolic expressions are legitimate interpretive practices. They are clearly "in the book," and while others may want to force them "off the page" — suggesting they have taken leave of it — they are able to claim the book's most vital space as their own: the interpretive edge of the margins.

Learning to creatively engage tradition is an important educational movement in the life of marginal Christian communities. However, it by no means dulls their critically suspicious verve. For these communities, the interpretive space of the margins still retains its sharp, dangerous, cutting-edge character. The edge of the book represents the place where we notice most what has not been written, what lies blank and silent, what has been excluded, *"outside the book," from the position of deep suspicion and critique; yet we must nevertheless recognize that it is the book to which we belong that we are rewriting and that we are ultimately responsible for. . . . Welch speaks of these prophetic gatherings as "communities of resistance and solidarity," releasing the voices of subjugated knowledge — all those voices exiled and marginalized by the centers of control and power that systematically dominate, regulate, and exclude.*

In Bernstein's view, deconstruction represents an ethical-political openness to the claim of the other and the different, the rebellious, and the absent. It has the quality of an "exile bearing witness" to all those who have been excluded and banished from the mainstream discourses of Western tradition. . . . "At the heart of what we take to be familiar, native, at home — where we think we can find our center — lurks (is concealed and repressed) what is unfamiliar, strange, uncanny."

Our situation is one of a crisis or passage of history — the passing of a dominant Western Enlightenment culture. . . . We live in the postmodern times of a great dismantling of a world constructed through the privilege of a white, patriarchal, Western, colonial hegemony: "it feels as though we are reaching the end of a historical era, since we find ourselves in the midst of cognitive, historical, political, and religious changes of vast importance, shattering the monolithic character and hegemony of the Western church as a whole."

repressed, unacknowledged. As intentional communities learn ways of entering a renewed dialogue with their tradition, they also need to learn ways of dealing with the distortions and ambiguities of tradition, with those elements that create structures of exclusion and nonbelonging.

I find that intentional Christian communities resonate passionately with this function of marginal hermeneutics. Their readings of texts and situations — and no less — their readings of society, usually contain strong moments of critique and suspicion. They tune in very readily with words of prophets, mystics, artists, poets, dissenters, visionaries. These words seem to name how they see themselves and their vocation as intentional communities. They are positive, creative words that point to the transformative and emancipatory interest of critical suspicion.

Intentional Christian communities characteristically address issues concerning oppression and injustice. Their critical readings lead them into difficult considerations about the function of domination and exclusion and about how established ways of doing things can be challenged — what things might look like if they could be reimagined and done differently. Theories of critical and emancipatory education suggest that interpretive conversation must pass through profound moments of suspi-

These "interruptions" place us in the realm of the postmodern age, an age whose description is still being written. According to Tracy, it is an age that now recognizes the differences between errors that can be corrected, and systematic distortions which are so deep that we cannot help but sense our exilic condition. . . . Retrieval now demands both critique and suspicion. Indeed, retrieval can now often come best through critique and suspicion.

cion, not to impede the conversation, but to develop it in such ways that fuller, more fruitful possibilities may emerge in front of us to shape new, liberative futures. Intentional Christian communities reflect a deep passion toward forging redemptive relations in the church and in society. As *intentional* communities, they have strong purposes that motivate their coming together, particularly their desire to tackle the pressing social issues of our time, to effect a critical transformation of societal and ecclesial structures. They are engaged in what Walter Brueggemann calls the task of funding the postmodern imagination: "to provide the pieces, materials, and resources out of which a new world can be imagined."

Because they are such passionate protesters against "more of the same," mar-

Whereas we are inclined to think of belonging to tradition in terms of its familiarity to us, as that which is always the same, Gadamer suggests that if we truly listen to tradition we will hear it more according to its strange "otherness" than its familiar "sameness."

ginal Christian communities often need to learn that the tradition to which they belong can actually be a surprisingly dangerous conversation partner — "dangerous" in the sense that tradition can be as much a provocative questioner of our habits

and assumptions as we are of its. There are subversive memories in tradition that refuse to be tamed and that jar our complacent worlds, that act against us and our own distorted practices.

Tradition becomes not a refuge of belonging, nor a purely presupposed familiarity, nor something that we can keep under control by making it fit our preconceptions or prevailing viewpoints; rather, it becomes something that refuses the same and impinges as other. As Gadamer says, openness to the otherness of tradition means "allowing tradition's claim. . . that it is has something to say to me. . . that I myself must accept that some things are against me." In this sense, tradition is

Many intentional communities are rediscovering the importance of hearing tradition's claims, of recognizing that this presumably familiar book of belonging is actually quite strange, that its words can wreak havoc on our accustomed habits. Hermeneutics often works against us, such that the familiar is put at risk and is never felt the same way again. Suddenly, we find ourselves drawn into the book's uncanny ability to stun and provoke.

"that which says no to me," and hermeneutics is the "yes" to this "no."

As communities of interpretation, intentional communities have much to learn from the ancient practice of rabbis gathering around an open book. For these sage interpreters, "what matters is that they belong to the Book, and through the Book they belong together. The Book is the world and the world is the Book; to live is to interpret and to interpret is to live. But they can only do it together, not alone."

"If we are to approach a text," writes Derrida, "it must have an edge." On the side of the written appears what is stable, familiar, privileged, reverberating, and enduring. On the side of the unwritten appears what is wandering, strange, excluded, secret, and haunting. Between the two, in the margins, there is "writing": interpretation that listens to the written and the unwritten, interpretation that continually shifts and oscillates in and out of the book, moving between what is and what is not to explore possibilities of what could be.

All that we once took as "home" becomes strange, different, provocatively mysterious again, evocative once more of new, unthought possibilities.

In my experience of belonging to an intentional Christian community, I have always sensed that this represents a time and space that is marked with an essential quality. This is conversation that matters. It is where people are bound together to speak of experiences that count, questions that weigh, issues that matter. The conversation is characterized by stories, commentaries, questions, responses, debates, disputes, digressions, reflections. All this takes place in the open space between text and situation, past and present, present and future, the written and the unwritten. Marginal hermeneutics offers a range of interpretive responses that intentional communities can learn from. For example: (i) We say "yes!" We feel a power of resonance with the text, a disclosive nature. We feel the power of its enduring and reverberating quality. (ii) We say "no!" We sense some distortion or lie in the text that rouses our critical and suspicious attention. (iii) We feel challenged or provoked. The text seems to be saying "no" to our current ways of thinking, perceiving, acting. We are alerted to rethink and reevaluate our position and practices. (iv) We listen to what has not been written, what has been excluded or left unsaid. We give the unwritten a chance to play in the margins of the text, to claim its share of interpretive practice. (v) We write it differently. We scribble our own thoughts and feelings that reflect our contemporary situation. We expand the text, or evoke new text, that says better where we are and what we believe is important. (vi) We note similarities and differences with other texts. We place other texts alongside our own to create an even wider, interactive margin.

Tradition is dependent on those who read it, and every reader is a potential writer. Tradition is always written differently. This is what wounds it so — it resists what it seeks: a book of pure transparency and clarity, a book that is no need of further commentary and questioning. Yet this wound insures its life — a book continually making itself, resisting impossible closures for the sake of its openness to the possible.

Marginal hermeneutics affirms the imaginative, productive, creative process of interpretive writing. It is free, playful, generous, and generative writing. It does not seek sterile stability but rather yearns for movement — to get going, to be underway, to break free, to move in wider and wider circles, to weave and create, enlarge and extend.

Margin writing is scribbling at its best — scribbling that dares to write new commentaries because it knows itself to stand in a long line of descendants who have felt the same interpretive power that issues forth when commentary becomes the very life and breath of a text. The pages of tradition are crowded with interpretive scribblers who have run with the wind in the field as their pens have run with the words of writing. Marginal hermeneutics shifts the role of interpretive communities from that of "consumers" of a text to that of "producers" of the text. This is a performative hermeneutic directed toward the future of the text; it opens it out, sets it going, and "gathers it up as play, activity, production, practice."

Writing in the margins is excessive and indulgent writing that scribbles madly anything and everything that

The margins, which we typically think of as thin, insignificant space, are actually the very space upon which the book's life is dependent. It is in the margins that the book either spills its borders to enlarge and expand itself or shrinks into virtual nonexistence through lack of provocation, questioning, commentary. It is in the margins that the book will become either a book of great size or a book of little measure. The success of the book depends largely on how much its margins are filled with commentary, question, and response; in other words, how much it provokes new interpretive reading and writing among intentional communities of interpretation.

When we think of the argument, commentary, play, and questioning that characterizes marginal hermeneutics, we need not think of them as undermining the book. Rather, they bring a decision to bear; they place the book "underway." As intentional communities grapple and question, listen and respond, they are "taken up" into the book, and out of this grappling something "comes to be" — a world is evoked for them. This revelation, this coming to be, this unconcealment, this world that rises up — this happens because it is grounded or "earthed" in the book's elusive fullness, its earth-like concealment that is the spring or well from which interpretive worlds rise up.[4]

Marginal hermeneutics sinks into the depths of words written and their *wells up and wants to be written. It is "vitally engaged with the living situations of men and women: it is concrete rather than abstract, displays life in all its rich variousness, and rejects barren conceptual enquiry for the feel and taste of what it is to be alive."*

Instead of banishing the poet/prophet/ margin writer, can we linger in their company long enough to allow their words a place along the liminal edges of our texts? If we can, we might realize, as Bruns suggests, that "in its heart of hearts hermeneutics is prophetic rather than nostalgic."

Intentional Christian communities are vibrant communities of interpretation — scribbling in the margins of tradition — enacting hermeneutical practices informed by an interpretive wisdom that represents a dramatic, playful, transformative performance of reading and writing in the margins of the book.

unfathomable source, yet it also sinks into the depths of words left unsaid and their unfathomable yearning. Margin space, far from being narrow and constricting, suddenly becomes large and expanding. One perceives a great movement as this narrow, edged space finds itself taken into expanding, ever-widening spirals of commentary and writing.

There is a "spirituality" that has emerged for me in my reflections on hermeneutics. I am almost inclined to call this spirituality a "textuality" — for it has much to do with the texture of life and the process of "reading" and "writing" — learning that life is lived in large measure by a careful, attentive reading of what is before us, and a tentative, yet hopeful writing of what we must comment on, repair, or celebrate in life.

Notes

1. The texts cited throughout this commentary are taken directly from the previous chapters.

2. Herman Hesse, *The Glass Bead Game.*

3. Margaret Hebblethwaite, *Basic Is Beautiful*, p. 10.

4. For this theme, see Heidegger, "The Origin of the Work of Art," in *Basic Writings*, esp. pp. 167–87. See also "The Nature of Language," in *On the Way to Language*, pp. 57–108.

AFTERWORD

by
Bernard J. Lee

Under Two Hats

When it comes to small Christian communities, I wear two hats. Under whichever of those two hats I regard this book, I am profoundly interested. It is a remarkable work by a new young scholar.

The one hat belongs to me as a long-time member of a small Christian community, without which my own faith would be deprived beyond measure. The other hat has under it a theologian engaged in research on small Christian communities in the U.S. Catholic church, looking for the data, and pondering an adequate ecclesiological understanding of a phenomenon no one saw coming, and whose future no one knows for sure.

Not coincidentally, perhaps, that is the way the Spirit is described in John's Gospel. It is like the wind: you don't know where it comes from and you don't know where it's going. There is an incipient theology of church embedded in Terry Veling's hermeneutical approach to marginal communities. Such an ecclesiology might help chart the windflow of small Christian communities.

Since my word is an afterword, I will share a few reflections that have stayed with me long after my reading of the text, first under the community-member hat, then under the theologian hat.

First the One Hat . . .

If Terry Veling's reflections help us understand that marginal means being on the page, and if we remember that alone, the tour through the difficult terrain with which he deals will have been worthwhile.

If we remember further that in times of great societal change, the margins are often more important than the main text, since futures lurk there, then it will have been doubly worthwhile.

Finally, if these understandings—shall we say "interpretations"—are able to guide and energize the movement of small Christian communities, then church is doubly blessed as well.

Some small Christian communities are nearer to mainline status, such as those—and there are many of them—located within parish life. Their presence is a great blessing to parish life. They often help restructure the parish, for example, those communities that are motivated by the National Alliance of Communities Restructuring the Parish, inspired by the work of Father Art Baranowski of the Detroit Archdiocese. But this is not the way most parishes have functioned or do function. This is a real alternative for a future. These communities and the parishes in which they live also have a marginal character. They speak with a voice that is not like the "standard" parish voice.

There are also some grassroots communities, fewer in number, whose members have religious needs and hungers that they do not find adequately met in parish experience. There are also some grassroots communities whose members are alienated from parish or church. They are not just looking for something more, but for something different. Some remember that the house church was the only way of being church in the early centuries. These are marginal in a different way. They are less tied, and often there is a wider imagination at work in the exploration of churchhood.

With the metaphor of "margins" Terry Veling does a great service to these latter kinds of grassroots communities. In popular usage, marginal often means "flaky," "spacey," or "out in left field," where there is rarely any significant action. What Veling establishes is that marginal life is essential life, and that societies without it atrophy, for futures are often being incubated there in the margins. The margin is, as Veling says, "an area of freedom where an interpretive community is partially released from the burden of prescribed meanings and weighty, dominant reception of a text [for 'text' read 'church']." In times of profound transformation, like our own, when many received meanings are under suspicion, and when many strategic early memories are being retrieved, the grassroots communities are playing seriously with new life. Veling's *Living in the Margins* celebrates the vocation of grassroots imagination, commitment, and energy.

And Then the Other Hat . . .

What excites the "me" that is underneath the theologian's hat is what I perceive to be some incipient ecclesiology. The hermeneutical framework of Veling's work reminds us that when anyone tells a story, her/his social location has a lot of impact on how the story gets told. The official Catholic story has almost exclusively been told by those in positions of power, rarely from history's underside, and more rarely from people who live in the margins. The small Christian communities in Latin America began to tell the Catholic story from the underside and the margins by people who did not belong to the official guild of interpreters. And, not surprisingly, the official guild had problems with the new storytellers. The story sounded a little messy, a little political, in short, a little marginal. But the storytellers keep on telling the story in some new ways that actually have the ring of ancient ways.

The Second Vatican Council has recalled the radical truth that all the people are the People of God, that People of God is another name for Church, and that this entire People of God is anointed by God's Spirit to speak truth. Telling the story from the margins can speak truth no less than telling the story from the places of power. I sometimes hear marginal communities claim their churchhood under the rubric of church with a small "c" rather than Church with a large "C."

The incipient ecclesiology that lurks in Terry Veling's work suggests that a space is needed where the interpretations from above and from below can coexist in mutually critical, mutually caring dialogue. The "space" needs some kind of validation, and maybe even a facilitator or referee. I do not mean this suggestion as a cute remark. Historical consciousness instructs us that pluralism is not a temporary stopping point on the way to agreement (it can also be that, of course), but a normative condition that needs a normative structure to maintain community in the midst of the many voices of the People of God. Small Christian communities are not themselves the needed dialogic space. They are a story-forming space and a story-forming activity. As such, they lay claim to reliable insight into the Catholic story—not all the truth, but some genuine truth. The SCC experience, whether relatively mainstream or decidedly grassroots, calls for a place where its marginal voice need not elbow its way in, but already has membership and a place at the table.

And I think we should keep our eyes on the Veling name. I can't imagine that a fertile, playful mind like that wouldn't have a lot more in store!

BIBLIOGRAPHY: WORKS CITED
AND SOURCES CONSULTED

Alcoff, Linda. "Cultural Feminism Versus Poststructuralism: The Identity Crisis in Femi-nist Theory." *Signs* (Spring 1988): 405–36.

Altizer, Thomas et. al. *Deconstruction and Theology.* New York: Crossroad, 1982.

Aman, Kenneth, ed. *Border Regions of Faith: An Anthology of Religion and Social Change.* Maryknoll, NY: Orbis, 1987.

Arbuckle, Gerald. *Out of Chaos: Refounding Religious Congregations.* New York: Paulist Press, 1988.

————. *Refounding the Church: Dissent for Leadership.* Maryknoll, NY: Orbis, 1993.

Arendt, Hannah. "The Public and the Private Realm." In *The Human Condition,* 22–78. Chicago: University of Chicago Press, 1958.

Atkins, Elaine. "Reframing Curriculum Theory in Terms of Interpretation and Practice: A Hermeneutical Approach." *Curriculum Studies* 20/5 (1988): 437–48.

Banks, Robert. *Paul's Idea of Community: The Early House Churches in Their Historical Setting.* Homebush, Australia: Lancer/Anzea, 1979.

Banks, Robert, and Julia Banks. *The Home Church.* Sutherland, Australia: Albatross Books, 1986.

Baranowski, Arthur. *Creating Small Faith Communities: A Plan for Restructuring the Parish and Renewing Catholic Life.* Cincinnati, OH: St. Anthony Messenger Press, 1988.

Barciauskas, Rosemary Curran, and Debra Beery Hull. *Loving and Working: Reweaving Women's Public and Private Lives.* Bloomington, IN: Meyer Stone Books, 1989.

Barnes, Michael. "Tracy in Dialogue: Mystical Retrieval and Prophetic Suspicion." *The Heythrop Journal* 34/1 (January 1993): 60–65.

Barthes, Roland. *The Pleasure of the Text,* trans. Richard Miller. New York: The Noon-day Press, 1975.

Baynes, Kenneth, James Bohman, and Thomas McCarthy, eds. *After Philosophy: End or Transformation?* Cambridge, MA: MIT Press, 1987.

Becker, Ernest. *The Denial of Death.* New York: The Free Press, 1973.

Belenky, Mary Field, et al. *Women's Ways of Knowing.* New York: Basic Books, 1986.

Bellah, Robert. "Small Face-to-Face Christian Communities in a Mean-Spirited and Polarized Society." *New Oxford Review* (June 1992): 17–22.

Bellah, Robert, et al. *The Good Society*. New York: Alfred A. Knopf, 1991.
_____. *Habits of the Heart*. New York: Harper & Row, 1985.
Benhabib, Seyla, and Drucilla Cornell, eds. *Feminism as Critique*. Minneapolis: University of Minnesota Press, 1987.
Berger, Peter L. *The Heretical Imperative: Contemporary Possibilities of Religious Affirmation*. New York: Anchor Books, 1979.
_____. *The Sacred Canopy: Elements of a Sociological Theory of Religion*. New York: Anchor Books, 1967.
Berger, Peter, and Thomas Luckmann. *The Social Construction of Reality: A Treatise on the Sociology of Knowledge*. New York: Anchor Books, 1966.
Berger, Peter, and Richard Neuhaus. *To Empower People: The Role of Mediating Structures in Public Policy*. Washington, DC: American Enterprise Institute, 1977.
Bernasconi, Robert. "The Ethics of Suspicion." *Research in Phenomenology* 20 (1990): 3–18.
Bernstein, Richard J. *Beyond Objectivism and Relativism: Science, Hermeneutics, and Praxis*. Philadelphia: University of Pennsylvania Press, 1983.
_____. *The New Constellation: The Ethical-Political Horizons Of Modernity/Postmodernity*. Cambridge, MA: MIT Press, 1991.
Bernstein, Richard J., ed. *Habermas and Modernity*. Cambridge, MA: MIT Press, 1985.
Bevans, Stephen B. *Models of Contextual Theology*. Maryknoll, NY: Orbis Books, 1992.
Biale, David. *Gershom Scholem: Kabbalah and Counter-History*. Cambridge, MA: Harvard University Press, 1979.
Bianchi, Robert, and Rosemary Radford Ruether, eds. *A Democratic Catholic Church: The Reconstruction of Roman Catholicism*. New York: Crossroad, 1993.
Bilimoria, Purushottoma. "The Dismantling of 'Radical' Religious Pluralism." *Australian Religion Studies Review* 7/2 (Spring 1994): 69–77.
Birch, Charles. *A Purpose for Everything: Religion in a Postmodern Worldview*. Mystic, CT: Twenty-Third Publications, 1990.
Blake, William. *William Blake*, ed. J. Bronowski. Harmondsworth, Middlesex, England: Penguin Books, 1958.
Blanchot, Maurice. *The Space of Literature*, trans. Ann Smock. Lincoln: University of Nebraska Press, 1982.
Bleicher, Josef. *Contemporary Hermeneutics*. London: Routledge, 1980.
Bloom, Harold, et al. *Deconstruction and Criticism*. New York: Seabury Press, 1979.
Boff, Leonardo. *Ecclesiogenesis: The Base Communities Reinvent the Church*. London: Collins, 1986.
Bonsor, Jack. "Irreducible Pluralism: The Transcendental and Hermeneutical as Theological Options." *Horizons* 16/2 (Fall 1989): 316–45.
Boys, Mary C. *Educating In Faith: Maps & Visions*. New York: Harper & Row, 1989.
_____. "Teaching: The Heart of Religious Education." *Religious Education* 79 (1984): 252–72.
Boys, Mary C, ed. *Education for Citizenship and Discipleship*. New York: Pilgrim Press, 1989.
Braaten, Jane. *Habermas' Critical Theory of Society*. Albany: State University of New York Press, 1991.

Britt, Mary. *In Search of New Wineskins: An Exploration of Models of Christian Community.* Melbourne: Collins Dove, 1988.

Brookfield, Stephen D. *Developing Critical Thinkers: Challenging Adults to Explore Alternate Ways of Thinking and Acting.* San Francisco: Jossey-Bass, 1987.

_____. *The Skillful Teacher.* San Francisco: Jossey-Bass, 1990.

_____. *Understanding and Facilitating Adult Learning.* San Francisco: Jossey-Bass, 1986.

Brueggemann, Walter. *The Creative Word: Canon as a Model for Biblical Education.* Philadelphia: Fortress Press, 1982.

_____. *Hope within History.* Atlanta: John Knox Press, 1987.

_____. *Interpretation and Obedience.* Minneapolis: Fortress Press, 1991.

_____. *The Prophetic Imagination.* Philadelphia: Fortress Press, 1978.

_____. *Texts under Negotiation: The Bible and Postmodern Imagination.* Minneapolis: Fortress Press, 1993.

Bruns, Gerald. *Hermeneutics Ancient and Modern.* New Haven, CT: Yale University Press, 1992.

Buber, Martin. *Eclipse of God.* Atlantic Highlands, NJ: Humanities Press, 1952; 1988.

_____. *I and Thou.* Translated by Ronald Gregor Smith. New York: Scribners/Collier, 1958.

_____. *Tales of the Hasidim.* New York: Schocken Books, 1947.

Bultmann, Rudolf. *New Testament and Mythology,* trans. and ed. Schubert Ogden. Philadelphia: Fortress Press, 1984.

Burton-Christie, Douglas. *The Word in the Desert: Scripture and the Quest for Holiness in Early Christian Monasticism.* New York: Oxford University Press, 1993.

Byrne, Patrick. "*Ressentiment* and the Preferential Option for the Poor." *Theological Studies* 54 (1993): 213–41.

Cady, Linell E. "Resisting the Postmodern Turn: Theology and Contextualization." In *Theology at the End of Modernity,* ed. Sheila Greeve Davaney, 81–98. Philadelphia: Trinity Press International, 1991.

Capps, Donald. *Pastoral Care and Hermeneutics.* Philadelphia: Fortress Press, 1984.

Caputo, John. "Beyond Aestheticism: Derrida's Responsible Anarchy." *Research in Phenomenology* 18 (1988): 59–73.

_____. "Gadamer's Closet Essentialism: A Derridean Critique." In *Dialogue and Deconstruction: The Gadamer-Derrida Encounter,* ed. Diane P. Michelfelder and Richard E. Palmer, 258–64. Albany: State University of New York Press, 1989.

_____. "Hyperbolic Justice: Deconstruction, Myth, and Politics." *Research in Phenomenology* 21 (1991): 3–20.

_____. *Radical Hermeneutics: Repetition, Deconstruction, and the Hermeneutic Project.* Bloomington: Indiana University Press, 1987.

_____. "Three Transgressions: Nietzsche, Heidegger, Derrida." *Research in Phenomenology* 15 (1985): 61–78.

Cargas, Harry James, and Bernard Lee, eds. *Religious Experience and Process Theology.* New York: Paulist Press, 1976.

Carmille, Michael. *Image on the Edge: The Margins of Medieval Art.* London: Reaktion Books, 1992.

Charlesworth, James H., ed. *Jesus' Jewishness: Exploring the Place of Jesus in Early Judaism*. New York: Crossroad, 1991.

Chopp, Rebecca. *The Power to Speak: Feminism, Language, God.* New York: Crossroad, 1989.

Christ, Carol P. *Laughter of Aphrodite: Reflections on a Journey to the Goddess*. San Francisco: Harper & Row, 1987.

Christ, Carol, and Judith Plaskow. *Womanspirit Rising: A Feminist Reader in Religion*. San Francisco: Harper & Row, 1979.

Clooney, Francis X. "Christianity and World Religions: Religion, Reason, and Pluralism." *Religious Studies Review* 15/3 (1989): 197–204.

Code, Lorraine. *What Can She Know? Feminist Theory and the Construction of Knowledge*. Ithaca, NY: Cornell University Press, 1991.

Collins, Paul. *Mixed Blessings: The Crisis in World Catholicism and the Australian Church*. Ringwood, Victoria, Australia: Penguin Books, 1986.

_____. *No Set Agenda: Australia's Catholic Church Faces an Uncertain Future*. Melbourne: David Lovell Publications, 1991.

Conn, Joann Wolski, ed. *Women's Spirituality: Resources for Christian Development*. New York: Paulist Press, 1986.

Cook, Guillermo. *The Expectation of the Poor: Latin American Basic Ecclesial Communities in Protestant Perspective*. Maryknoll, NY: Orbis Books, 1985.

Cook, Michael. "Jesus and the Pharisees — The Problem as It Stands Today." *Journal of Ecumenical Studies* 15/3 (1978): 441–60.

Corbett, Maura, and Diarmuid O'Murchu. "Movement into Small Communities." *Religious Life Review* 29/143 (July/August 1990): 190–95.

Cowan, Michael A. "Conversation with a Text." Unpublished paper, Loyola University Institute for Ministry, New Orleans.

_____. Gathering National Conference. Keynote addresses presented by Michael Cowan, September 1989, Sydney. Sponsored by the Paulian Association, Croydon Park, N.S.W.

_____. "Seeking the Welfare of the City: The Public Life of Small Communities of Faith." *Chicago Studies* 31/2 (1992): 205–14.

_____. "Small Communities and Parish Life in the United States: Possibilities, Tensions, Questions." Unpublished paper, July-September, 1988. School of Theology, St. John's University; School of Divinity, College of St. Thomas, St. Paul, MN.

Cowan, Michael A., ed. *Alternative Futures for Worship:* Volume 6: *Leadership Ministry in Community*. Collegeville, MN: Liturgical Press, 1987.

Coward, Harold, and Toby Foshay, eds. *Derrida and Negative Theology*. Albany: State University of New York Press, 1992.

Craighead, Meinrad. *The Mother's Songs: Images of God the Mother*. New York: Paulist Press, 1986.

Crick, Bernard. *In Defense of Politics*. Chicago: University of Chicago Press, 1962.

Crisp, Jill, et al., eds. *The Church That Meets in the Home*. Conference Notes and Papers, April 1993, Canberra, Australia. Published by Canberra Home Churches, Canberra.

Crossan, John Dominic. *The Historical Jesus: The Life of a Mediterranean Jewish Peasant*. San Francisco: Harper & Row, 1991.

Cully, Iris V., and Kendig Brubaker, eds. *Harper's Encyclopedia of Religious Education.* San Francisco: Harper & Row, 1990.

Cutter, William. "Reading for Ethics — Renouncing Simplicity." *Religious Education* 88/2 (Spring 1993): 212–25.

Dahl, Robert A. *Democracy and Its Critics.* New Haven: Yale University Press, 1989.

Daly, Mary. *Gyn/Ecology: The Metaethics of Radical Feminism.* Boston: Beacon Press, 1978 (2d ed. 1990).

————. *Pure Lust: Elemental Feminist Philosophy.* Boston: Beacon Press, 1984.

Davaney, Sheila Greeve, ed. *Theology at the End of Modernity.* Philadelphia: Trinity Press International, 1991.

Dean, William. *American Religious Empiricism.* Albany: State University of New York Press, 1986.

Dean, William, and Larry E. Axel, eds. *The Size Of God: The Theology of Bernard Loomer in Context.* Macon, GA: Mercer University Press, 1987.

deC. Azevedo, Marcello. *Basic Ecclesial Communities in Brazil.* Washington, DC: Georgetown University Press, 1987.

Derrida, Jacques. *A Derrida Reader: Between the Blinds*, ed. Peggy Kamuf. New York: Columbia University Press, 1991.

————. *Of Grammatology.* Translated by G. Spivak. Baltimore, MD: Johns Hopkins University Press, 1976.

————. "How to Avoid Speaking: Denials," and "Post-Scriptum: Aporias, Ways and Voices." In *Derrida and Negative Theology*, ed. Harold Coward and Toby Foshay. Albany: State University of New York Press, 1992.

————. "The Principle of Reason: The University in the Eyes of Its Pupils." *Diacritics* 13/3 (Fall 1983): 3–20.

————. *Writing and Difference.* Translated by Alan Bass. Chicago: University of Chicago Press, 1978.

Dewey, John. *Experience and Education.* New York: Collier, 1938.

Driver, Tom. *The Magic of Ritual: Our Need for Liberating Rites that Transform Our Lives and Our Communities.* San Francisco: Harper & Row, 1991.

Eagleton, Terry. *Literary Theory: An Introduction.* Minneapolis: University of Minnesota Press, 1983.

Eckardt, A. Roy. *Reclaiming the Jesus of History.* Minneapolis: Fortress Press, 1992.

Edgerton, W. Dow. *The Passion of Interpretation.* Louisville, KY: Westminster/John Knox Press, 1992.

Edwards, Denis. *Called to be Church in Australia.* Slough, England: St. Paul Publications, 1987.

Egan, Harvey. "Christian Apophatic and Kataphatic Mysticisms." *Theological Studies* 39/3 (September 1978): 399–426.

Elbow, Peter. "Methodological Doubting and Believing: Contraries in Inquiry." In *Embracing Contraries: Explorations in Teaching and Learning*, 254–300. New York: Oxford University Press, 1986.

Erickson, Joyce Quiring. "On Being at Home." *Cross Currents* 43/2 (Summer 1993): 235–46.

Falk, Harvey. *Jesus the Pharisee.* New York: Paulist Press, 1985.

Farley, Margaret. "Feminist Ethics in the Christian Education Curriculum." In *Main-*

streaming: Feminist Research for Teaching Religious Studies, ed. Arlene Swidler and Walter Conn, 65–83. Lanham, NY: University Press of America, 1985.

Faur, José. "The Limits of Readerly Collusion in Rabbinic Tradition." *Soundings* 76 (Spring 1993): 153–61.

Feyerabend, Paul. *Against Method: Outline of an Anarchistic Theory of Knowledge.* London: NLB, 1975.

_____. *Farewell to Reason.* London: Verso, 1987.

Fiorenza, Elisabeth Schüssler. *Bread Not Stone: The Challenge of Feminist Biblical Interpretation.* Boston: Beacon Press, 1984.

_____. *But She Said: Feminist Practices of Biblical Interpretation.* Boston: Beacon Press, 1992.

_____. *In Memory of Her: A Feminist Theological Reconstruction of Christian Origins.* New York: Crossroad, 1983.

_____. "Justified by All Her Children: Struggle, Memory, and Vision." *Concilium: On the Threshold of the Third Millennium,* 19–38. London: SCM Press, 1990/1.

Fiorenza, Elisabeth Schüssler, and David Tracy, eds. *Concilium: The Holocaust as Interruption.* Edinburgh: T. & T. Clark, 1984.

Fiorenza, Francis Schüssler. "The Crisis of Hermeneutics and Christian Theology," in *Theology at the End of Modernity,* ed. Sheila Greeve Davaney, 117–40. Philadelphia: Trinity Press International, 1991.

_____. "The Crisis of Scriptural Authority." *Interpretation* 44 (1990): 353–68.

_____. "The Influence of Feminist Theory on My Theological Work" (and other respondents). *Journal of Feminist Studies in Religion* 7/1 (Spring 1991): 95–126.

_____. "Systematic Theology: Tasks and Methods." In *Systematic Theology: Roman Catholic Perspectives,* ed. Francis Schüssler Fiorenza and John P. Galvin, 1–87. Minneapolis: Fortress Press, 1991.

_____. "Theology in the University." The Council of Societies for the Study of Religion, *Bulletin* 22/2 (April 1993): 34–40.

_____. "Theory and Practice: Theological Education as a Reconstructive, Hermeneutical, and Practical Task." *Theological Education* 23 (Supplement 1987): 112–41.

Foucault, Michel. *The Foucault Reader,* ed. Paul Rabinow. New York: Pantheon, 1984.

Fowler, James W. *Becoming Adult Becoming Christian: Adult Development and Christian Faith.* Blackburn, Victoria: Dove Communications, 1984.

Frakenberry, Nancy. *Religion and Radical Empiricism.* Albany: State University of New York Press, 1987.

Frank, Manfred. *What Is Neostructuralism?* Translated by Sabine Wilke and Richard Gray. Minneapolis: University of Minnesota Press, 1989.

Fraser, Ian. "Liberating Faith: Basic Christian Communities and the Eucharist." *Ecumenical Review* 44 (January 1992): 58–64.

_____. *Living a Countersign: From Iona to Basic Christian Communities.* Glasgow: Wild Goose Publications, 1990.

_____. *Reinventing Theology as the People's Work.* Glasgow: Wild Goose Publications, 1988.

_____. "Use the Space." *Open House* (April 1992): 3–4.

Fraser, Ian, and Margaret Fraser. *Wind and Fire: The Spirit Reshapes the Church in Basic*

Christian Communities. Dublane: Scottish Churches House, Basic Communities Resource Centre, 1986.

Freire, Paulo. *Pedagogy of the Oppressed.* Harmondsworth, Middlesex, England: Penguin Books, 1972.

Frost, Robert. *Robert Frost: Selected Poems,* ed. Ian Hamilton. Harmondsworth, Middlesex, England: Penguin Books, 1969.

Gadamer, Hans-Georg. "The Hermeneutics of Suspicion." In *Hermeneutics: Questions and Prospects,* ed. Gary Shapiro and Alan Sica, 54–65. Amherst: University of Massachusetts Press, 1984.

_____. "Letter to Dallmayr." In *Dialogue and Deconstruction,* ed. Diane P. Michelfelder and Richard E. Palmer, 93–101. Albany: State University of New York Press, 1989.

_____. *Philosophical Hermeneutics.* Translated and edited by David E. Linge. Berkeley: University of California Press, 1976.

_____. "The Problem of Historical Consciousness." In *Interpretive Social Science,* ed. Paul Rabinow and William Sullivan, 103–62. Berkeley: University of California Press, 1979.

_____. *Reason in the Age of Science.* Translated by Frederick G. Lawrence. Cambridge, MA: MIT Press, 1981.

_____. "Religious and Poetical Speaking." In *Myth, Symbol and Reality,* ed. Alan M. Olson, 86–98. Notre Dame, IN: Notre Dame University Press, 1980.

_____. "Reply to Jacques Derrida." In *Dialogue and Deconstruction,* ed. D. Michelfelder and R. Palmer, 55–57. Albany: State University of New York Press, 1989.

_____. "Reply to My Critics." In *The Hermeneutic Tradition: From Ast to Ricoeur,* ed. Gayle Ormiston and Alan Schrift, 273–97. Albany: State University of New York Press, 1990.

_____. "Text and Interpretation." In *Dialogue and Deconstruction,* ed. D. Michelfelder and R. Palmer, 21–51. Albany: State University of New York Press, 1989.

_____. *Truth and Method.* Translated by Joel Weinsheimer & Donald Marshall. 2d rev. ed. New York: Crossroad, 1989.

_____. "What Is Truth?" In *Hermeneutics and Truth,* ed. Brice R. Wachterhauser, 33–46. Evanston, IL: Northwestern University Press, 1994.

Gadon, Elinor W. *The Once and Future Goddess.* San Francisco: Harper & Row, 1989.

Gallagher, Shaun. *Hermeneutics and Education.* Albany: State University of New York Press, 1992.

Geertz, Clifford. *The Interpretation of Cultures.* New York: Basic Books, 1973.

Gerhart, Mary, and Allan Russell. *Metaphoric Process: The Creation of Scientific and Religious Understanding.* Fort Worth: Texas Christian University Press, 1984.

Gilligan, Carol. *In a Different Voice: Psychological Theory and Women's Development.* Cambridge, MA: Harvard University Press, 1982.

Gimbutas, Marija. *The Language of the Goddess.* San Francisco: Harper & Row, 1989.

Goldberg, Natalie. *Writing Down the Bones.* Boston: Shambhala, 1986.

Goldenberg, Naomi R. *Changing of the Gods: Feminism and the End of Traditional Religions.* Boston: Beacon Press, 1979.

Gould, Eric, ed. *The Sin of the Book: Edmond Jabès.* Lincoln: University of Nebraska Press, 1985.

Grant, Robert, and David Tracy. *A Short History of the Interpretation of the Bible.* 2d ed. Philadelphia: Fortress Press, 1984.

Griffin, David Ray, ed. *Spirituality and Society: Postmodern Visions.* Albany: State University of New York Press, 1988.

Groome, Thomas H. *Christian Religious Education: Sharing Our Story and Vision.* Melbourne: Dove, 1980.

_____. "Identity and Change in Religious Education." *The Way* 34/1 (January 1994): 36–45.

_____. *Language for a "Catholic" Church.* Kansas City: Sheed & Ward, 1991.

_____. *Sharing Faith: A Comprehensive Approach to Religious Education and Pastoral Ministry: The Way of Shared Praxis.* San Francisco: Harper & Row, 1991.

_____. "Theology on Our Feet: A Revisionist Pedagogy for Healing the Gap Between Academia and Ecclesia." In *Formation and Reflection,* ed. Lewis Mudge and James Poling, 55–78. Philadelphia: Fortress Press, 1987.

Guarino, Thomas. "Between Foundationalism and Nihilism: Is *Phronesis* the *Via Media* for Theology?" *Theological Studies* 54 (1993): 37–54.

Gutiérrez, Gustavo. *A Theology of Liberation: History, Politics and Salvation.* Fifteenth-Anniversary edition. Translated by Caridad Inda and John Eagleson. Maryknoll, NY: Orbis Books, 1988.

Habermas, Jürgen. "The Hermeneutic Claim to Universality." In *The Hermeneutic Tradition: From Ast to Ricoeur,* ed. Gayle Ormiston and Alan Schrift, 245–72. Albany: State University of New York Press, 1990.

_____. *Knowledge and Human Interests.* Translated by Jeremy Shapiro. Boston: Beacon Press, 1971.

_____. "Modernity — An Incomplete Project." In *Postmodernism,* ed. Patricia Waugh, 160–70. London: Edward Arnold, 1992.

_____. "A Review of Gadamer's *Truth and Method.*" In *The Hermeneutic Tradition,* ed. G. Ormiston and A. Schrift, 213–44. Albany, NY: State University of New York Press, 1990.

_____. "Towards a Theory of Communicative Competence." *Inquiry* 13 (1970): 360–75.

Haight, Roger. *Dynamics of Theology.* New York: Paulist Press, 1990.

_____. "The Case for Spirit Christology." *Theological Studies* 53 (1992): 257–85.

Hall, Gerard Vincent. "Raimon Panikkar's Hermeneutics of Religious Pluralism." Ph.D. diss., The Catholic University of America, 1994.

Handelman, Susan. "*Emunah:* The Craft of Faith." *Cross Currents* (Fall 1992): 293–313.

_____. *The Slayers of Moses: The Emergence of Rabbinic Interpretation in Modern Literary Theory.* Albany: State University of New York Press, 1982.

Hanson, Paul. *The People Called: The Growth of Community in the Bible.* New York: Harper & Row, 1986.

Harding, Sandra. *The Science Question in Feminism.* Ithaca, NY: Cornell University Press, 1986.

Harris, Maria. *Fashion Me a People: Curriculum in the Church.* Louisville, KY: Westminster/John Knox Press, 1989.

Harrison, Beverly Wildung. *Making the Connections: Essays in Feminist Social Ethics,* ed. Carol S. Robb. Boston: Beacon Press, 1985.

Hart, Kevin. *The Trespass of the Sign: Deconstruction, Theology and Philosophy.* Cambridge: Cambridge University Press, 1989.

Haughey, John C. "The Eucharist and Intentional Communities." In *Alternative Futures for Worship.* Volume Three: *The Eucharist,* ed. Bernard Lee, 49–84. Collegeville, MN: Liturgical Press, 1987.

Haughton, Rosemary, principle contributor. *A New Heart for a New World.* Sydney: St. Paul Publications, 1986.

_____. *There Is Hope for a Tree.* Sydney: Catholic Commision of Justice and Peace, Occasional Paper no. 4, 1984.

Healey, Joseph. "Today's New Way of Being Church: Pastoral Implications of the Small Christian Communities." *The Catholic World* (July-August, 1991): 185–91.

Hebblethwaite, Margaret. "Base Communities and the Parish." *The Tablet* (a three-part series: 16, 23, 30 April, 1988).

_____. *Basic Is Beautiful: Basic Ecclesial Communities From Third World to First World.* London: Fount, 1993.

Heidegger, Martin. *Basic Writings,* ed. David Farrell Krell. New York: HarperCollins, 1977.

_____. "Language." In *Hermeneutical Enquiry,* ed. D. Klemm, 141–55. Atlanta: Scholars Press, 1986.

_____. *On the Way to Language.* Translated by Peter D. Hertz. San Francisco: Harper, 1971.

Heider, John. *The Tao of Leadership.* Aldershot, Hants., England: Wildwood House, 1985.

Heilman, Samuel C. *The People of the Book.* Chicago: University of Chicago Press, 1983.

Hess, Ernest. "Practical Biblical Interpretation." *Religious Education* 88/2 (Spring 1993): 190–211.

Hesse, Herman. *The Glass Bead Game.* Harmondsworth, Middlesex, England: Penguin Modern Classics.

Heyward, Carter. *Speaking of Christ: A Lesbian Feminist Voice.* New York: Pilgrim Press, 1989.

Hick, John, and Paul Knitter, eds. *The Myth of Christian Uniqueness: Toward a Pluralistic Theology of Religions.* Maryknoll, NY: Orbis Books, 1987.

Hines, Virginia. "Self-generated Ritual: Trend or Fad?" *Worship* 55 (1981): 410–22.

Hodgson, Peter. *Revisioning the Church: Ecclesial Freedom in the New Paradigm.* Minneapolis: Fortress Press, 1988.

Hodgson, Peter, and Robert King, eds. *Christian Theology: An Introduction to Its Traditions and Tasks.* 2d ed. Philadelphia: Fortress Press, 1985.

Holland, Joe, and Peter Henriot. *Social Analysis: Linking Faith and Justice.* Rev. ed. Maryknoll, NY: Orbis Books & Center of Concern, 1983.

Holtz, Barry W, ed. *Back to the Sources: Reading the Classic Jewish Texts.* New York: Simon & Schuster, 1984.

Horsley, Richard, and John Hanson. *Bandits, Prophets and Messiahs: Popular Movements at the Time of Jesus.* San Francisco: Harper & Row, 1985.

Hug, James, ed. *Tracing the Spirit: Communities, Social Action, and Theological Reflection.* New York: Paulist Press, 1983.

Hull, Thomas-Patrick, ed. *Basic Christian Communities: The United States Experiment.* Chicago: National Federation of Priests' Councils, no date.

Huyssen, Andreas. "Mapping the Postmodern." *New German Critique* 33 (Fall 1984): 5–52.

Jabès, Edmond. *From the Book to the Book.* Translated by Rosmarie Waldrop. Hanover: University Press of New England/Wesleyan University Press, 1991.

————. *The Book of Dialogue.* Translated by Rosmarie Waldrop. Middletown, CT: Wesleyan University Press, 1987.

————. *The Book of Margins.* Translated by Rosmarie Waldrop. Chicago: University of Chicago Press, 1993.

————. *The Book of Questions.*

I, II, III. *The Book of Questions: The Book of Questions, The Book of Yukel, Return to the Book.* Published as Volume 1. Translated by Rosmarie Waldrop. Hanover: University Press of New England/ Wesleyan University Press, 1972.

IV, V, VI. *The Book of Questions: Yaël, Elya, Aely.* Volume 2. Translated by Rosmarie Waldrop. Middletown, CT: Wesleyan University Press, 1983.

VII. *El (or the last book).* Translated by Rosmarie Waldrop. Middletown, CT: Wesleyan University Press, 1984.

————. *The Book of Resemblances.* Volume 1. Translated by Rosmarie Waldrop. Hanover: University Press of New England/ Wesleyan University Press, 1990.

————. *The Book of Resemblances: Intimations, The Desert.* Volume 2. Translated by Rosmarie Waldrop. Hanover: University Press of New England/Wesleyan University Press, 1991.

————. *The Book of Resemblances: The Ineffaceable, The Unperceived.* Volume 3. Translated by Rosmarie Waldrop. Hanover: University Press of New England/ Wesleyan University Press, 1991.

————. *The Book of Shares.* Translated by Rosmarie Waldrop. Chicago: University of Chicago Press, 1989.

Jabès, Edmond, with Marcel Cohen. *From the Desert to the Book.* Translated by Pierre Joris. Barrytown: Station Hill, 1990.

Janik, Allan, and Stephen Toulmin. *Wittgenstein's Vienna.* New York: Touchstone/Simon & Schuster, 1973.

Jeanrond, Werner G. *Text and Interpretation: As Categories of Theological Thinking.* New York: Crossroad, 1988.

————. *Theological Hermeneutics: Development and Significance.* New York: Crossroad, 1991.

Jeanrond, Werner G., and Jennifer L. Rike, eds. *Radical Pluralism and Truth: David Tracy and the Hermeneutics of Religion.* New York: Crossroad, 1991.

Johnson, Elizabeth A. *She Who Is: The Mystery of God in Feminist Theological Discourse.* New York: Crossroad, 1992.

Johnson, Luke. *The Writings of the New Testament: An Interpretation.* Philadelphia: Fortress, 1986.

Joy, Morny, and Penelope Magee, eds. *Claiming Our Rites: Studies in Religion by Australian Women Scholars.* Adelaide: The Australian Association for the Study of Religions, 1994.

Junkin, Edward Dixon. "Up from the Grassroots: The Church in Transition." *Interpretation* 3 (July 1992): 271–80.

Kant, Immanuel. "What Is Enlightenment?" In *Critique of Practical Reason.* Translated and edited by Lewis White Beck, 286–92. Chicago: University of Chicago Press, 1949.

Kearney, Richard, ed. *Dialogues with Contemporary Continental Thinkers: The Phenomenological Heritage.* Manchester: Manchester University Press, 1984.

Killian, David. "Developing the Kinds of Small Communities Your Parish or Diocese Needs." *Pace 13* (1982–1983): 1–6.

King, Paul, et al. *Risking Liberation: Middle Class Powerlessness and Social Heroism.* Atlanta: John Knox Press, 1988.

Klenicki, Leon, and Geoffrey Wigoder, eds. *A Dictionary of the Jewish-Christian Dialogue,* New York: Paulist Press, 1984.

Klenicki, Leon, and Gabe Huck, eds. *Spirituality and Prayer: Jewish and Christian Understandings.* New York: Paulist Press, 1983.

Knowles, Malcom. *The Modern Practice of Adult Education.* Rev. ed. New York: Cambridge Book Company, 1980.

Kristeva, Julia. *The Kristeva Reader,* ed. Toril Moi. New York: Columbia University Press, 1986.

Kugel, James, and Rowan Greer. *Early Biblical Interpretation.* Philadelphia: Westminster Press, 1986.

Kuhn, Thomas. *The Structure of Scientific Revolutions.* 2d ed. Chicago: University of Chicago Press, 1970.

Küng, Hans. *On Being a Christian.* Translated by Edward Quinn. London: Collins, 1976.

————. "Dialogability and Steadfastness: On Two Complementary Virtues." In *Radical Pluralism and Truth,* ed. Werner Jeanrond and Jennifer Rike, 237–49. New York: Crossroad, 1991.

LaCugna, Catherine Mowry, ed. *Freeing Theology: The Essentials of Theology in Feminist Perspective.* San Francisco: Harper & Row, 1993.

Lane, Dermot. *Foundations for a Social Theology.* New York: Paulist Press, 1983.

Lash, Nicholas. *Easter in Ordinary: Reflections on Human Experience and the Knowledge of God.* Charlottesville: University Press of Virginia, 1988.

————. "Conversation in Gethsemane." In *Radical Pluralism and Truth,* ed. Werner Jeanrond and Jennifer Rike, 51–61. New York: Crossroad, 1991.

Lawrence, Fred. "The Fragility of Consciousness: Lonergan and the Postmodern Concern for the Other." *Theological Studies,* 54 (1993): 55–94.

Lee, Bernard J. "Christians and Jews in Dialogic Community? A Question to Jacob Neusner." *Journal of Ecumenical Studies,* 28/1 (Winter 1991): 101–8.

————. *The Galilean Jewishness of Jesus: Retrieving the Jewish Origins of Christianity.* New York: Paulist Press/Stimulus Books, 1988.

————. "Intentional Christian Communities in the U.S. Church." *The Catholic World* July/August (1991): 180–84.

————. *Jesus and the Metaphors of God: The Christs of the New Testament.* New York: Paulist Press/Stimulus Books, 1993.

————. "Practical Theology: Its Character and Possible Implications for Higher Education." *Current Issues in Catholic Higher Education,* 14/2 (Winter 1994): 25–36.

_____. "A Socio-Historical Theology of Charism." *Review for Religious* (January-February 1989): 124–35.

_____. "Theological Reflections on Ambiguity." *Communitas* 3 (1988): 27–40.

_____. "The Two Process Theologies." *Theological Studies* 45 (1984): 307–19.

Lee, Bernard J., ed. *Alternative Futures for Worship:* Volume 3: *The Eucharist.* Collegeville, MN: Liturgical Press, 1987.

Lee, Bernard J., and Michael A. Cowan. *Dangerous Memories: House Churches and Our American Story.* Kansas City: Sheed & Ward, 1986.

Leech, Christopher. "Intentional Christian Community and Education." *Journal of Christian Education,* Papers 94 (April 1989): 33–39.

Legrand, Herve-Marie. "The Presidency of the Eucharist According to Ancient Tradition." *Worship* 53/5 (1979): 413–38.

Lerner, Gerder. *The Creation of Patriarchy.* New York: Oxford University Press, 1986.

Leunig, Michael. *Everyday Devils and Angels.* Ringwood, Victoria: Penguin Books Australia, 1992.

Levenson, Jon. "Is There a Counterpart in the Hebrew Bible to New Testament Anti-Semitism?" *Journal of Ecumenical Studies* 22/2 (Spring 1985): 242–60.

Levinas, Emmanuel. *The Levinas Reader,* ed. Sean Hand. Oxford: Blackwell, 1989.

_____. "To Love the Torah More Than God." *Judaism* 28 (1979): 216–23.

_____. *Totality and Infinity.* Translated by Alphonso Lingis. Pittsburgh: Duquesne University Press, 1969.

Lindbeck, George A. *The Nature of Doctrine: Religion and Theology in a Postliberal Age.* Philadelphia: Westminster, 1984.

Lodahl, Michael E. "Christo-Praxis: Foundations for a Post-Holocaust Ethical Christology." *Journal of Ecumenical Studies* 30/2 (Spring 1993): 213–25.

_____. *Shekinah/Spirit: Divine Presence in Jewish and Christian Religion.* New York: Paulist Press, 1992.

Lohfink, Gerhard. *Jesus and Community.* Translated by John Galvin. Philadelphia: Fortress Press, 1984.

Loomer, Bernard. "Process Theology: Origins, Strengths, Weaknesses." *Process Studies* 16/4 (Winter 1987): 245–54.

_____. "Two Kinds of Power." *Criterion* (Winter 1976): 11–29.

_____. "The Size of God." In *The Size of God,* ed. William Dean and Larry E. Axel, 20–51. Macon, GA: Mercer University Press, 1987.

Lovat, Terence J. *What Is This Thing Called Religious Education?* Wentworth Falls, N.S.W.: Social Science Press, 1989.

Lyotard, Jean-François. *The Postmodern Condition: A Report on Knowledge.* Translated by Geoff Bennington and Brian Massumi. Minneapolis: University of Minnesota Press, 1984.

McCarthy, Thomas. *The Critical Theory of Jürgen Habermas.* Cambridge, MA: MIT Press, 1978.

McFague, Sallie. *Metaphorical Theology.* Philadelphia: Fortress Press, 1982.

_____. *Models of God.* Philadelphia: Fortress Press, 1987.

McGovern, Arthur. *Liberation Theology and Its Critics.* Maryknoll, NY: Orbis Books, 1989.

Mackay, Hugh. *Reinventing Australia: The Mind and Mood of Australia in the 90s.* Sydney: Angus and Robertson, 1993.

Macquarrie, John. *Martin Heidegger.* Richmond, VA: John Knox Press, 1968.

Malone, Peter, ed. *Discovering an Australian Theology.* Sydney: St. Paul Publications, 1988.

Mann, Thomas. *The Book of Torah.* Atlanta: John Knox Press, 1988.

Mannheim, Karl. *Ideology and Utopia.* Translated by Louis Wirth and Edward Shils. San Diego: Harvest/HBJ, 1936.

Maranhao, Tullio, ed. *The Interpretation of Dialogue.* Chicago: University of Chicago Press, 1990.

Maréchal, Paul. *Dancing Madly Backwards.* New York: Crossroad, 1982.

Marins, Jose, et al. *Basic Ecclesial Communities: The Church from the Roots.* Quezon City, Philippines: Claretian Publications, 1983.

Markey, John. "Religious Communities' Prophetic Role." *Religious Life Review* 29/143 (July/August 1990): 206–12.

Mason, Michael. "Nurturing Small Faith Communities." Workshop notes from the *Gathering National Conference,* September 1989, Sydney.

Meeks, Wayne. *The First Urban Christians.* New Haven, CT: Yale University Press, 1983.

Meier, John. *A Marginal Jew: Rethinking the Historical Jesus.* New York: Doubleday, 1991.

Meister Eckhart: Teacher and Preacher. In *The Classics of Western Spirituality,* ed. Bernard McGinn. New York: Paulist Press, 1986.

Meland, Bernard. "The Appreciative Consciousness." In *Higher Education and the Human Spirit,* 48–78. Chicago: University of Chicago Press, 1953.

Meskin, Jacob. "In the Flesh: Embodiment and Jewish Existence in the Thought of Emmanuel Levinas." *Soundings* 76 (Spring 1993): 173–90.

Metz, Johann-Baptist, "Facing the Jews: Christian Theology after Auschwitz." In *Concilium: The Holocaust as Interruption,* ed. Elisabeth Schüssler Fiorenza and David Tracy, 26–33. Edinburgh: T. & T. Clark, 1984.

————. *Faith in History and Society.* Translated by D. Smith. New York: Crossroad, 1980.

————. "The 'One World': The Challenge to Western Christianity." In *Radical Pluralism and Truth,* ed. Werner G. Jeanrond and Jennifer L. Rike, 203–14. New York: Crossroad, 1991.

————. "Suffering from God: Theology as Theodicy." *Pacifica* 5 (1992): 274–87.

Michelfelder, Diane P., and Richard E. Palmer, eds. *Dialogue and Deconstruction: The Gadamer-Derrida Encounter.* Albany: State University of New York Press, 1989.

Minnich, Elizabeth Kamarck. *Transforming Knowledge.* Philadelphia: Temple University Press, 1990.

Mollenkott, Virginia Ramey, ed. *Women of Faith in Dialogue.* New York: Crossroad, 1987.

Monette, Maurice. "Basic Christian Communities: Parish with a Difference." *Pace* 10 (1979): 1–5.

Moore, Mary Elizabeth Mullino. *Education for Continuity and Change: A New Model for Christian Religious Education.* Nashville, TN: Abingdon Press, 1983.

_____. *Teaching from the Heart: Theology and Educational Method.* Minneapolis: Fortress Press, 1991.

Moran, Gabriel. *Religious Body: Design for a New Reformation.* New York: Seabury, 1974.

_____. *Uniqueness: Problem or Paradox in Jewish and Christian Traditions.* Maryknoll, NY: Orbis Books, 1992.

Motte, Warren. *Questioning Edmond Jabès.* Lincoln: University of Nebraska Press, 1990.

Mudge, Lewis, and James Poling, eds. *Formation and Reflection: The Promise of Practical Theology.* Philadelphia: Fortress Press, 1987.

Murphy, Frederick. *The Religious World of Jesus: An Introduction to Second Temple Palestinian Judaism.* Nashville, TN: Abingdon Press, 1991.

Nelson, Gertrud Mueller. *To Dance with God: Family Ritual and Community Celebration.* New York: Paulist Press, 1986.

Neusner, Jacob. "Can People Who Believe in Different Religions Talk to Each Other?" *Journal of Ecumenical Studies* 28/1 (Winter 1991): 88–100.

_____. "The Formation of Rabbinic Judaism: Yavneh (Jamnia) from A.D. 70 to 100." *Aufstieg und Niedergang der römischen Welt* 11.19.2.

_____. *Foundations of Judaism.* Philadelphia: Fortress Press, 1989.

_____. *Judaism in the Matrix of Christianity.* Philadelphia: Fortress Press, 1985.

_____. *Torah: From Scroll to Symbolism in Formative Judaism.* Philadelphia: Fortress Press, 1985.

_____. *What Is Midrash?* Philadelphia: Fortress Press, 1987.

Nicholson, Carol. "Postmodernism, Feminism, and Education: The Need for Solidarity." *Educational Theory* 39/3 (Summer 1989): 197–205.

Nietzsche, Friedrich. *Basic Writings of Nietzsche.* Translated by Walter Kaufmann. New York: Random House, 1968.

_____. "Interpretation." In *Transforming the Hermeneutic Context,* ed. Gayle L. Ormiston and Alan D. Schrift, 43–57. Albany: State University of New York Press, 1990.

_____. *On the Genealogy of Morals* and *Ecce Homo.* Translated and edited by Walter Kaufmann. New York: Vintage Books/Random House, 1967.

Nisbet, Robert. *The Quest for Community: A Study in the Ethics of Order and Freedom.* San Francisco: ICS Press, 1990 (first published by Oxford University Press, 1953).

Norris, Christopher. *Deconstruction: Theory and Practice.* Rev. ed. London: Routledge, 1991.

Ochs, Peter. "Borowitz and the Postmodern Renewal of Theology." *Cross Currents* 43/2 (Summer 1993): 164–83.

_____. "Compassionate Postmodernism: An Introduction to Rabbinic Semiotics." *Soundings* 76 (Spring 1993): 139–52.

O'Halloran, James. *Signs of Hope: Developing Small Christian Communities.* Maryknoll, NY: Orbis Books, 1991.

O'Leary, Joseph S. *Questioning Back: The Overcoming of Metaphysics in Christian Tradition.* Minneapolis: Winston Press, 1985.

O'Murchu, Diarmuid. *Sharing the Vision: A Report on the Christian Community Movement in the United Kingdom.* Birmingham: The National Centre for Christian Communities and Networks, 1987.

Ong, Walter. *Orality and Literacy: The Technologizing of the Word.* London: Routledge, 1982.

Ormiston, Gayle L., and Alan D. Schrift, eds. *The Hermeneutic Tradition: From Ast to Ricoeur.* Albany: State University of New York Press, 1990.

_____, eds. *Transforming the Hermeneutic Context: From Nietzsche to Nancy.* Albany: State University of New York Press, 1990.

Overman, J. Andrew. *Matthew's Gospel and Formative Judaism.* Minneapolis: Fortress Press, 1990.

Pagels, Elaine. *The Gnostic Gospels.* New York: Vintage Books, 1979.

Palmer, Parker. *The Company of Strangers: Christians and the Renewal of America's Public Life.* New York: Crossroad, 1981.

_____. *To Know as We Are Known: Education as a Spiritual Journey.* San Francisco: Harper, 1983.

Palmer, Richard E. *Hermeneutics: Interpretation Theory in Schleiermacher, Dilthey, Heidegger, and Gadamer.* Evanston, IL: Northwestern University Press, 1969.

Pawlikowski, John. *What Are They Saying about Christian-Jewish Relations?* New York: Paulist Press, 1980.

Plaskow, Judith. *Standing Again at Sinai: Judaism from a Feminist Perspective.* San Francisco: Harper & Row, 1990.

Plaskow, Judith, and Carol Christ, eds. *Weaving the Visions: New Patterns in Feminist Spirituality.* San Francisco: Harper & Row, 1989.

Plato. *The Dialogues of Plato.* New York: Bantam Books, 1986.

Poovey, Mary. "Feminism and Deconstruction." *Feminist Studies* 14/1 (Spring 1988): 51–65.

Pope, Stephen. "Proper and Improper Partiality and the Preferential Option for the Poor." *Theological Studies* 54 (1993): 242–71.

Postman, Neil. *Technopoly: The Surrender of Culture to Technology.* New York: Vintage Books/Random House, 1992.

Power, David. "Households of Faith in the Coming Church." *Worship* 57/3 (1983): 237–55.

Prior, David. *The Church in the Home.* Basingstoke, England: Marshalls, 1983.

Rabinow, Paul, and William Sullivan, eds. *Interpretive Social Science.* Berkeley: University of California Press, 1979.

Rahner, Karl. "Church from the Roots." In *The Shape of the Church to Come.* New York: Seabury, 1974.

Randall, John Herman. "On the Importance of Being Unprincipled." *The American Scholar* 7/2 (Spring 1938): 1–11.

Reagan, Charles, and David Stewart, eds. *The Philosophy of Paul Ricoeur: An Anthology of His Work.* Boston: Beacon Press, 1978.

Rice, Philip, and Patricia Waugh, eds. *Modern Literary Theory.* 2d ed. London: Edward Arnold, 1992.

Ricoeur, Paul. *Essays on Biblical Interpretation,* ed. Lewis Mudge. Philadelphia: Fortress Press, 1980.

_____. *Freud and Philosophy: An Essay on Interpretation.* New Haven, CT: Yale University Press, 1970.

232 *Living in the Margins*

_____. *Hermeneutics and the Human Sciences*. Translated and edited by John B. Thompson. Cambridge: Cambridge University Press, 1981.

_____. *Interpretation Theory: Discourse and the Surplus of Meaning*. Fort Worth: Texas Christian University Press,1976.

_____. "Love and Justice." In *Radical Pluralism and Truth*, ed. Werner Jeanrond and Jennifer Rike, 187–202. New York: Crossroad, 1991.

_____. "The Metaphorical Process as Cognition, Imagination, and Feeling." *Critical Inquiry* 5 (Autumn 1978): 143–59.

_____. "The Model of the Text: Meaningful Action Considered as a Text." In *Interpretive Social Science*, ed. Paul Rabinow and William Sullivan, 73–102. Berkeley: University of California Press, 1979.

_____. *The Symbolism of Evil*. Translated by Emerson Buchanan. Boston: Beacon Press, 1967.

Rilke, Rainer Maria. *Letters to a Young Poet*. Translated by M. D. Herter Norton. New York: W. W. Norton, 1934.

_____. *Selected Poems of Rainer Maria Rilke*. Translated and edited by Robert Bly. New York: Harper & Row Perennial Library, 1981.

Rodin, Samuel. "Midrash, Morality and Social Inquiry." In *Encounters with Judaism: Jewish Studies in a Non-Jewish World*, 88–107. Hamilton, N.Z.: Waikato University and Colcom Press, 1991.

Rorty, Richard. "Derrida on Language, Being, and Abnormal Philosophy." *Journal of Philosophy* 74 (1977): 673–81.

_____. *Philosophy and the Mirror of Nature*. Princeton, NJ: Princeton University Press, 1979.

Rosenak, Michael. *Commandments and Concerns: Jewish Religious Education in Secular Society*. Philadelphia: Jewish Publication Society, 1987.

Rudolf, Anthony. "A Translator's Tribute" (to Edmond Jabès). *The Jewish Quarterly* 38/2 (Summer 1991): 41–43.

Ruether, Rosemary Radford. *Gaia and God: An Ecofeminist Theology of Earth Healing*. San Francisco: Harper & Row, 1992.

_____. *Sexism and God-Talk: Toward a Feminist Theology*. Boston: Beacon Press, 1983.

_____. *Womanguides: Readings Toward a Feminist Theology*. Boston: Beacon Press, 1985.

_____. *Women-Church: Theology and Practice*. San Francisco: Harper & Row, 1986.

Rush, Ormond. "Reception Hermeneutics and the 'Development' of Doctrine: An Alternative Model." *Pacifica* 6 (June 1993): 125–40.

Russell, Anthony J. "Theology in Context and 'The Right to Think' in Three Contemporary Theologians: Gutiérrez, Dussel, and Boff." *Pacifica* 2/3 (October 1989): 282–322.

Saldarini, Anthony. "The Gospel of Matthew and Jewish-Christian Conflict." In *Social History of the Matthean Community: Cross-Disciplinary Approaches to an Open Question*, 36–59. Minneapolis: Fortress Press, 1991.

_____. "Judaism and the New Testament." In *The New Testament and Its Modern Interpreters*, ed. Eldon Epp and George MacRae, 27–53. Atlanta: Scholars Press, 1989.

————. "Rabbinic Literature and the N.T." *Anchor Bible Dictionary.* Vol. 5, pp. 602–4. New York: Macmillan, 1992.

————. "Reconstructions of Rabbinic Judaism." In *Early Judaism and Its Modern Interpreters,* ed. Robert A. Kraft and George W. E. Nickelsburg, 437–77. Atlanta: Scholars Press, 1986.

Sanders, E. P. *Jesus and Judaism.* Philadelphia: Fortress Press, 1985.

Sanders, James A. "First Testament and Second." *Biblical Theology Bulletin* 17/2 (April 1987): 47–49.

————. *From Sacred Story to Sacred Text.* Philadelphia: Fortress Press, 1987.

Sanks, T. Howland. "David Tracy's Theological Project: An Overview and Some Implications." *Theological Studies* 54 (1993): 698–727.

Schaffran, Janet, and Pat Kozak. *More Than Words: Prayer and Ritual for Inclusive Communities.* Rev. ed. Oak Park, IL: Meyer Stone Books, 1988.

Schillebeeckx, Edward. *Church: The Human Story of God.* Translated by John Bowden. New York: Crossroad, 1990.

————. *The Church with a Human Face.* Translated by John Bowden. London: SCM Press, 1985.

————. *God Is New Each Moment.* In conversation with Huub Oosterhuis and Piet Hoogeveen. Translated by David Smith. New York: Seabury Press, 1983.

————. *Jesus: An Experiment in Christology.* Translated by Hubert Hoskins. New York: Crossroad, 1979.

————. *Jesus in Our Western Culture: Mysticism, Ethics and Politics.* Translated by John Bowden. London: SCM Press, 1987.

————. *The Schillebeeckx Reader,* ed. Robert Schreiter. New York: Crossroad, 1987.

Schillebeeckx, Edward, and Johann-Baptist Metz, eds. *Concilium: The Right of the Community to a Priest.* New York: Seabury Press, 1980.

Schneiders, Sandra M. *The Revelatory Text: Interpreting the New Testament as Sacred Scripture.* San Francisco: Harper & Row, 1991.

Schoenherr, Richard. "Power and Authority in Organized Religion: Disaggregating the Phenomenological Core." *Sociological Analysis* 47 (1987): 52–71.

Scholem, Gershom. *Kabbalah.* New York: Dorset Press, 1974.

————. "Tradition and Commentary as Religious Categories in Judaism." *Judaism* 15 (Winter 1966): 23–39.

Schreiter, Robert. *Constructing Local Theologies.* Maryknoll, NY: Orbis Books, 1985.

Scott, Charles. "Beginning with Belonging and Nonbelonging in Derrida's Thought: A Therapeutic Reflection." *Soundings* 74 (Fall/Winter, 1991): 399–409.

Scott, Joan. "Deconstructing Equality-versus-Difference: Or, The Uses of Poststructuralist Theory for Feminism" *Feminist Studies* 14/1 (Spring 1988): 33–50.

Scott, Kieran. "Three Traditions of Religious Education." *Religious Education* 79 (Summer 1984): 323–39.

Scott, Nathan A. "Hermeneutics and the Question of the Self." In *Radical Pluralism and Truth,* ed. Werner Jeanrond and Jennifer Rike, 81–94. New York: Crossroad, 1991.

Segal, Alan F. *Rebecca's Children: Judaism and Christianity in the Roman World.* Cambridge, MA: Harvard University Press, 1986.

Sells, Michael A. *Mystical Languages of Unsaying.* Chicago: University of Chicago Press, 1994.

Seltzer, Robert M. *Jewish People, Jewish Thought: The Jewish Experience in History.* New York: Macmillan Publishing Co., 1980.

Seymour, Jack, et al. *Contemporary Approaches to Christian Education.* Nashville, TN: Abingdon Press, 1982.

Shanks, Herschel, ed. *Christianity and Rabbinic Judaism: A Parallel History of Their Development.* Washington, DC: Biblical Archaeology Society, 1992.

Shea, John. *Stories of Faith.* Chicago: Thomas More Press, 1980.

Shor, Ira, and Paulo Freire. *A Pedagogy for Liberation: Dialogues on Transforming Education.* New York: Bergin & Garvey, 1987.

Silverman, Hugh, ed. *Gadamer and Hermeneutics.* New York: Routledge, 1991.

Skinner, Quentin, ed. *The Return of Grand Theory in the Human Sciences.* Cambridge: Cambridge University Press, 1985.

Smith, Christopher. "The Ethical Dimensions of Gadamer's Hermeneutical Theory." *Research in Phenomenology* 18 (1988): 75–91.

Smith, Dennis, and Hal Taussig. *Many Tables: The Eucharist in the New Testament and Liturgy Today.* London: SCM Press, 1990.

Starhawk. *The Spiral Dance: A Rebirth of the Ancient Religion of the Great Goddess.* 10th Anniversary Edition. San Francisco: Harper & Row, 1979/1989.

Stephens, Mitchell. "Jacques Derrida." *The New York Times Magazine,* January 23, 1994, 22–25.

Stern, David. "Midrash and Indeterminacy." *Critical Inquiry* 15/3 (Autumn, 1988): 132–61.

Stewart, John. "Interpretive Listening: An Alternative to Empathy." *Communication Education* 32 (October 1983): 379–91.

_____. "Martin Buber's Central Insight: Implications for His Philosophy of Dialogue." In *Dialogue,* ed. Marcelo Dascal, 325–39. Amsterdam: John Benjamins, 1985.

_____. "A Postmodern Look at Traditional Communication Postulates." *Western Journal of Speech and Communication* 55 (Fall 1991): 354–79.

_____. "Speech and Human Being: A Complement to Semiotics." *Quarterly Journal of Speech* 72 (1986): 55–73.

Stewart, John, and Milt Thomas. "Dialogic Listening: Sculpting Mutual Meanings." In *Bridges Not Walls,* ed. John Stewart, 192–210. 5th ed. New York: McGraw-Hill, 1990.

Stone, Merlin. *When God Was a Woman.* New York: Dorset Press, 1976.

Strauss, Jennifer. *Boundary Conditions: The Poetry of Gwen Harwood.* Queensland: University of Queensland Press, 1992.

Sweetser, Thomas. "The Parish of the Future: Beyond the Programs." *America* (March 10, 1990): 238–40.

Sweetser, Thomas, and Patricia Forster. "A Festschrift on Small Faith Communities." *Chicago Studies* 31/2 (1992): 173–81.

Swidler, Leonard. *After the Absolute: The Dialogical Future of Religious Reflection.* Minneapolis: Fortress Press, 1990.

_____. *Yeshua: Model for Moderns.* Kansas City: Sheed & Ward, 1988.

Swidler, Leonard, et al. *Bursting the Bonds? A Jewish-Christian Dialogue on Jesus and Paul.* Maryknoll, NY: Orbis Books, 1990.

Taylor, Mark C. *Erring: A Postmodern A/theology.* Chicago: University of Chicago Press, 1984.

_____. *Nots.* Chicago: University of Chicago Press, 1993.

_____. "Text as Victim." In *Deconstruction and Theology,* ed. Thomas J. J. Altizer et al., 58–78. New York: Crossroad, 1982.

Theissen, Gerd. *The Shadow of the Galilean.* Philadelphia: Fortress Press, 1986.

Thiselton, Anthony. *The Two Horizons: New Testament Hermeneutics and Philosophical Description.* Grand Rapids, MI: William B. Eerdmans, 1980.

Thoma, Clemens, and Michael Wyschogrod, eds. *Understanding Scripture: Explorations of Jewish and Christian Traditions of Interpretation.* New York: Paulist Press/Stimulus Books, 1987.

Thompson, William. *The Jesus Debate.* New York: Paulist Press, 1985.

Thornhill, John. *Making Australia: Exploring Our National Conversation.* Sydney: Millennium Books, 1992.

Tracy, David. *The Analogical Imagination: Christian Theology and the Culture of Pluralism.* New York: Crossroad, 1981.

_____. *Blessed Rage for Order: The New Pluralism in Theology.* San Francisco: Harper & Row, 1988 (originally published by Seabury Press, 1975).

_____. "On Naming the Present." *Concilium: On the Threshold of the Third Millennium,* 66–85. London: SCM Press, 1990/1.

_____. *Plurality and Ambiguity: Hermeneutics, Religion, Hope.* San Francisco: Harper & Row, 1987.

_____. "Practical Theology in the Situation of Global Pluralism." In *Formation and Reflection,* ed. Lewis Mudge and James Poling, 139–54. Philadelphia: Fortress Press, 1987.

_____. "Theological Method." In *Christian Theology: An Introduction to Its Traditions and Tasks,* ed. Peter Hodgson and Robert King, 35–60. Philadelphia: Fortress Press, 1985.

_____. "The Uneasy Alliance Reconceived: Catholic Theological Method, Modernity, and Postmodernity." *Theological Studies* 50 (1989): 548–70.

Trepp, Leo. *Judaism: Development and Life.* Belmont, CA: Wadsworth Publications, 1982.

Turner, Victor. *The Ritual Process: Structure and Anti-Structure.* Ithaca, NY: Cornell University Press, 1969.

van Beeck, Frans Jozef. *Loving the Torah More than God?* Chicago: Loyola University Press, 1989.

van Buren, Paul. *A Theology of the Jewish-Christian Reality. Part Three: Christ in Context.* San Francisco: Harper & Row, 1988.

Vanier, Jean. *Community and Growth.* Slough, England: St. Paul Publications,1979.

Vermes, Geza. *The Dead Sea Scrolls in English.* London: Penguin Books, 1962/1987.

_____. *Jesus the Jew.* Philadelphia: Fortress Press, 1973.

_____. *Jesus and the World of Judaism.* Philadelphia: Fortress Press, 1983.

_____. "Jewish Studies and New Testament Interpretation." *Journal of Jewish Studies* 31 (1980): 1–17.

Veverka, Fayette B. "Re-imagining Catholic Identity: Toward an Analogical Paradigm of Religious Education." *Religious Education* 88/2 (Spring 1993): 238–54.

Visotzky, Burton. *Reading the Book.* New York: Anchor/Doubleday, 1991.

Vogel, Linda Jane. *Teaching and Learning in Communities of Faith: Empowering Adults Through Religious Education.* San Francisco: Jossey-Bass, 1991.

Vogelsang, John D. "A Hermeneutics of Reconstruction." *Religious Education* 88/2 (Spring 1993): 167–77.

Wachterhauser, Brice R., ed. *Hermeneutics and Truth.* Evanston, IL: Northwestern University Press, 1994.

Warnke, Georgia. *Gadamer: Hermeneutics, Tradition and Reason.* Stanford, CA: Stanford University Press, 1987.

Waugh, Patricia. "Stalemates?: Feminists, Postmodernists and Unfinished Issues in Modern Aesthetics." In *Postmodernism,* ed. Patricia Waugh, 341–60. London: Edward Arnold, 1992.

Waugh, Patricia, ed. *Postmodernism.* London: Edward Arnold, 1992.

Weber, Max. *The Sociology of Religion,* trans. Ephraim Fischoff. Boston: Beacon Press, 1963.

Weinsheimer, Joel. *Gadamer's Hermeneutics: A Reading of Truth and Method.* New Haven, CT: Yale University Press, 1985.

Welch, Sharon D. *Communities of Resistance and Solidarity.* Maryknoll, NY: Orbis Books, 1985.

_____. *A Feminist Ethic of Risk.* Minneapolis: Fortress Press, 1990.

Wells, Harry L. "Taking Pluralism Seriously: The Role of Metaphorical Theology Within Interreligious Dialogue." *Journal of Ecumenical Studies* 30/1 (Winter 1993): 20–33.

Westerhoff, John. *Living the Faith Community.* Minneapolis: Winston Press, 1985.

Whitehead, Alfred North. *Adventures of Ideas.* New York: Free Press, 1933.

_____. *Process and Reality.* Corrected edition edited by David Ray Griffin and Donald W. Sherburne. New York: Free Press, 1978.

_____. *Science and the Modern World.* New York: Free Press, 1925.

Whitehead, James D., and Evelyn E. Whitehead. *Community of Faith.* New York: Seabury Press, 1982. (New edition: *Community of Faith: Crafting Christian Communities.* Mystic, CT: Twenty-Third Publications, 1992).

_____. *The Emerging Laity: Returning Leadership to the Community of Faith.* New York: Doubleday/Image, 1986.

_____. *The Promise of Partnership: Leadership and Ministry in an Adult Church.* San Francisco: Harper & Row, 1991.

Wieman, Henry Nelson. "Creative Good." In *The Source of Human Good,* 54–83. Southern Illinois University Press, 1946.

Wiesel, Elie. *Night.* New York: Bantam Books, 1960.

Wilder, Amos. "Story and Story-World." *Interpretation* 37 (1983): 353–64.

Winquist, Charles E. *Desiring Theology.* Chicago: University of Chicago Press, 1995.

Wood, David, ed. *Derrida: A Critical Reader.* Oxford: Blackwell, 1992.

Woodward, Evelyn. "Uses of Power in Community." *Human Development* 4/2 (Summer 1983): 24–32.

Wyschogrod, Edith. *Saints and Postmodernism.* Chicago: University of Chicago Press, 1990.

_____. "Trends in Postmodern Jewish Philosophy." *Soundings* 76 (Spring 1993): 129–37.

Yeats, William Butler. *Yeats: Selected Poetry*, ed. A. Norman Jeffares. London: Pan Books, 1962.

Yob, Iris M. "Teaching in the Language of Religion." *Religious Education* 88/2 (Spring 1993): 226–37.

Yoder, John Howard. *The Politics of Jesus*. Grand Rapids, MI: William B. Eerdmans, 1972.

Young, Iris Marion. "The Ideal of Community and the Politics of Difference." *Social Theory and Practice* 12/1 (Spring 1986): 1–26.

——————. "Impartiality and the Civic Public: Some Implications of Feminist Critiques of Moral and Political Theory." In *Feminism and Critique*, ed. Seyla Benhabib and Drucilla Cornel, 56–95. Minneapolis: University of Minnesota Press, 1987.

Zohar: The Book of Enlightenment. Translated and introduced by Daniel Chanan Matt. Mahwah, NJ: Paulist Press, 1983.

INDEX

alienation, 121, 203
androcentric bias, 106
application, 37
Aristotle, 179
Augustine, 156
authorial intent, 33, 46n. 42, 67–68
authority
  and reason, 29
  rejection of, 11–12

Banks, Robert, 6
base communities, 7
belief, 53
Bellah, Robert, 14, 120, 125
Bernstein, Richard, 82–83, 84, 87, 91, 93
biblical tradition, 108–9
Boff, Leonardo, 12, 13, 119–20
bottom-up approach, 6–7, 11–12
broken book, 79–80
Brookfield, Stephen, 66, 117–19, 124, 179–80
Brueggemann, Walter
  analysis of canon, 187–88
  and funding the postmodern imagination, 103
  on the Enlightenment, 29–30
  on the exodus, 184–85
  on Jewish exile, 150
  on margin and center, 10
  on margin writing, 145
Bruns, Gerald
  hermeneutical question of, 28

and margin writing, 140
on rabbinic interpretation, 160
on Torah, 147
on tradition, 32, 40, 41
Buber, Martin, 67
Bultmann, Rudolf, 33

canon, 187
canonical hermeneutics, 188
Caputo, John
  on community, 123–24
  on deconstruction, 90, 91, 104
  on law and justice, 182–83
  on *phronesis*, 178–79
  on reason, 180–81
  on Western metaphysics, 89–90
Cartesianism, 29–30
charism and renewal, 12
Chopp, Rebecca, 10, 11
Christianity
  birth of, 151
  central hermeneutical distinction of, 156
  relationship to Judaism, 90, 151–52
  tendency of, to solidify, 167
  view of Judaism, 156–57
Christian Reformists, 17
church, 22n. 18
classics, 57–58, 71n. 34, 72n. 38, 80
commanding presence, 95
communal meaning, 65–66

false consensus, 81, 191
feminism
  ethics of, 110, 113, 114
  hermeneutics of, 107–8
  and postmodernism, 116–17
  theologies of, 105
  value of community in, 113
feminist Judaism, 106
Feyerabend, Paul, 116
Fiorenza, Elisabeth Schüssler
  on evaluation of tradition, 107
  hermeneutical principles of, 127n. 25
  on patriarchy, 105
  on women's history, 106
Fiorenza, Francis Schüssler, 91, 194–95
Foucault, Michel, 96n. 14
Frankfurt school, 96n. 7
Freire, Paulo, 119
Freud, Sigmund, 80
fusion of horizons, 37–38

Gadamer, Hans-Georg
  dialogical hermeneutics of, 36–39, 189
  and domination, 85–86
  and effective-historical consciousness, 45n. 25
  on experience, 41–42
  false consensus in, 81–82
  hermeneutical circle of, 34–35
  and hermeneutical experience, 47n. 85
  on language, 39, 47n. 74
  on listening, 40
  on the other, 92
  on prejudices, 31, 34, 45n. 28
  on questioning, 42–43, 54, 144
  on romanticism, 33
  and self-criticism, 85
  on tradition, 27–28, 35, 39–41
  on understanding, 47n. 62
Gallagher, Shaun, 51, 53–54, 55–56, 179
game playing, 59
God
  absence of, 164–65, 176n. 170
  and creation, 165
  naming, 137
  self-exile of, 165
  and suffering, 185

Greek views
  on political theory, 131n. 114
  of words, 156
Groome, Thomas, 63–64, 181–82
Gutiérrez, Gustavo, 102

Habermas, Jürgen
  communicative competence theory of, 84
  and critical reason, 117
  critique of Gadamer, 79, 80
  on distortion, 80, 83
  and the Enlightenment, 82–83
  and false consensus, 191
Handelman, Susan, 70n. 6, 152, 153, 155–57, 158, 163
Harding, Sandra, 65
Haughton, Rosemary, 22n. 18
haunted interpretation, 138
Heidegger, Martin
  on belonging, 40
  critique of Cartesianism, 30
  on fore-structures, 30–31
Heilman, Samuel, 147
hermeneutical circle, 34–35
hermeneutical engagement
  approaches for, 62–64
  of tradition, 61
hermeneutics
  a central concern, 15–16, 32
  concerns of, 27–28
  as dialogue, 35–36, 37
  and marginal space, 18
  productive approach, 68
  reproductive approach, 67–68
  value of, 202
hermeneutics of suspicion
  and exile, 78–79
  feminist use of, 105, 109
Hermes, 141
Hess, Ernest, 63–64
hierarchical oppositions, 111, 112
historical conditioning, 115
historical consciousness, 31–32, 49
historical context, 33, 46n. 42
historicist hermeneutics, 46n. 42
Hodgson, Peter, 8
Holocaust, 164

Lightning Source UK Ltd.
Milton Keynes UK
19 October 2009

145173UK00003B/10/P